Fungibility Capacitance of Carburet Alkylators

Nike G

Fungibility Capacitance of Carburet Alkylators

First Edition December 2025

Written by Nike G

INDEX

CH.NO.	TITLE	PAGE NO.
1	OVERVIEW OF OIL INDUSTRY	1 - 46
2	RESEARCH METHODOLOGY	47 – 61
3	SAMPLE PROFILE	62 – 91
4	ANALYSIS OF PROFITABILITY	92 – 128
5	ANALYSIS OF LIQUIDITY	129 – 166
6	PROFITABILITY VIS A VIS LIQUIDITY ANALYSIS	167 - 208
7	SUMMARY, FINDINGS AND CONCLUSIONS	209 - 256
	ABBREVIATIONS	257 - 257
	BIBLIOGRAPHY	258 - 261

List of tables

SR. NO.	TABLE TITLE	PAGE NO.
1	TABLE 1.1 CHRONOLOGICAL EVENTS OF DEVELOPMENT OF GLOBAL OIL INDUSTRY	5
2	TABLE 1.2 WORLD PROVED RESERVES OF CRUDE OIL	8
3	TABLE 1.3 WORLD CRUDE OIL PRODUCTION (MTS.)	9
4	TABLE 1.4 WORLD CRUDE OIL CONSUMPTION (MTS.)	10
5	TABLE 1.5 CHRONOLOGY OF EXPLORATION & PRODUCTION OF OIL IN INDIA	15
6	TABLE 1.6 DIFFERENCE BETWEEN EARLIER ROUNDS AND NELP	22
7	TABLE 1.7 BLOCK OFFERED UNDER PRE – NELP EXPLORATION ROUNDS	23
8	TABLE 1.8 FOREIGN INVESTMENT IN INDIA DURING NELP	24
9	TABLE 1.9 A BARREL OF CRUDE OIL MAKES.	32
10	TABLE 1.10 WORLD TOP LARGEST OIL REFINERIES	37
11	TABLE 1.11 PETROLEUM REFINERY CAPACITY IN INDIA	40
12	TABLE 1.12 ANNUAL GROWTH OF FDI IN REFINERY IN INDIA	44

13	TABLE 1.13 ESTIMATES OF CRUDE OIL PRODUCTION IN 12TH PLAN (2012-17)	45
14	TABLE 3.1 ANALYSIS OF VARIANCE TABLE FOR ONE WAY ANOVA	57
15	TABLE NO. 4.1 GROSS PROFIT RATIO OF THE SELECTED REFINERY INDUSTRY UNDER THE STUDY FOR THE PERIOD OF (2007-08 TO 2012-13)	107
16	TABLE NO. 4.2 ANALYSIS OF VARIANCE TEST (ANOVA) ON CURRENT RATIO AMONG THE REFINERIES INDUSTRY	109
17	TABLE NO. 4.3 NET PROFIT RATIO OF THE SELECTED REFINERY INDUSTRY UNDER THE STUDY FOR THE PERIOD OF (2007-08 TO 2012-13)	110
18	TABLE NO. 4.4 ANALYSIS OF VARIANCE TEST (ANOVA) ON NETP PROFIT RATIO AMONG THE REFINERIES INDUSTRY	112
19	TABLE NO. 4.5 RETURN ON CAPITAL EMPLOYED OF THE SELECTED REFINERY INDUSTRY UNDER THE STUDY FOR THE PERIOD OF (2007-08 TO 2012-13)	114
20	TABLE NO. 4.6 ANALYSIS OF VARIANCE TEST (ANOVA) ON RETURN ON CAPITAL EMPLOYED AMONG THE REFINERIES INDUSTRY	116

21	TABLE NO. 4.7 RETURN ON NET WORTH OF THE SELECTED REFINERY INDUSTRY UNDER THE STUDY FOR THE PERIOD OF (2007-08 TO 2012-13)	117
22	TABLE NO. 4.8 ANALYSIS OF VARIANCE TEST (ANOVA) ON RETURN ON NET WORTH AMONG THE REFINERIES INDUSTRY	120
23	TABLE NO. 4.9 DIVIDEND PER SHARE OF THE SELECTED REFINERY INDUSTRY UNDER THE STUDY FOR THE PERIOD OF (2007-08 TO 2012-13)	122
24	TABLE NO. 4.10 ANALYSIS OF VARIANCE TEST (ANOVA) ON DIVIDEND PER SHARE AMONG THE REFINERIES INDUSTRY	124
25	TABLE NO. 4.11 EARNING PER SHARE OF THE SELECTED REFINERY INDUSTRY UNDER THE STUDY FOR THE PERIOD OF (2007-08 TO 2012-13)	125
26	TABLE NO. 4.12 ANALYSIS OF VARIANCE TEST (ANOVA) ON EARNING PER SHARE AMONG THE REFINERIES INDUSTRY	127
27	TABLE NO. 5.1 CURRENT RATIO OF THE SELECTED REFINERY INDUSTRY UNDER THE STUDY FOR THE PERIOD OF (2007-08 TO 2012-13)	143

28	TABLE NO. 5.2 ANALYSIS OF VARIANCE TEST (ANOVA) ON CURRENT RATIO AMONG THE REFINERIES INDUSTRY	145
29	TABLE NO. 5.3 STOCK TURNOVER RATIO OF THE SELECTED REFINERY INDUSTRY UNDER THE STUDY FOR THE PERIOD OF (2007-08 TO 2012-13)	147
30	TABLE NO. 5.4 ANALYSIS OF VARIANCE TEST (ANOVA) ON STOCK TURNOVER RATIO AMONG THE REFINERIES INDUSTRY	149
31	TABLE NO. 5.5 DEBTORS TURNOVER RATIO OF THE SELECTED REFINERY INDUSTRY UNDER THE STUDY FOR THE PERIOD OF (2007-08 TO 2012-13)	151
32	TABLE NO. 5.6 ANALYSIS OF VARIANCE TEST (ANOVA) ON DEBTORS TURNOVER RATIO AMONG THE REFINERIES INDUSTRY	153
33	TABLE NO. 5.7 QUICK RATIO OF THE SELECTED REFINERY INDUSTRY UNDER THE STUDY FOR THE PERIOD OF (2007-08 TO 2012-13)	155
34	TABLE NO. 5.8 ANALYSIS OF VARIANCE TEST (ANOVA) ON QUICK RATIO AMONG THE REFINERIES INDUSTRY	157
35	TABLE NO. 5.9 DEBT EQUITY RATIO OF THE SELECTED REFINERY INDUSTRY	159

	UNDER THE STUDY FOR THE PERIOD OF (2007-08 TO 2012-13)	
36	TABLE NO. 5.10 ANALYSIS OF VARIANCE TEST (ANOVA) ON DEBT EQUITY RATIO AMONG THE REFINERIES INDUSTRY	161
37	TABLE NO. 5.11 FIXED ASSETS TURNOVER RATIO OF THE SELECTED REFINERY INDUSTRY UNDER THE STUDY FOR THE PERIOD OF (2007-08 TO 2012-13)	163
38	TABLE NO. 5.12 ANALYSIS OF VARIANCE TEST (ANOVA) ON FIXED ASSETS TURNOVER RATIO AMONG THE REFINERIES INDUSTRY	165
39	TABLE NO. 6.1 LIQUIDITY PROFITABILITY STATUS OF THE SELECTED REFINERY INDUSTRIES BASED ON THE COMBINATION OF CURRNET RATIO AND GROSS PROFIT RATIO	170
40	TABLE NO. 6.2 LIQUIDITY PROFITABILITY STATUS OF THE SELECTED REFINERY INDUSTRIES BASED ON THE COMBINATION OF CURRNET RATIO AND NET PROFIT RATIO	171
41	TABLE NO. 6.3 LIQUIDITY PROFITABILITY STATUS OF THE SELECTED REFINERY INDUSTRIES BASED ON THE COMBINATION OF CURRNET RATIO AND EARNING PER SHARE	172
42	TABLE NO. 6.4 LIQUIDITY PROFITABILITY STATUS OF THE SELECTED REFINERY INDUSTRIES BASED ON THE COMBINATION OF CURRNET RATIO AND	173

	DIVIDEND PER SHARE	
43	TABLE NO. 6.5 LIQUIDITY PROFITABILITY STATUS OF THE SELECTED REFINERY INDUSTRIES BASED ON THE COMBINATION OF CURRNET RATIO AND RETURN ON NET WORTH	174
44	TABLE NO. 6.6 LIQUIDITY PROFITABILITY STATUS OF THE SELECTED REFINERY INDUSTRIES BASED ON THE COMBINATION OF CURRNET RATIO AND RETURN ON CAPITAL EMPLOYED	175
45	TABLE NO. 6.7 LIQUIDITY PROFITABILITY STATUS OF THE SELECTED REFINERY INDUSTRIES BASED ON THE COMBINATION OF STOCK TURNOVER RATIO AND GROSS PROFIT RATIO	176
46	TABLE NO. 6.8 LIQUIDITY PROFITABILITY STATUS OF THE SELECTED REFINERY INDUSTRIES BASED ON THE COMBINATION OF STOCK TURNOVER RATIO AND NET PROFIT RATIO	177
47	TABLE NO. 6.9 LIQUIDITY PROFITABILITY STATUS OF THE SELECTED REFINERY INDUSTRIES BASED ON THE COMBINATION OF STOCK TURNOVER RATIO AND EARNING PER SHARE	178
48	TABLE NO. 6.10 LIQUIDITY PROFITABILITY STATUS OF THE SELECTED REFINERY INDUSTRIES BASED ON THE COMBINATION OF STOCK TURNOVER RATIO AND DIVIDEND PER SHARE	179
49	TABLE NO. 6.11 LIQUIDITY PROFITABILITY STATUS OF THE	180

	SELECTED REFINERY INDUSTRIES BASED ON THE COMBINATION STOCK TURNOVER RATIO AND RETURN ON NET WORTH	
50	TABLE NO. 6.12 LIQUIDITY PROFITABILITY STATUS OF THE SELECTED REFINERY INDUSTRIES BASED ON THE COMBINATION OF STOCK TURNOVER RATIO AND RETURN ON CAPITAL EMPLOYED	181
51	TABLE NO. 6.13 LIQUIDITY PROFITABILITY STATUS OF THE SELECTED REFINERY INDUSTRIES BASED ON THE COMBINATION OF DEBTORS TURNOVER RATIO AND GROSS PROFIT RATIO	182
52	TABLE NO. 6.14 LIQUIDITY PROFITABILITY STATUS OF THE SELECTED REFINERY INDUSTRIES BASED ON THE COMBINATION OF DEBTORS TURNOVER RATIO AND NET PROFIT RATIO	183
53	TABLE NO. 6.15 LIQUIDITY PROFITABILITY STATUS OF THE SELECTED REFINERY INDUSTRIES BASED ON THE COMBINATION OF DEBTORS TURNOVER RATIO AND EARNING PER SHARE	184
54	TABLE NO. 6.16 LIQUIDITY PROFITABILITY STATUS OF THE SELECTED REFINERY INDUSTRIES BASED ON THE COMBINATION OF DEBTORS TURNOVER AND DIVIDEND PER SHARE	185
55	TABLE NO. 6.17 LIQUIDITY PROFITABILITY STATUS OF THE SELECTED REFINERY INDUSTRIES BASED ON THE COMBINATION OF DEBTORS TURNOVER RATIO AND RETURN ON NET WORTH	186

56	TABLE NO. 6.18 LIQUIDITY PROFITABILITY STATUS OF THE SELECTED REFINERY INDUSTRIES BASED ON THE COMBINATION OF DEBTORS TURNOVER RATIO AND RETURN ON CAPITAL EMPLOYED	187
57	TABLE NO. 6.19 LIQUIDITY PROFITABILITY STATUS OF THE SELECTED REFINERY INDUSTRIES BASED ON THE COMBINATION OF QUICK RATIO AND GROSS PROFIT RATIO	188
58	TABLE NO. 6.20 LIQUIDITY PROFITABILITY STATUS OF THE SELECTED REFINERY INDUSTRIES BASED ON THE COMBINATION OF QUICK RATIO AND NET PROFIT RATIO	189
59	TABLE NO. 6.21 LIQUIDITY PROFITABILITY STATUS OF THE SELECTED REFINERY INDUSTRIES BASED ON THE COMBINATION OF QUICK RATIO AND EARNING PER SHARE RATIO	190
60	TABLE NO. 6.22 LIQUIDITY PROFITABILITY STATUS OF THE SELECTED REFINERY INDUSTRIES BASED ON THE COMBINATION OF QUICK RATIO AND DIVIDEND PER SHARE	191
61	TABLE NO. 6.23 LIQUIDITY PROFITABILITY STATUS OF THE SELECTED REFINERY INDUSTRIES BASED ON THE COMBINATION OF QUICK RATIO AND RETURN ON NET WORTH	192
62	TABLE NO. 6.24 LIQUIDITY PROFITABILITY STATUS OF THE SELECTED REFINERY INDUSTRIES BASED ON THE	193

	COMBINATION OF QUICK RATIO AND RETURN ON CAPITAL EMPLOYED	
63	TABLE NO. 6.25 LIQUIDITY PROFITABILITY STATUS OF THE SELECTED REFINERY INDUSTRIES BASED ON THE COMBINATION OF DEBT EQUITY RATIO AND GROSS PROFIT RATIO	194
64	TABLE NO. 6.26 LIQUIDITY PROFITABILITY STATUS OF THE SELECTED REFINERY INDUSTRIES BASED ON THE COMBINATION OF DEBT EQUITY AND NET PROFIT RATIO	195
65	TABLE NO. 6.27 LIQUIDITY PROFITABILITY STATUS OF THE SELECTED REFINERY INDUSTRIES BASED ON THE COMBINATION OF DEBT EQUITY AND EARNING PER SHARE	196
66	TABLE NO. 6.28 LIQUIDITY PROFITABILITY STATUS OF THE SELECTED REFINERY INDUSTRIES BASED ON THE COMBINATION OF DEBT EQUITY RATIO AND DIVIDEND PER SHARE	197
67	TABLE NO. 6.29 LIQUIDITY PROFITABILITY STATUS OF THE SELECTED REFINERY INDUSTRIES BASED ON THE COMBINATION OF DEBT EQUITY RATIO AND RETURN ON CAPITAL EMPLOYED	198
68	TABLE NO. 6.30 LIQUIDITY PROFITABILITY STATUS OF THE SELECTED REFINERY INDUSTRIES BASED ON THE COMBINATION OF DEBT EQUITY RATIO AND RETURN ON NET WORTH	199
69	TABLE NO. 6.31	200

	LIQUIDITY PROFITABILITY STATUS OF THE SELECTED REFINERY INDUSTRIES BASED ON THE COMBINATION OF FIXED ASSETS TURNOVER RATIO AND GROSS PROFIT RATIO	
70	TABLE NO. 6.32 LIQUIDITY PROFITABILITY STATUS OF THE SELECTED REFINERY INDUSTRIES BASED ON THE COMBINATION OF FIXED ASSETS TURNOVER RATIO AND NET PROFIT RATIO	201
71	TABLE NO. 6.33 LIQUIDITY PROFITABILITY STATUS OF THE SELECTED REFINERY INDUSTRIES BASED ON THE COMBINATION OF FIXED ASSETS TURNOVER RATIO AND EARNING PER SHARE	202
72	TABLE NO. 6.34 LIQUIDITY PROFITABILITY STATUS OF THE SELECTED REFINERY INDUSTRIES BASED ON THE COMBINATION OF FIXED ASSETS TURNOVER RATIO AND DIVIDEND PER SHARE	203
73	TABLE NO. 6.35 LIQUIDITY PROFITABILITY STATUS OF THE SELECTED REFINERY INDUSTRIES BASED ON THE COMBINATION OF FIXED ASSETS TURNOVER RATIO AND RETURN ON NET WORTH	204
74	TABLE NO. 6.36 LIQUIDITY PROFITABILITY STATUS OF THE SELECTED REFINERY INDUSTRIES BASED ON THE COMBINATION OF CURRNET RATIO AND RETURN ON CAPITAL EMPLOYED	205

List of figures

SR.NO.	NAME OF FIGURES	PAGE NO.
1	FIGURE1.1 DRAKE'S WELL AT TITUSVILLE, PENNSYLVANIA	3
2	FIGURE 1.2 MAP OF OIL PRODUCING COUNTRIES	11
3	FIGURE 1.3 DIGBOI SITE	12
4	FIGURE 1.4 PRODUCTION OF CRUDE OIL AND ITS GROWTH	19
5	FIGURE 1.5 IMPORTS OF CRUDE OIL AND AVERAGE CRUDE OIL PRICES	20
6	FIGURE 1.6 PROCESS OF REFINING	31
7	FIGURE 1.7 MAJOR REFINERIES IN INDIA	39
8	FIGURE 1.8 SHARE PETROLEUM SECTOR COMPANIES	41
9	FIGURE 1.9 REFINERY CAPACITY AND ITS GROWTH	41
10	FIGURE 1.10 PRODUCTION AND CONSUMPTION (INDIGENOUS SALES) OF PETROLEUM PRODUCTS	42
11	FIGURE 1.11 IMPORTS AND EXPORTS OF PETROLEUM PRODUCTS	43
12	FIGURE 4.1 DU – PONT CHART	101

13	FIGURE 4.2 GROSS PROFIT RATIO OF REFINERY INDUSTRY	107
14	FIGURE 4.3 NET PROFIT RATIO OF REFINERY INDUSTRY	110
15	FIGURE 4.4 RETURN ON CAPITAL EMPLOYED OF REFINERY INDUSTRY	114
16	FIGURE 4.5 RETURN ON NET WORTH OF REFINERY INDUSTRY	117
17	FIGURE 4.6 DIVIDEND PER SHARE OF THE REFINERY INDUSTRY	122
18	FIGURE 4.7 EARNING PER SHARE OF THE REFINERY INDUSTRY	125
19	FIGURE 5.1 CIRCULAR FLOW OF WORKING CAPITAL CYCLE	131
20	FIGURE 5.2 OPERATING CYCLE OF MANUFACTURING CONCERN	139
21	FIGURE 5.3 CURRENT RATIO OF REFINERY INDUSTRY	143
22	FIGURE 5.4 INVENTORY TURNOVER RATIO OF REFINERY INDUSTRY	147
23	FIGURE 5.5 DEBTORS TURNOVER RATIO OF REFINERY INDUSTRY	151
24	FIGURE 5.6	155

	QUICK RATIO OF REFINERY INDUSTRY	
25	FIGURE 5.7 DEBT EQUITY RATIO OF REFINERY INDUSTRY	159
26	FIGURE 5.8 FIXED ASSETS TURNOVER RATIO OF REFINERY INDUSTRY	163
27	FIGURE 5.9 LIQUIDITY – PROFITABILITY TRADE OFF MATRIX	178

INDEX

Sr.no.	Title	Page no.
1.1	Introduction	3
1.2	Chronology of worldwide exploration and development of oil industry	4
1.3	Overview of worldwide crude oil industry • world proved reserves of crude oil • world crude oil production • world crude oil consumption	6
1.4	Overview of oil industry in India • chronology of exploration and production of oil • growth and development of oil sector in India • production of crude oil and its growth • imports of crude oil and Average crude oil price	12
1.5	History of Pre – NELP Licensing Policy overview • difference between earlier rounds and NELP • evolution of NELP • NELP rounds	21
1.6	Operating of oil markets • Concept • Benchmark • effects of oil prices on economy	26
1.7	Overview of refinery industry • meaning • process • World's top largest refinery	29
1.8	Basic Refinery Economics • New builds V/s Upgrades • cost of inputs – price of outputs • Crack spread • Determinants of profitability • 8.5 Refinery size, configuration and complexity	34

1.9	Refining capacity in India	38
1.10	Production and consumption of petro products	42
1.11	Import and export of petro products	43
1.12	Annual growth of FDI in P& NG sector	44
1.13	Estimates of crude oil production in 12TH PLAN (2012-17)	45

1.1 Introduction

We all know that products such as motor oil and gasoline are derived from crude oil. However, many people are unaware that crude oil also serves as the raw material for a wide range of everyday products, including clothing, vitamin capsules, tyres, and numerous synthetic materials. Crude oil is found deep beneath the earth's surface, both on land and under the ocean. It is formed from the remains of plants and animals that lived millions of years ago and were gradually subjected to intense heat and pressure over long periods of time. Typically blackish in colour, crude oil has a distinctive odour due to the presence of small quantities of sulphur- and nitrogen-containing compounds. Crude oil exists in different grades, each having a unique composition determined by the original organic material and the geological characteristics of the surrounding soil and rock formations. Based on density, crude oil may be classified as light or heavy.

Petroleum, also known as crude oil, is a naturally occurring, oily and flammable liquid found in underground reservoirs. It is composed mainly of hydrocarbons, along with trace amounts of nitrogenous and sulphur-based compounds. The term "petroleum" is derived from the words petro, meaning rock, and oleum, meaning oil. Natural oil seeps and pools have been known for thousands of years. Historical records indicate that the Chinese extracted oil from wells as deep as 800 feet using bamboo pipes as early as 347 AD, primarily to evaporate brine and produce salt. American Indians used petroleum for medicinal purposes, while ancient Persians, Macedonians, and Egyptians applied it for waterproofing ships. The Babylonians used asphalt as early as the 8th century to construct city walls, towers, and roads.

1.2 Chronology of worldwide crude oil industry

Oil has been used for lighting purposes for many thousands of years. In areas where oil is found in shallow reservoirs, seeps of crude oil or gas may naturally develop, and some oil could simply be collected from seepage or tar ponds. Historically we know the tales of eternal fires where oil and gas seeps ignited and burned. For e.g. famous oracle of Delphi was built around 1,000 B.C. written sources from 500 B.C. describe how Chinese used natural gas to boil water. It was not until 1859 that "Colonel" Edwin Drake drilled the first successful oil well, with the sole purpose of finding oil. The Drake well was located in the middle of quiet farm country in northwestern Pennsylvania, and sparked the international search for an industrial use for petroleum. Electricity did not emerge as an illuminant till the Edison Electric Light Company was founded in 1878. Well into the 20th century, kerosene, gas and electricity continued to compete as illuminants. Whilst the use of gas as an illuminant has virtually disappeared, a large population, especially in India, continues to use kerosene as illuminant. In 1890 Canadian Geologist Abraham Gesner has found Kerosene, which was extracted from coal and oil. Kerosene was most common energy source during that time as was used in lighting of the lamp which would in return the increase the value of kerosene.

The invention of the motor car by Karl Friedrich Benz in 1885 created a market for petrol, anew refined product (petrol is called Benzin after Karl Benz in Germany). In 1898, Rudolf Diesel invented an engine in which oil was ignited by compression, the diesel engine he invented came to power larger vehicles, after this, the production and use of motor vehicles spread rapidly in the United States, especially after 1908 when Henry Ford began mass manufacture of his Model T, and petroleum and diesel oil became the most important refined precuts, first in the Us and progressively across the world.

Table 1.1 chronological events of development of global oil industry

Year	*Events*
1264	Marco polo visited Persian city and oil was found from Caspian sea
1500	Oil extracted from the mountains of Carpathian
1816	Inception of oil industry in U.S.A.
1821	First time Commercial production of gas in Fiona
1857	First oil well digging at north west Butchrest
1858	First oil well was dig in North America
1859	Colonel Edwin Drake found out oil at 69ft. under earth
1870	J.D.Rockfeller established Standard Oil Co.
1885	Royal Dutch Co. has expanded oil sector
1895	Bitumen was found
1901	Birth of Texas oil industry
1905	Fire spread at Baku oil sector during Russian revolution
1907	Merger of Shale and Royal Dutch company
1908	Establishment of Persian Oil Company
1911	Dissolution of Standard Oil trust
1930	Dad Joiner had found out oil in Western Texas
1932	Oil was found in Behrin
1938	Oil was found in Kuwait and Saudi Arabia
1951	Nationalization of Iranian Oil Company
1956	Oil was found in Algeria and Nigeria
1959	Natural gas was found in Denmark, Arab Oil Congress agreed on production and marketing of oil
1968	Oil was found in Northern Alaska
1969	Oil was found in Santa Barbara
1971	Libya, Saudi Arabia, Algeria, and Iraq increase the price of oil – Iraq declared oil reserve as national assets
1975	Nationalization of oil industry in Venezuela
1977	Completion of oil pipeline at Alaska
1982	First time OPEC declared its oil quota
1991	Due to Gulf war, reduction in oil supply

1997	Qatar has introduced first meaningful export of LNG (Liquid Natural Gas)
2006	Oil hits a record high of $78.40/bbl on New York Mercantile Exchange on supply and world political concerns - nuclear tensions in Iran and supply concerns in Iraq, Nigeria, Gulf of Mexico; missile testing by North Korea and flare ups between Israel and Lebanon.
2007	Russia turns off flow of oil through Belarus to Eastern Europe on accusations that Belarus was illegally taking their oil. Venezuela planning to nationalize oil refineries.
2008	Crude oil hits a record high over $147.27 per barrel on continued concern over supplies and the weak US dollar. Global recession fears.
2010	China National Oil Corp (CNOC) to spend $2.2Billion to acquire an interest in the Eagle Ford Shale (liquids rich gas) in South Texas.
2011	Unrest in various countries of the Arab world creates concern over energy supply and boosts oil prices.
2011	Australian parliament passes carbon emissions law - forcing the 500 top polluters to pay for carbon emission.
2012	Chinese company Sinopec agrees to invest $US2.2Billion in five plays owned by Devon Energy Corp. An electrical power failure in India left a reported 600milliion people without electricity

1.3 Overview of World wide Crude oil industry

In 2011, global crude oil demand increased to 88 million barrel per day (mbpd) from 87.4 mbpd in 2010. The demand growth slowed down to meager 0.7% after registering a growth of 3.3% in 2010. This was mainly due to slowdown in global GDP growth rate to 3.9% in 2011 from 5.3% in 2010.

Global oil production is increased by 1.3% in 2011. In 2011 annual global oil production increased by 1.1 mbpd or 1.3%. Virtually, the entire incremental supply came from OPEC, with large increases in Saudi Arabia (1.2 million barrels per day), the UAE, Kuwait and Iraq more than offsetting a loss of Libyan supply (1.2 million barrels per day). Output reached record levels in Saudi Arabia, the UAE and Qatar. Non OPEC output was broadly flat, with increase in the US, Canada, Russia and Columbia offsetting continued declines in mature provinces such as the UK and

Norway, as well as unexpected outages in number of other countries. ***The US (2,85,000 barrels/day) had the largest increase among non OPEC producers for the third consecutive year. Driven by continued strong growth in onshore production of shale liquids, US output reached the highest levels since 1998.***

World proved reserves of crude oil

Crude oil supply from OPEC increased to 35.8 mbpd in 2011 form 35 mbpd in 2006. Global dependence on OPEC crude oil, which is currently at 36%, is expected to remain stable over the next few years. This is due to incremental supply from new fields in non OPEC countries to counter structural decline in their existing matured fields. In addition, many small and marginal fields in non – OPEC which were earlier considered unviable have now become viable at higher oil prices. Also, production of OPEC is expected to increase over the next five years.

Since may 2012, crude oil prices have declined sharply below $100 per barrel from $120.5 per barrel in April 2012 mainly because of increased concerns over the recovery of stressed European economies as well as fears of slowdown in global crude oil demand. Also, production form many countries, including the US, Iraq, Libya, Saudi Arabia, etc, has increased significantly since the last one year.

Prices have declined after remaining persistently high for almost two years. Crude oil prices had increased to $120 per barrel in April 2012 from $85 per barrel in April 2010. Prices surged mainly because crude oil demand rebounded by 3.3% in 2010 post the economic downturn, and also due to intensifying of geo – political tensions in various Middle Eastern and North African (MENA) countries like Egypt, Libya, Syria, Yemen and Sudan. Additionally, January 2012, the US and European Union enforced sanctions against importing of crude oil from Iran. In response, Iran threatened to block the Gulf of Hormuz. This added a significant risk premium to crude oil prices, which traded at around $120 per barrel since February 2012.

Table 1.2 world's proved reserve of crude oil

World Proved Reserves of Crude Oil (at the end 2013)			
Country / Region	**Thousand million tonnes**	**Thousand million barrels**	**R/P ratio**
US	5.4	44.2	12.1
Canada	28.1	174.3	*
Mexico	1.5	11.1	10.6
Argentina	0.3	2.4	9.8
Brazil	2.3	15.6	20.9
Ecuador	1.2	8.2	5.7
Venezuela	46.6	298.3	*
Kazakhstan	3.9	30.0	46.5
Russia	12.7	93.0	23.9
Iran	21.6	157.0	*
Iraq	20.2	150.0	*
Kuwait	14.0	101.5	92.5
Oman	0.7	5.5	15.2
Qatar	2.6	25.1	30.9
Sarudi Arabia	36.5	265.9	67.3
Syria	0.3	2.5	*
U.A.E	13.0	97.8	78.5
Yemen	0.4	3.0	54.1
Libya	6.3	48.5	*
China	2.5	18.1	12.0
India	0.8	5.7	19.0

***more than 100 years**

R/P ratio – Reserve to Production means reserves remaining at the end of any year are divided by the production in that year, the result is the length of time that those remaining reserves would last if production were to contiune at that rate.

The consumption in Organization for Economic Co – operation and Development (OECD) countries declined by 1.2% (6,00,000 barrels per day), the fifth decrease in the past six years, reaching the lowest level since 1995. The major decline was witnessed in the US and Europe, where the consumption went down by more than 3,00,000 barrels/day. In non – OECD countries, consumption grew by 1.2 million barrels per day, or 2.8%. ***China again recorded the highest increment to global consumption growth (5,05,000 barrels per day)*** followed by Russia (1,56,000 barrels per day), India (1,40,000 barrels per day) and Saudi Arabia (1,08,000 barrels per day)

Table 1.3 world's crude oil production (million tonnes)

World Crude Oil Producion (Million Tonnes)						
Country/Region	**2008**	**2009**	**2010**	**2011**	**2012**	**2013**
US	302.30	322.40	332.90	345.70	394.10	446.20
Canada	152.90	152.80	160.30	169.80	182.60	193.00
Mexico	156.90	146.70	145.60	144.50	143.90	141.80
Argentina	36.50	34.90	34.00	32.20	31.10	30.50
Brazil	98.80	105.60	111.40	26.80	112.20	109.90
Ecuador	27.20	26.10	26.10	114.20	27.10	28.20
Venezuela	165.60	155.70	145.70	141.50	136.60	135.10
Kazakhstan	72.05	78.21	81.65	82.37	81.30	83.80
Russia	493.68	500.82	511.78	518.48	526.23	531.40
Iran	214.50	205.53	208.84	208.23	174.92	166.10
Iraq	119.32	119.93	121.48	136.68	152.45	153.20
Kuwait	136.12	121.23	122.51	139.67	152.49	151.30
Oman	37.71	40.35	42.93	44.13	45.80	46.10
Qatar	65.03	62.39	72.13	78.21	83.35	84.20
Sarudi Arabia	509.87	456.72	473.82	525.95	547.03	542.30
Syria	20.29	19.97	19.17	16.29	8.19	2.80
U.A.E	141.37	126.19	133.34	151.26	154.13	165.70
Yemen	14.76	14.30	13.55	10.57	8.33	7.40
Libya	85.52	77.37	77.73	22.49	71.07	46.50
China	190.44	189.49	203.01	202.88	207.47	208.10
India	37.93	37.20	40.85	42.32	42.03	42.00

Table 1.4 world's crude oil consumption (million tonnes)

World Crude Oil Consumption				(Million Tonnes)		
Country/Region	**2008**	**2009**	**2010**	**2011**	**2012**	**2013**
US	875.4	833.2	850.1	834.9	817.0	831.0
Canada	101.2	95.0	101.3	105.0	104.3	103.5
Mexico	91.6	88.5	88.5	90.3	92.3	89.7
Argentina	24.7	24.0	26.9	26.9	28.5	29.4
Brazil	108.6	109.1	118.1	121.9	125.8	132.7
Ecuador	8.7	8.9	10.3	10.5	10.9	11.6
Venezuela	33.8	34.2	32.1	31.9	33.0	36.2
Kazakhstan	11.0	8.9	9.3	12.3	13.1	13.8
Russia	133.9	128.2	134.3	143.5	148.9	153.1
Iran	93.3	95.5	86.7	88.2	89.5	92.9
Kuwait	19.0	20.4	21.6	20.4	21.6	21.8
Qatar	6.1	6.0	6.5	7.8	8.0	8.5
Saudi Arabia	106.7	115.8	124.2	125.1	131.3	135.0
U.A.E	29.4	27.7	30.1	33.0	34.3	35.6
China	377.6	391.0	440.4	464.1	490.1	507.4
India	144.7	152.6	155.4	163.0	173.6	175.2
Japan	226.3	201.8	204.1	204.9	217.8	208.9
South korea	103.1	103.7	105.0	105.8	108.8	108.4

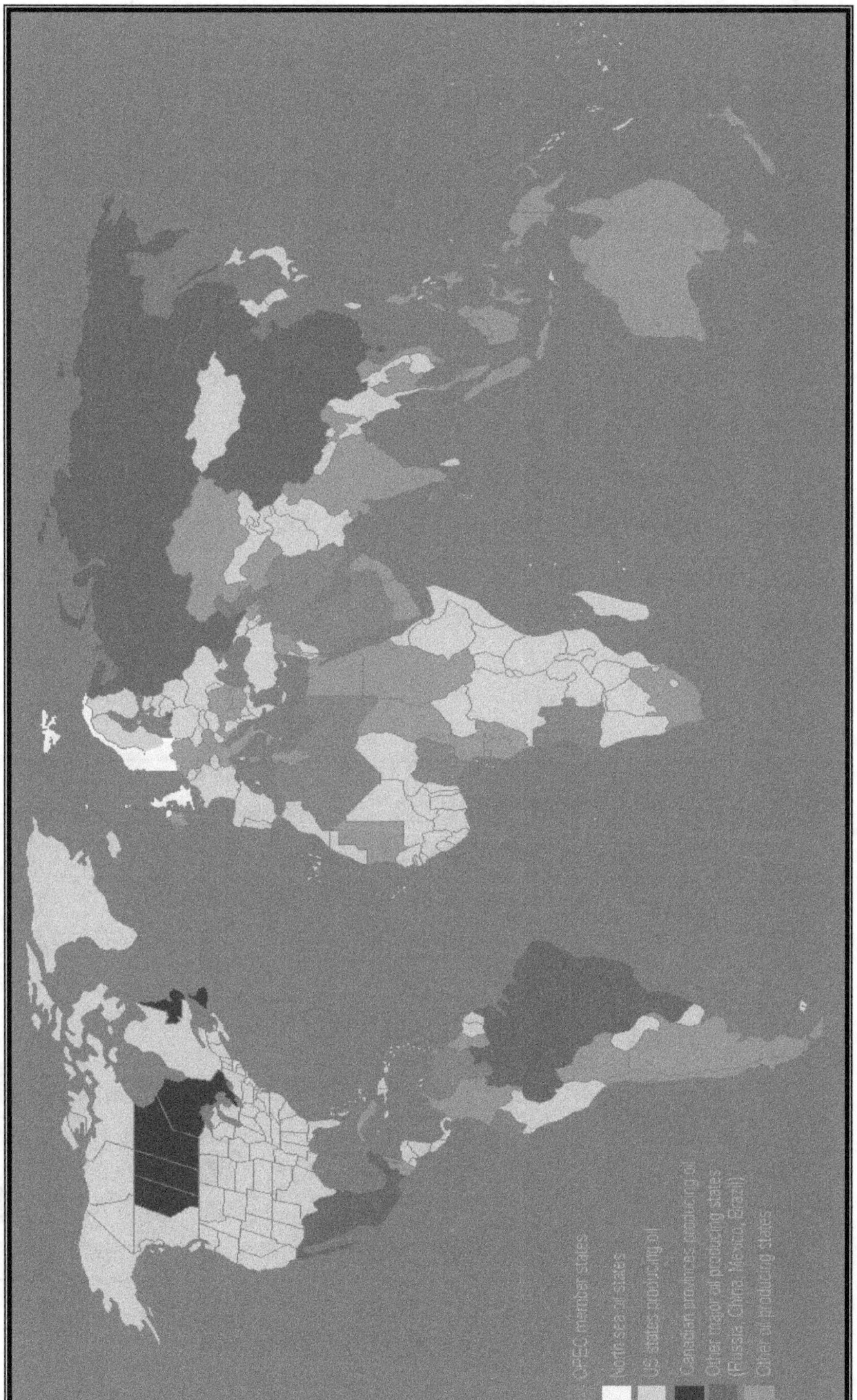

Figure 1.2 Map of Oil Producing Countries

1.4. Overview of oil industry in India

Growth and Development of Oil industry in India

As in the US, China and Iran, oil seeped out of the soil in India as well, British travelers in Assam reported such pools from 1825 onwards. Once fractionation technology was proved in the US, industrial refining of oil became feasible. Assam Railway and Trading Company Ltd was registered in London in 1881 to exploit Assam's natural resources. It struck oil in exploitable volume near Digboi in 1889, at that point it transferred its oil interests to separate company, Assam Oil Company. AOC built a refinery in Digboi in 1901. AOC was taken over in 1917 by Burmah Oil Company, which later became Burmah Shell and then Shell. Expanded and modernized a number of times, the Digboi refinery continues to function till today that shows its importance.

Figure 1.3 Digboi site

In 1938, AOC took a prospecting license for 6,290 square miles in Assam, it ceded the concession after the war started in 1939, and resumed it in 1947. AOC struck oil in Naharkotia in 1953. By that time, however, the government of India had become paranoid about foreign ownership of business, there was a long standoff between it and AOC over the exploitation of the new oilfield. Finally in 1959, AOC and the government set up Oil India ltd, a 67:33 joint venture, to exploit the Naharkotiya oilfield, in 1961 it became a 50:50 joint venture.

Apart from the small refinery in Digboi, India did not produce refinery products when it became independent in 1947; it depended almost entirely on imports, mostly from Anglo-Iranian Oil Company's refinery in Abadan. Three companies sold the products through their distribution networks –Burmah Shell, Standard Vacuum and Caltex (now merged into Shell, Exxon and Chevron respectively). Burmah Shell was the largest, with an almost 50% share of the market.

In December 1953, the Indian government entered a 25:75 joint venture with Standard Vacuum for survey of 10,000 square miles in West Bengal. The company did some gravimetric and seismic survey, and drilled seven holes. It found some gas in some which it considered non commercial; it did not find any oil. The general impression was that Standard Vacuum put little effort into prospecting in West Bengal. This could have been due to the incentive structure. Standard Vacuum had access to cheap crude from the Gulf, if it found oil in India; the government would force it to exploit it. Its cost was likely to be higher, and the company would either have earned lower profit margins or the government would have had to protect domestic refining. The negotiations between Standard Vacuum and the government on the refinery threw up a large number of issues. The government suspected that the oil companies were happy with the import of refined products from Abadan refinery, which they sold in India at certain and high profits. But after Iran nationalized the Abadan refinery in May 1951, India looked a safer country to operate in.

The government was frustrated with the experience of negotiations with three oil companies in the 1950s; the government took a number of steps to reduce dependence on foreign oil companies. In 1956, it set up Oil and Natural Gas Commission to explore for oil, and brought in Soviet and Rumanian rigs and crews to prospect for oil. The two areas chosen were the Cambay area in Gujarat and the

Jawalpuri – Janaur area in what is now Himachal Pradesh. The Soviet crew considered Gujarat more promising and drilled there first. The first well was found on 25th July 1958, on 24th September it struck oil under at 7000 feet. Further exploratory drilling led to the discovery of Ankleshwar and Kalol oilfields in 1960, and suggested that the oil bearing strata extended offshore to what came to be known as Bombay High. Oil from this area was the foundation of ONGC's emergence as an oil producer.

The Soviet survey had shown the oil bearing structures of Gujarat extending into the sea in 1964-67, but the soviet did not have the technology for offshore exploration or production. In 1974, a Japanese survey ship leased by ONGC discovered the prolific Bombay High offshore field. It has been mainstay of ONGC's business since then.

In 1976, India nationalized the three refineries owned by Shell, Caltex and Esso. In 1981, the government bought out Burmah oil's 50% stake in Assam Oil Company, with the nationalizations, the entire Indian oil industry passed into government hands, and came to be run as a part of the government.

In 1977, the government introduced an Administered Price Mechanism (APM), to be operated by an Oil Coordinating Committee (OCC). The ministry of petroleum fixed so called retention prices designed to give oil producers 15% and refineries 12% of their net worth, and it set administered prices at which products were sold to consumers. The difference between the revenue and dues of an oil company went its account with OCC. So overall, the price level was cost plus, but the government could cross – subsidize individual products at will.

It was the companies practice to construct their own petrol pumps and give them to dealers to run. Under the private companies, dealerships were given to trusted associates, and they became a part of the companies. After nationalization, the government decided to set up a fairer system. In 1983 it set up four oil selection boards, each board had retired judge and one other member. Oil pumps made good profits with little investment on the part of the dealer and at low risk. So many more people wanted pumps than could get them, and recommendations and corruption were rampant in their allocation. Prime Minister Vajpayee cancelled all the 3850 allotments made. There has been no public scandal then, but that does not necessarily mean that the system works any better now.

Table 1.5 chronology of exploration and production of crude oil in India

Year	Chronology of Events
1889	W. L. Lake of Assam Railway and Trading Co. (AR & T Co) started Digboi Well No-1
1899	AR&T Co formed a new company Assam Oil Company (AOC) and set up a small refinery at Margharita (Upper Assam) with a capacity of 500 bopd to refine the Digboi-oil.
1901	Digboi refinery commissioned
1911	Entry of Burmah Oil Company (BOC) in India
1921	BOC takes over AOC
1937-39	Seismic surveys were initiated in and a major 'High' was located at Nahorkatiya in Assam
1948	Geological Survey of India (GSI) started geophysical surveys in Cambay area
1956	Moran oil field discovered by AOC.
August 14, 1956	Oil & Natural Gas Commission (ONGC) was established.
October 15, 1959	'ONGC' becomes autonomous body, under an act of parliament
1959	Oil India Private Ltd (OIL) incorporated and registered as a Rupee Company
1960	Oil struck at Ankleswar in Gujarat and Rudrasagar in Assam
1962	The first public sector refinery comes up at Guwahati
1963	- World's first crude oil conditioning plant commissioned at Nahorkatiya. - India's first deviated well NHK122 drilled by OIL.
1968	Oil discovered in Geleki by ONGC.
1970	India's first offshore well spudded in the Gulf of Cambay
1974	Drillship Sagar Samrat strikes oil in Bombay High
1981	First well spudded in Godavari offshore
October 14, 1981	'OIL' becomes a Government of India enterprise
1983-84	Gas struck at Razole in Andhra Pradesh and Gotaru in Rajasthan
1984	First Early Production system (EPS) commences in Gujarat
1984-85	Oil struck in kutch offshore, Godavari offshore and Changmaigam in Assam
1986-87	ONGC strikes oil in the Tapti offshore area and Namti structure (Assam)
1988-89	Commercial gas finds in Rajasthan by OIL Nada field in Gujarat discovered
1989-90	- Western offshore production reaches a peak of 21.72 MMT - South Heera field discovered in Mumbai offshore
1998	New Exploration Licensing Policy (NELP) launched and 48 Exploration blocks offered under round-I.
2000	Second round of New Exploration Licensing Policy launched and 25 Exploration blocks offered
2002	Third round of New Exploration Licensing Policy launched and 27 Exploration blocks offered
2003	Fourth round of New Exploration Licensing Policy launched and 24 Exploration blocks offered
2005	Fifth round of New Exploration Licensing Policy launched and 20 Exploration blocks offered
2006	Sixth round of New Exploration Licensing Policy launched and 55 Exploration blocks offered
2007	Seventh round of New Exploration Licensing Policy launched and 57 Exploration blocks offered

Source: Directorate General of Hydrocarbons

The origin of oil & gas industry in India can be traced back to 1867 when oil was struck at Makum near Margherita in Assam. At the time of Independence in 1947, the Oil & Gas industry was controlled by international companies. India's domestic oil production was just 250,000 tonnes per annum and the entire production was from one state - Assam.

This small amount of production made the oil experts from different countries predict the future of the oil industry as a dull one and also doubted India's ability to search for new oil reserves. But the Government of India declared the Oil industry in India as the core sector industry under the Industrial Policy Resolution bill in the year 1954, which helped the Oil Industry in India vastly.

Oil exploration and production in India is done by companies like NOC or National Oil Corporation, ONGC or Oil and Natural Gas Corporation and OIL who are actually the oil companies in India that are owned by the government under the Industrial Policy Rule. The National Oil Corporation during the 1970s used to produce and supply more than 70 percent of the domestic need for the petroleum but by the end of this amount dropped to near about 35 percent. This was because the demand on the one hand was increasing at a good rate and the production was declining at a steady rate.

Size of the Industry	**India today has total reserves of 775 million metric tonnes (MMT) of crude oil and 1074 billion cubic metres**
Geographical distribution	**Assam, Rajasthan, Mumbai, Vishakhapatnam, Chennai, Nagapatinam, Kochi, Bongaigaon, Numaligarh, Mangalore, Tatipaka**
Output per annum	**India produced roughly 880 thousand barrels per day (bbl/d) of total oil in 2009 from over 3,600 operating oil wells**
Percentage in world market	**India has approximately 5.6 billion barrels of proven oil reserves as of January 2010, the second-largest amount in the Asia-Pacific region after China.**

Oil Industry in India during the year 2004-2005 fulfilled most of demand through importing oil from multiple oil producing countries. The Oil Industry in India itself produced nearly 35 million metric tons of Oil from the year 2001 to 2005. The Import that is done by the Oil Industry in India comes mostly from the Middle East Asia.

The Oil that is produced by the Oil Industry in India provides more than 35 percent of the energy that is primarily consumed by the people of India. This amount is expected to grow further with both economic and overall growth in terms of production as well as percentage. The demand for oil is predicted to go higher and higher with every passing decade and is expected to reach an amount of nearly 250 million metric ton by the year 2024.

OIL SECTOR IN INDIA

Oil accounts for about 30% of India's total energy consumption. According to the 2008 BP Statistical Energy Survey, India had proved oil reserves of 5.459 billion barrels at the end of 2007, the majority of which are allocated in the Mumbai High, Upper Assam, Cambay, Krishna-Godavari, and Cauvery basins.

According to the 2008 BP Statistical Energy Survey, India produced an average of 800.7 thousand barrels of crude oil per day in 2007 and consumed an average of 2748.17 thousand barrels a day, 3.25% of the world total . Because of its growing economy, India is an increasingly significant `consumer of oil and natural gas.

Although a net importer of oil, India is attempting to limit its dependence on oil imports by expanding domestic exploration and production. The Indian government is pursuing the New Exploration Licensing Policy (NELP), first announced in 1997, which permits foreign involvement in exploration, an activity that was once restricted to Indian state-owned firms and between 2000 and 2005, awarded 110 oil and natural gas concessions in five separate licensing rounds. The sixth bidding round (known as NELP-VI) recently concluded, with 52 exploration blocks awarded.

The bulk of India's natural gas production comes from the western offshore regions, especially the Mumbai High complex. According to the 2008 BP Statistical Energy Survey, India had 2007 proved natural gas reserves of 1.05 trillion cubic meters, 0.59% of the world total. The onshore fields in Assam, Andhra Pradesh, and Gujarat states are also major producers of natural gas. According to the 2008 BP Statistical Energy Survey, India had 2007 natural gas production of 30.17 billion cubic meters while consuming 40.17 billion cubic meters of natural gas.

There have been several large natural gas finds in India over the last five years, predominantly in the offshore Bay of Bengal. It is still expected, however, that the demand for natural gas in India will outstrip any new supply in the years ahead. Indian natural gas consumption has risen faster than any other fuel over the last five years, leading India to consider the large-scale importation of natural gas via pipelines.

India is the world's second largest importer of Iranian crude after China, importing about 400 000 barrels a day in 2011. Indian refiners are, however, diversifying their oil supplies away from Iran as international sanctions intensify.

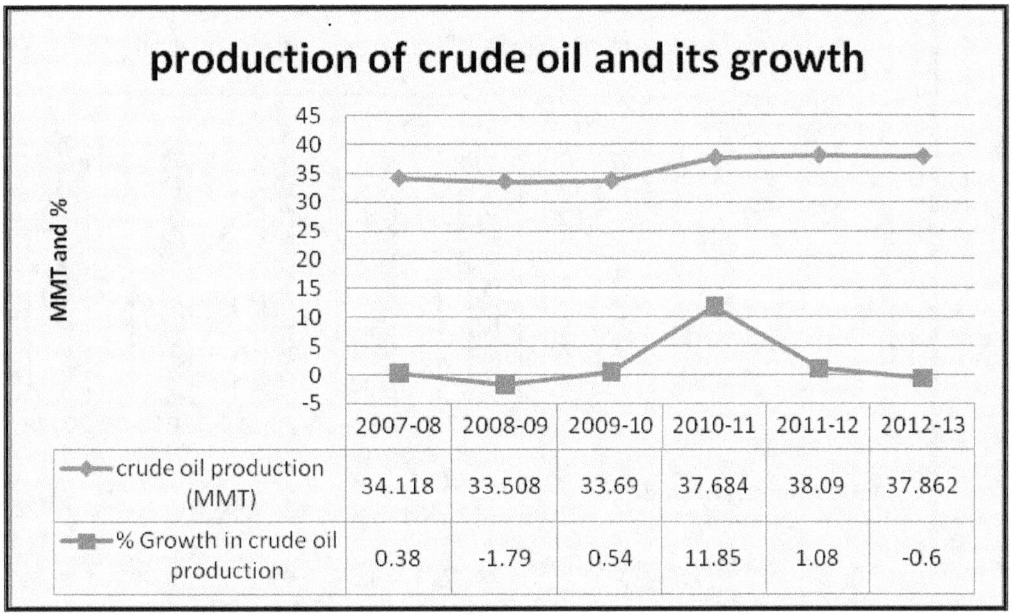

Figure 1.4 Production of crude oil and its growth

The estimated crude oil production for the year 2013-14 was 37,788 million tonnes (MMT) as against actual production 37.862 MMT for the year 2012-13, showing a marginal decrease of about 0.20%. the majority of curde oil production from ageing fields except new field viz., Rajasthan and KG deep – water blocks. Production of crude oil was affected due to environmental factors, bandhs/blockades in Assam, power diturbances in Gujarat, delay in production from wells in Andhra Pradesh, and lesser production from development/side track wells in Mumbai, poor reflux, under performance of producing wells and less base potential of major fields that affected production of Ahmedabad and Ankleshwar. Highest growth was noticed in the year 2010-11 of 11.85%, whereas it was negative during 2008-09 and 2012-13. The highest production was in 2012-13, i.e. 37.862 MMT, and the lowest in 2008-09 of 33.508 MMT.

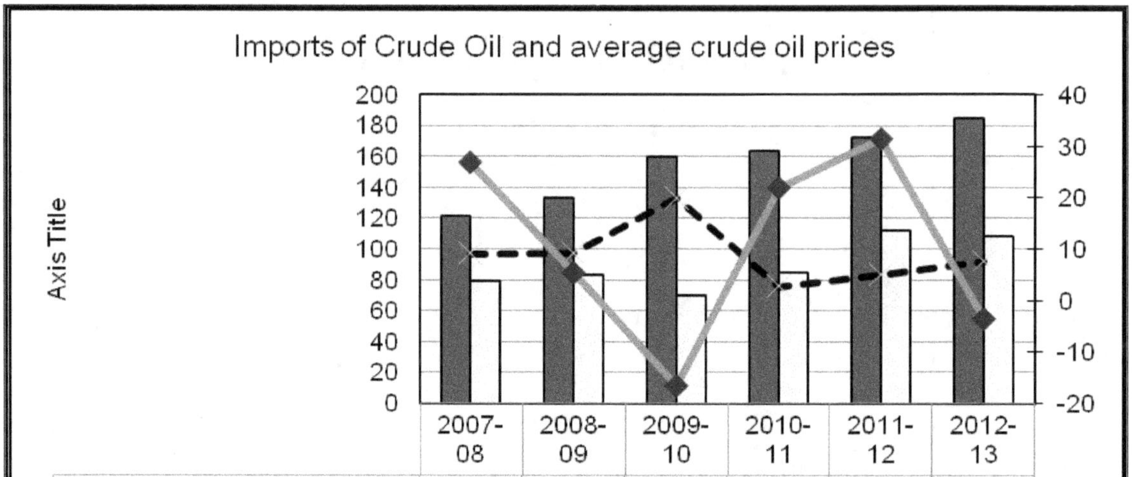

	2007-08	2008-09	2009-10	2010-11	2011-12	2012-13
imports of crude oil (MMT)	121.672	132.775	159.259	163.595	171.729	184.795
average crude oil porices (US$/bbl)	79.25	83.57	69.76	85.09	111.89	107.97
% growth in imports of crude oil	9.12	9.13	19.95	2.72	4.97	7.61
%growth in avg average crude oil prices	26.88	5.45	-16.53	21.98	31.5	-3.5

Figure 1.5 imports of crude oil and average crude oil prices

During the year 2013-14 the import of crude oil was 189.238 MMT valued at rs. 8,64,875 crore as against 184.795 MMT production in 2012-13 valued at rs. 7,84,652. An increase of about 2.40% in quantitiy terms and 10.22% in value terms has been observed during the year 2013-14 over 2012-13.

The average international crude oil price (indian basket) was US$ 105.52/bbl. In 2013-14 as compared to US$ 107.97/bbl. In 2012-13. Average price of International crude oil (Indian basket) during 2013-14 was lower by 2.27% as compared to the previous year 2012-13. The trend in growth of crude oil imorts and and crude oil international (indian basket) prices shown in above figure.

1. 5.HISTORY OF PRE – NELP LICENCING POLICY (New Exploration Licensing Policy)

OVERVIEW

The earliest effort at attracting foreign companies to invest was in the mid 1970s under the then Union Minister for Petroleum and Chemicals H. R. Gokhale. ONGC and OIL were the major players, except for Carlesberg (U.S.) and Reading and Bates of Canada, the government could not farm out any of the areas to other parties. The two also eventually pulled out without finding any oil but made their documentation available to the government. Failure to meet reserve accretion targets prompted the government to involve the private sector. Exploration bidding rounds were not successful. The first four rounds took 12 years to come (1979 – 91). The next five rounds came in two years (1994 -95) and succeeded in generating some interest in the international oil industry. An innovation was also introduced in 9th round known as the JV round (joint venture) to reduce the risk for the private investors by associating ONGC/OIL as partners in these exploration ventures. However, the rigid decision making structures of these National Oil Companies (NOCs) created problems of compatibility and reduced the attractiveness of this innovation.

To raise the interest of foreign companies in the E&P sector. The government decided to award some small and medium fields for development to the private and joint sectors respectively, and came out with two rounds in 1992 and 1993. These rounds evinced tremendous response from foreign players. Also in order to upgrade the information on the hydrocarbon potential of India's unexplored sedimentary basins, the government offered blocks for geophysical survey during 1993 to 1995.

Table 1.6 Difference between earlier rounds and NELP		
Terms	Earlier rounds	NELP
Royalty / cess	Companies exempt from payment of royalty. No cess. ONGC/OIL to bear these on private companies behalf, as per fiscal package approved by govt.	Companies to bear
Participating interest by NOCs	0% to 40% at their option, except for the joint venture exploration programme where they had to take 25% to 40% interest from the beginning.	No participation by NOCs as govt. nominee.
Carried interest of NOCs	NOCs had 30% carried interest, exercisable on commercial discovery, except in JVEP where they have working interest from the start.	No carried interest by NOCs.
Level playing field for NOCs	NOCs carried the burden on behalf of private companies and for their own operations they did not get the same terms available to private investor.	NOCs get international price on their production of oil and gas and exemption from payment of custom duty and cess
NOCs to compete for acreage	NOCs got acreage on preferential basis.	NOCs to compete for acreage.
Incentive for exploration	No special incentive	Only half royalty for deep water to be paid in the initial seven years

Evolution of NELP

It was the most important step that the Government has taken to strengthen oil industry. The series of new, attractive fiscal and contractual terms is designed to attract international operators to the Indian oil sector. Oil companies from private and public sectors will be treated at par and all new explorations will be given market driven price of crude oil and natural gas produced.

Table 1.7 Block offered under Pre – NELP Exploration Rounds.

Year	Round	No. of blocks offered			Bids received	Contracts signed		
		Offshore	Onshore	Total		Offshore	Onshore	Total
1980	One	17	15	32	4	1	0	1
1982	Two	42	8	50	Nil	0	0	0
1986	There	27	0	27	13	0	0	0
1991	Four	39	33	72	24	2	3	5
1993	Five	29	16	45	15	4	2	6
1993	Six	17	29	46	20	2	3	5
1994	Seven	17	28	45	12	2	3	5
1994	Eight	15	19	34	38	1	3	4
1995	Ninth JV round	10	18	28	22	1	1	2

(source : paper on 'Review of E & P licencing policy ' – petrofed)

Table 1.8 Foreign investment in India during NELP

Sr no	NELP	Year	About	Foreign investment
1	NELP I	1999	First round of new explorations licensing Received 45 bids for the 27 blocks 16 discoveries have been made World class discovery made by the RIL – Niko Resources consortium (KG basin)	Foreign company included are Enron Copro. U.S., Petronas Carigali –Malaysia, OAO Gazprom – Russia, Energy Equity India petroleum Pvt. Ltd. – Aus., Cairn energy – Aus., Niko resources, Canada., Out of 10 companies only 5 were successful in bagging a block.
2	NELP II	2000	For the first time blocks on west coast were put on offer. A total of 3 discoveries have been made in two blocks located in Cambay basin.	GOI appointed HIS energy group of USA as the marketing consultant. Participants were Niko resources, Petrobas, Exxon mobil, premier oil, pan Canadian.
3	NELP III	2002	GOI undertook a comprehensive promotional exercise campaigning at new Delhi, Singapore, London, Houston and Calgary. A total of 45 bids were received for the 23 blocks.	From 11 companies submitted bids, 4 were foreign companies. Cairn, premier oil,Hardy exploration and Geo global resources.
4	NELP IV	2003	Total 19 companies submitted their bids for 24 blocks, 12 were domestic (six PSU, six PVTs), and seven were foreign ,others are JVs. Provision made for fast track arbitration. Surcharge on income tax for foreign company abolished. Bank guarantee to be returned after minimum work programme completed.	Seven companies participated were Enpro finance, Niko resources, Canoro resources, Cairn energy, Geoglobal resources, Zarubenzneftgaz (Russia), BG, Hardy.

5	NELP V	2005	For the first time Maharashtra was included for exploration. Total 69 bids for 20 blocks. All geo scientific data was made available on internet. Details of all operational blocks from earlier rounds available on internet. Overwhelming response generated as compared to previous NELP rounds can be attributed to the professional and extensive promotional exercise.	Total of 26 foreign companies and 21 indian companies submitted their bids.Out of 26 foreign companies 17 companies submitting bids for the first time. These companies are British petroleum, Petrobras, ENI, Hunt oil, Beach petroleum, KUFPEC, Norwest energy, suntera resources ltd., Zakros holding ltd, foresight, providence resources,Birkbeck investment ltd., Exspan, Istech, jubilant energy, Welwyn resources.

1.6 Operating of Oil markets

Crude oil and refined products are commodities that trade on global commodity markets, such as those in London, New York and Singapore. Arguably, crude oil is the most actively traded and watched commodity in the world. Refined products, such as petrol and diesel, do not receive the same public profie, but are actively traded.

The market prices for curde oil and refined produts at any time are a function of current and future supply and demand conditons, and are asessed on a variety of scenarios. For crude oil, these include overall economic conditions, natural disasters and geopolitical or militiary events, especially in mojor oil producing regions. The price of curde oil affects the price of refined products (e.g. petrol and diesel) is often far important in influencing trading decisions, and determining the wholesale price of these commodities. Refinery outages, inclment weather, temporary surges or declines in demand – all have the potential to impact the supply and demand balance, and the resulting wholesale commodity price. As a result, wholesale (and consequently retail) petrol price can be increasing even when crude prices are decreasing and vice versa.

Benchmark

Because there are som many different varieities and grades of crude oil, buyers and sellers have established a number of 'benchmark' crude oils. Other crudes are prices at a discount or premium relative to these benchmark prices based on their quality. According to the International Petroleum Exchange, the price of Brent crude oil is used to price 2/3rd of the world's internationally traded crude oils. Brent is a light blend of four key crude oils from the North sea, and is generally accepted to be the world benchmark for oil, although sales volumes of Brent itself are far below those of some Saudi Arabian crudes. If no other information is given, reference to an oil price likelu cites the Brent price.

Effects of oil prices on economy

Crude oil price plays a very significant role on the economy of any country. India's growth story moves around the import of oil as India imports 70% of its crude oil requirements. This in turn results in spending huge amount of foreign exchange. The increasing quantum of imports of petroleum products has a significant effect on the Indian economy especially when crude oil prices are shooting up globally. Crude oil not only serves as a source of energy but also as major raw materials to various industries. Due to increase in oil prices, there will be a steep fall in current accounts, leads to further worsening of the treasury budgets, which will in turn further worsen balance between savings and investments also reducing tax revenues. In case of fixed nominal exchange rate, there is also an output gap, increase in oil price leads to increase in the general price level. ***According to RBI report (2005) for every unit dollar increase in crude oil prices, WPI (Wholesale Price Index) rises by 30 basis points.*** Historically there have been four oil shocks in past thirty years, in spite of this low inflationary pressure has been assisting the developed countries to counter the risk, on the other hand developing countries like India affected more due to absence of advanced technology to conserve more.

Future outlook of oil industry

Owing to the increasing use of shale gas and growing domestic production, US imports have been showing a decreasing trend and are likely to fall further also, ***the US became a net exporter of petroleum products in June 2011, for the first time since 1949.*** This development is likely to have a long term influence of moderating the price of sweet crude as reflected by benchmark such as Brent. The tentative upstick of economic activity in the US and Europe is unlikely to push up crude oil prices significantly, as such, the US has higher energy sufficiency and Europe has low crude oil dependence. Moderating growth in China could put downward pressure on crude oil prices. However the Organization of Petroleum Exporting countries (OPEC) may lower its output as it has done in the past, in the face of moderation in crude price. The Indian crude basket price may reduce the range of USD 2/bbl to USD 4/bbl. ***This along with moderation in consumption of petroleum products could beneficially impact India's 0il bill and the under recovery burden of Public Sector oil companies.***

OPEC is attributed to around 40% of global production, while the OPEC region is attributed around 60% of global traded crude volume. OPEC oil producers are essentially national oil companies which often adjust production levels to factors such global demand, oil production in non – OPEC field and global prices. The budgets of OPEC nations depend upon significantly on revenue from crude sales. As such, a crude price below USD 100/bbl may possibly draw a strong response from the OPEC nations, which may make downward adjustments to production level.

Geopolitical positives also going to benefit the future oil prices, improvements in political relations between the US and the two countries, IRAN and LIBYA, may improve the global supply of crude oil. However, Iran may not be able to immediately ramp up production to its historical levels. While in the past, Iran exported 2.2 million bpd, they fell to around 700,000 bpd in may 2013. ***India may benefit hugely from a sanction free Iran as the latter has been the second highest contributor to India's imports before sanctions were imposed.***

1. 7 OVERVIEW OF REFINERY INDUSTRY

Facilities and Processes

The oil and gas industry facilities and systems are broadly defined according to their use in the oil and gas industry production stream:

Exploration includes prospecting, seismic and drilling activities that take place before the development of a field is finally decided.

Upstream Typically refers to all facilities for production and stabilization of oil and gas. The reservoir and drilling community often uses upstream for the wellhead, well completion and reservoir only, and downstream of the wellhead as production or processing, Exploration and upstream production together is referred as E&P.

Midstream Broadly defined as gas treatment, LNG production and regasification plants, and oil and gas pipeline systems.

Refining where oil and condensates are processed into marketable products with defined specifications such as gasoline, diesel or feedstock for the petrochemical industry. Refinery offsites such as tank storage and distribution terminals are included in this segment, or may be part of as separate distribution operation.

Petrochemicals these products are chemical products where the main feedstock is hydrocarbons. Examples are plastics, fertilizers and a wide range of industrial chemicals.

REFINING

The easily available oil was not put to any mass use because the crude itself was not a good fuel, it gave out much soot and smoke. ***A distillation process using a retort was invented by Rhazes in Persia in the 9th century***, liquid heated in it vaporized, passed through a curved spout and condensed in another container. The process could be used to make kerosene, but it was more often used to make alcohol and essence of flowers for perfume. It was batch process, its fuel consumption was high, and it was not equally efficient at distilling kerosene from all crudes. A more efficient and reliable distillation processes came out of a series of inventions after 1846. ***The last invention was the invention of oil fractionation in 1854 by Benjamin Silman, a professor of Science in Yale***. It used a vertical column which separated components more efficiently, and which can be used continuously.

Refining aims to provide a defined range of products according to specifications. Simple refineries use a distillation column to separate crude into fractions, and the relative quantities are directly dependent on the crude uses. Therefore, it is necessary to obtain a range of crudes that can be blended to a suitable feedstock to produce the required quantity and quality of end products. The economic success of a modern refinery depends on its ability to accept almost any available crude. With a variety of processes such as cracking, reforming, additives and blending, it can provide product in quantity and quality to meet market demand. The refinery operations often include product distribution terminals for dispensing product to bulk customers such as air ports, petrol pumps, ports and industries.

Once discovered, drilled and brought to the earth's surface crude oil is transported to a refinery by pipeline, ship or both. At the refinery it is treated and converted into consumer and durable goods. There are three major refining processes that change crude oil into finished products.

.**Process of refining**

There are more than 150 different types of crude oil in the world. The basic choice of which crude to refine is between higher and heavier grades. Heavy grades have a higher proportion of heavier hydrocarbons composed of larger carbon chains. Heavy crude oils are cheaper and plenty, but more expensive to refine since they require significant investment and higher refining costs.

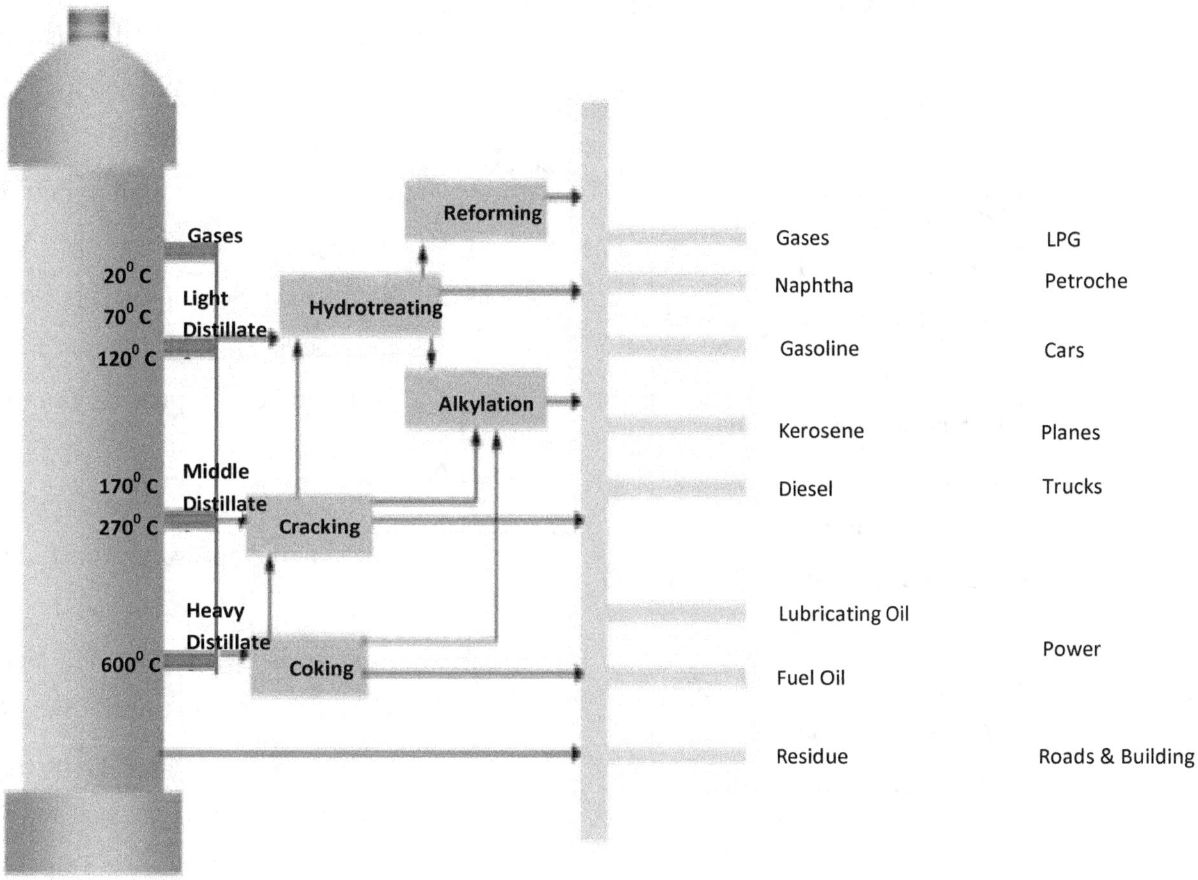

Figure 1.6 Process of refining

As Herrman observed, refining is "low return, low growth, capital intensive, politically sensitive and environmentally uncertain."

Once discovered, drilled and brought to the earth's surface, crude oil is transported to a refinery by pipeline, ship or both. At the refinery, it is treated and converted into consumer and industrial products. There are major refinery processes change crude oil into finished products:

Separation ⟶ Conversion ⟶ Purification

Separation

Table 1.9 What a barrel of crude oil makes.	
Product	**Gallons per Barrel**
Gasoline (petrol)	19.4
Distillate fuel oil *(includes domestic oil and diesel fuel)*	9.7
Kerosene type jet fuels	4.3
Coke	2.0
Residual fuel oil *(heavy oils used as fuels in industry, marine , transportation, and for electric power generation)*	1.9
Liquefied refinery gases	1.9
Still gas	1.8
Asphalt and road oil	1.4
Petrochemical feedstock	1.1
Lubricants	0.5
Kerosene	0.2
Others	0.4

The first step is to separate the crude oil into its naturally occurring components. This is known as separation and is accomplished by applying heat through a process is called distillation. Separation is performed in a series of distillation towers, with the bottom product from each tower feeding the next. A furnace in front of each distillation tower heats and vaporizes the crude oil mixture. The vapor and liquid mixture is then fed into the bottom section of the tower, the feed section is the hottest point in the distillation tower and can reach as high as 750 degrees Fahrenheit. Components that are still liquid at this elevated temperature become the tower's bottom product. Components that are in vapor form rise up the tower through a series of distillation stages. The temperature decreases as the vapors rise through the tower and components condense. The "yield" from a distillation tower refers to the relative percentage of each of the separated components, known as "product streams". This will vary according to the characteristics of the crude being processed. Because a liquid's boiling point decreases at lower pressure, the final distillation steps are performed in a vacuum to maximize liquid recovery. Products from the distillation tower range from gases at the top to the very heavy, viscous liquids at the bottom. In all cases, these product streams are still considered 'unfinished' and require further processing to become useful products.

Conversion

Distillation separates the crude oil into unfinished products. However, the products do not naturally exist in crude in the same proportions as the product mix that consumers demand. The biggest difference is that there is too little gasoline and too much heavy oil naturally occurring in crude oil. That is why conversion is so important. Their primary purpose is to convert low value heavy oil into high valued gasoline. All products in the refinery are based on the same building blocks, carbon and hydrogen chains, which are called hydrocarbons. The longer the carbon chain, the heavier the product will be. Converting heavier hydrocarbons to lighter hydrocarbons can be compared to cutting a link on a steel chain to make two smaller chains. In short it's a rearrangement of the molecules to add values.

Purification

Once crude oil has been through separation and conversion, the resulting products are ready for purification, which is principally sulfar removal. This is done by Hydrotreating, a process similar to hydrocracking but without converting heavy molecules into lighter ones. In hydrotreating, unfinished products are contacted with hydrogen under heat and high pressure in the presence of catalyst, resulting in hydrogen sulfide and desulfurized product. The catalyst accelerates the rate at which the sulfur removal occurs. In each case, sulfur removal is essential to meeting product quality specifications and environmental standards. Modern refinery and petrochemical technology can transform crude oil into literally thousands of useful products.

Meaning of Catalyst:

A material that helps to make a chemical reaction go faster, occur at lower temperature, or control which reactions occurred.

Oil does a lot more **than simple provide fuel for our cars and trucks. Keep our homes and offices comfortable, and power our industries. From lipstick to aspirin and diapers to roller blades, petrochemicals play a vital part here are few examples.**			
Antiseptics	Crayons	Golf Balls	Roofing
Aspirin	Dentures	House Paints	Shampoo
Baby strollers	Deodorant	Ink	Sunglasses
Balloons	Diapers	Jet fuel	Telephones
Cameras	DVDs	Medical Equipment	Tires
Candles	Footballs	Motor Oil	Toothpaste
CD players	Petrol	Perfumes	Toys
Clothing	Garbage bags	Photographs	Umbrellas
Compact Discs	Glue	Roller Blades	Vitamin Capsules

1.8 Basic Refinery Economics

In many businesses, profits or losses result primarily from the difference between costs of inputs and the price of outputs. In order to have a competitive edge, a business must make higher value products using lower cost inputs than competitors. In the oil refining business, the cost of inputs (crude oil) and the price of inputs (refined products) are both highly volatile, influenced by global, regional, and local supply and demand changes. Refineries must find the sweet spot against a backdrop of changing environmental regulation, changing demand patterns and increase global competition among refiners in order to profitable.

New builds V/s Upgrades

Oil refining is a capital intensive business. Planning, designing, permitting and building a new medium sized refinery is a 5-7 year process, and costs $ 7 billion, not counting acquiring the land (that's why Dhirubhai Ambani is legend, he started from grassroots). The cost varies depending on the locations, the type of crude to be processed and the range of outputs, both also affects the configuration and complexity of the refinery.

After the refinery is built, it is very expensive to operate. Fixed costs include personnel, maintenance, insurance, administration and depreciation. Variable costs include crude feedstock, chemicals and additives, catalysts, maintenance, utilities and purchased energy (such as natural gas and electricity). To be economically viable, the refinery must keep operating costs such as energy, labor and maintenance to a minimum. One should keep in mind that oil refineries are price takers: in setting their individual prices, they adapt to market prices.

Cost of inputs and Price of outputs

Since refineries have little or no influence over the price of their input or their output, they must rely on operational efficiency for their competitive edge. Because refining is caught between the volatile market segments of cost and price, it is exposed to significant risks. As ***Herman observed, refining is "low return, low growth, capital intensive, politically sensitive and environmentally uncertain."*** A refinery will close down if it cannot sustain its profitability. For e.g. in Canada more than 20 refineries have closed since 1970 due to shift to large more complex refineries and flat to declining prices. Following are the suggestions to improve the efficiency.

1. Select appropriate crude to fulfil anticipated product demand.
2. Increase the amount and value of product processed from the crude oil.
3. Reduce down time for maintenance, repair and investment.
4. Develop valuable by products or production inputs out of materials those are typically discarded.
5. Operating at a high utilization rate. When margins are high and conversely, reducing production and buying product from third parties when margins are low.

Crack spreads

The term 'Crack' comes from how a refinery makes money by breaking (or 'cracking') the long chain of hydrocarbons that make up crude oil into shorter chain petroleum products. The crack spread, therefore, is the difference between crude oil prices and wholesale petroleum product prices. Like most manufacturers, a refinery processes the raw materials it buys and the sells finished products. In the case of oil refining, both prices can fluctuate independently for short periods due to supply, demand, transportation and other factors. In 2008, for e.g. , crude oil prices increased almost 20% higher than the price of refined petroleum products. Since then, crude oil prices fell by nearly half, but prices for refined petroleum products are near their 2008 highs. Such short term volatility puts refiners at considerable risk when the price of one or the other rises or falls, narrowing profit margins and squeezing the crack spread. The crack spread is good approximation of the margin a refinery earns. Crack spreads are negative if the price of refined products falls below that of crude oil. A major determinant of a crack spread is the ratio of how much crude oil is processed into different refined petroleum products, because each type of crude more easily yields a different product, and each product has a different value. Some crude inherently produces more diesel or gasoline due its composition. These ratios and product combinations vary by region. The most common ratio in the US is 3 barrels of crude oil to produce 2 barrels of gasoline (petrol).

The determinants of profitability

For a common man, all refineries appear to be same. In reality each refinery is a unique and complex industrial facility, with some flexibility in the crude oils it can process and the mix of products it can refine. Each refinery constantly weighs a number of factors, including the type and amount of crude oil to process and the conditions under which various conversion units operate. However, there are limits to how flexible a refinery can be. The configuration and complexity of each facility determines the types of crude oil it can process and products it can produce. Location and transportation infrastructure further limit the degree to which a refinery can access various types of crude and other supplies. These factors impact energy and labor costs, as well as regulatory constraints and compliance costs.

Refinery size, configuration and complexity

Economies of scale are an important factor in refinery profitability – refinery size does matter. Larger facilities are more efficient, better able to withstand cyclical swings in business activity and they distribute fixed costs over a larger number of barrels. Refinery complexity also matters, especially since the trend is to heavier, more sour crudes and lighter products. There are several of complexities for refineries. The most publicly used is the Nelson Complexity Index (NCI) developed in the 1960s by Wilbur Nelson in a series of articles for the Oil and Gas Journal. The

NCI is a pure cost based index. It provides a relative measure of refinery construction costs based upon the distillation and upgrading capacity a refinery has. The increased demand for lighter petroleum products made from heavier crude oil requires more complex refineries. The complexity of a refinery refers to its ability to process crude oil into value added products. A simple refinery which is known as a 'topping' refinery is essentially limited to distilling crude oil. For e.g. making the raw material for gasoline and heavy fuel oil. A hydro – skimming refinery is also quite simple, with a NCI of about 2, and is mostly limited to processing light sweet crude into gasoline for motorists.

Table 1.10 World top largest oil refineries

Rank	Company	Location	Crude Capacity, barrels per calendar day (b/cd)
1.	Paraguana Refining Center	Cardon/Judibana, Falcon, Venezuela	940,000
2.	SK Corp.	Ulsan, South Korea	817,000
3.	GS Caltex Corp.	Yeosu, South Korea	750,000
4.	Reliance Petroleum Ltd. [merged with RIL since 2009]	Jamnagar, India	660,000
5.	ExxonMobil Refining & Supply Co.	Jurong/Pulau Ayer Chawan, Singapore	605,000
6.	Reliance Industries Ltd. [RIL]	Jamnagar, India	580,000
7.	S-Oil Corp.	Onsan, South Korea	565,000
8.	ExxonMobil Refining & Supply Co.	Baytown, Texas, USA	560,500
9.	Saudi Arabian Oil Co. (Saudi Aramco)	Ras Tanura, Saudi Arabia	550,000
10.	Formosa Petrochemical Co.	Mailiao, Taiwan	540,000
11.	ExxonMobil Refining & Supply Co.	Baton Rouge, Louisiana, USA	503,500

12.	Hovensa LLC	St. Croix, Virgin Islands, USA	500,000
13.	Kuwait National Petroleum Co.	Mina Al-Ahmadi, Kuwait	466,000
14.	Shell Eastern Petroleum (Pte) Ltd.	Pulau, Bukom, Singapore	462,000
15.	BP PLC	Texas City, Texas, USA	451,250

1.9 REFINING CAPACITY IN INDIA

The Indian refining industry has done exceedingly well in establishing itself as a major player globally. India is emerging as a refinery hub and refining capacity exceeds demand. The last decade has been tremendous growth in the sectors. The country's refining capacity has increased from a modest 62 million metric tonne per annum (MMPTA) in 1998 to 215.07 MMTPA as on 1st April 1014, and comprises of 22 refineries, with 17 under public sector, 3 under private and 2 under joint sectors, by the end of 12th five year plan refinery capacity is expected to reach 307.37 MMTPA. Refinery crude throughput (crude processed) for 2013-14 was about 222.70 MMT as against 219.21 MMT for the year 2012-13, showing a marginal increase of about 1.59%. During 2013-14, a total of 68.4 MMT for petroleum products, valued at Rs. 3,71,143 crore, was exported against 63.4 MMT, valued at rs. 3,20,000 crore, during 2012-13. Export of petroleum products during 2013-14 was higher by 7.9% and 16% in terms of quantity and value respectively, as compared to the previous year.

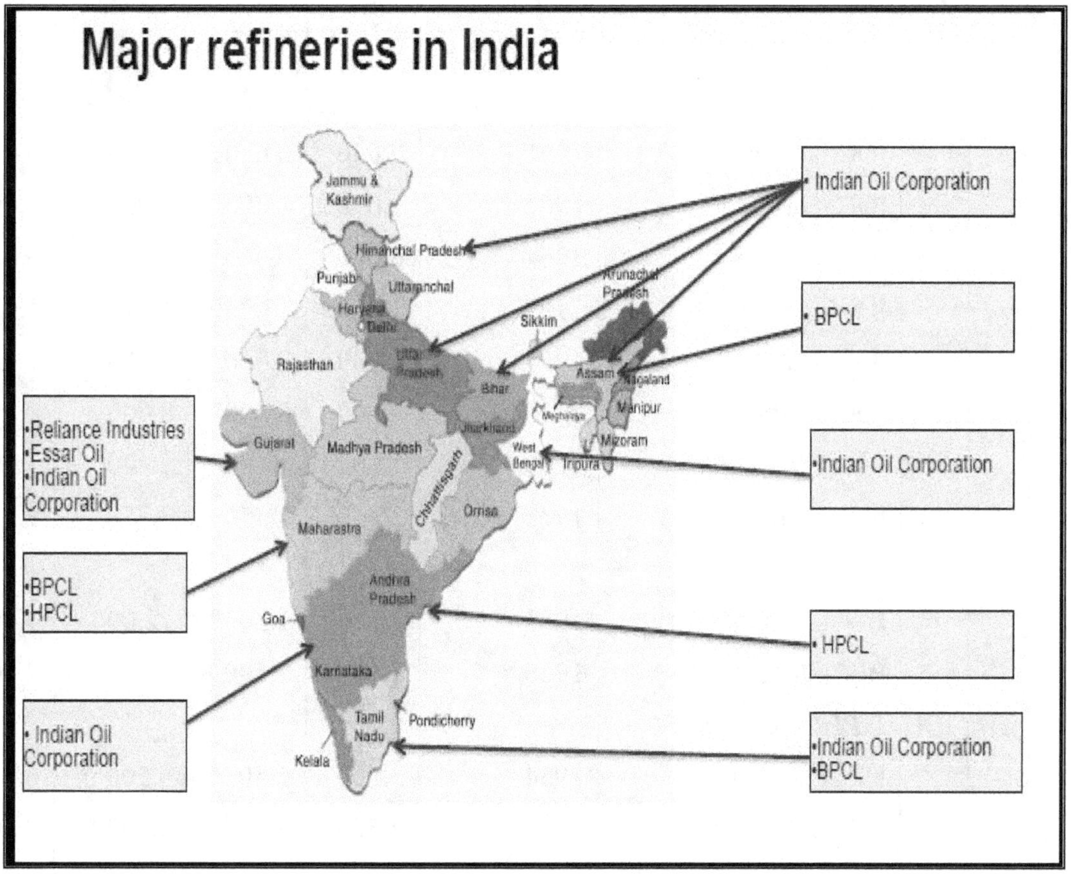

Figure 1.7 major refineries in India

TABLE 1.11 PETROLEUM REFINERY CAPACITY IN INDIA							
Sr. no.	**Refinery**	**Year of Estb.**	**31-3-2009**	**31-3-2010**	**31-3-2011**	**31-3-2012**	**31-3-2013**
A	**Public Sector**						
I	***IOCL Refineries***						
	IOC, Digboi	1901	0.650	0.650	0.650	0.650	0.650
	IOC, Guwahati	1962	1.000	1.000	1.000	1.000	1.000
	IOC, Barauni	1964	6,000	6,000	6,000	6,000	6,000
	IOC, Koyali	1965	13.700	13.700	13.700	13.700	13.700
	IOC, Haldia	1974	6.000	7.500	7.500	7.500	7.500
	IOC, Mathura	1982	8.000	8.000	8.000	8.000	8.000
	IOC, Panipat	1998	12.000	12.000	15.000	15.000	15.000
	IOC, Bongaigaon	1979	2.350	2.350	2.350	2.350	2.350
II	***BPCL Refineries***						
	BPCL, Mumbai	1955	12.000	12.000	12.000	12.000	12.000
	BPCl, Kochi	1966	7.500	9.500	9.500	9.500	9.500
III	***HPCL Refineries***						
	HPCL, Mumbai	1954	5.500	5.500	6.500	6.500	6.500
	HPCL, Visakh	1957	7.500	8.300	8.300	8.300	8.300
IV	***CPCL Refineries***						
	CPCL, Manali	1969	9.500	10.500	10.500	10.500	10.500
	CPCL, Nagapattinam	1993	1.000	1.000	1.000	1.000	1.000
V	***NRL, Numaligarh***	1999	3.000	3.000	3.000	3.000	3.000
VI	***ONGC, Tatipaka***	2002	0.066	0.066	0.066	0.066	0.066
VI	***MRPL, Mangalore***	1996	9.690	11.820	11.820	15.000	15.000
I	**Private Sector**						
B	***RPL Refineries***						
I	RIL, Jamnagar	1999	33.000	33.000	33.000	33.000	33.000
II	RIL (SEZ), Jamanagar	2008	27.000	27.000	27.000	27.000	27.000
	Essar Oil ltd., Vadinar	2006	10.500	10.500	10.500	18.000	20.000
C	**Joint Venture**						
I	BPCL, BORL – Bina	May, 2011				6.000	6.000
II	HMEL, Bathinda	April, 2012				9.000	9.000

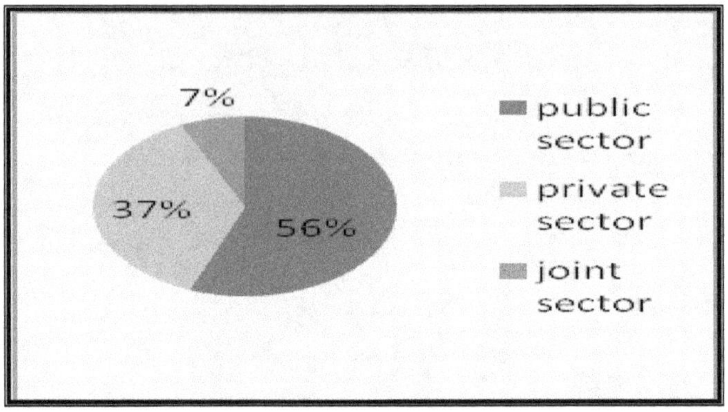

Figure 1.8 share of petroleum sectors companies in India

The above figure shows that public sector is dominating the refinery industry with 56% share in the total refining capacity. Whereas the share of joint venture is not much significant as it only consist of 7% of total refining. Private sector is playing a vital role and contributing significantly 37% in total refining capacity.

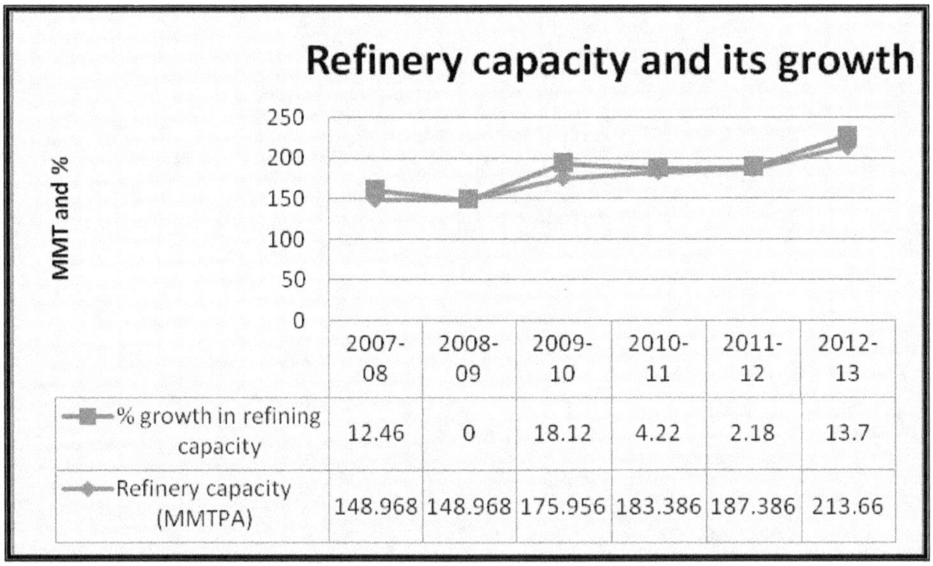

Figure 1.9 Refinery capacity and its growth

There has been considerabel increase in refining capapcity in the country over the years, although during 2013-14 there was no substantial capacity expansion. The refining capacity stood at 215.006 MMTPA. The growth was stable during 2008-09, after that it has turned table and noticed the highest growth of 18.12%

1.10. PRODUCTION AND CONSUMPTION OF PETRO PRODUCTS

With increase in refinery capacity, production of pertroleum products has increased substantially during last few years. During 2013-14, 67.864 MMT of petroleum products, valued at rs. 3,68,279 crore were exported. During the previous year 2012-13, export of these products was 63,408 MMT valued at Rs. 3,20,090 crore. Exports of petroleum products during 2013-14 were higher by 7.03% in terms of quantity and by 15.05% in terms of value,as compared to the previous year.

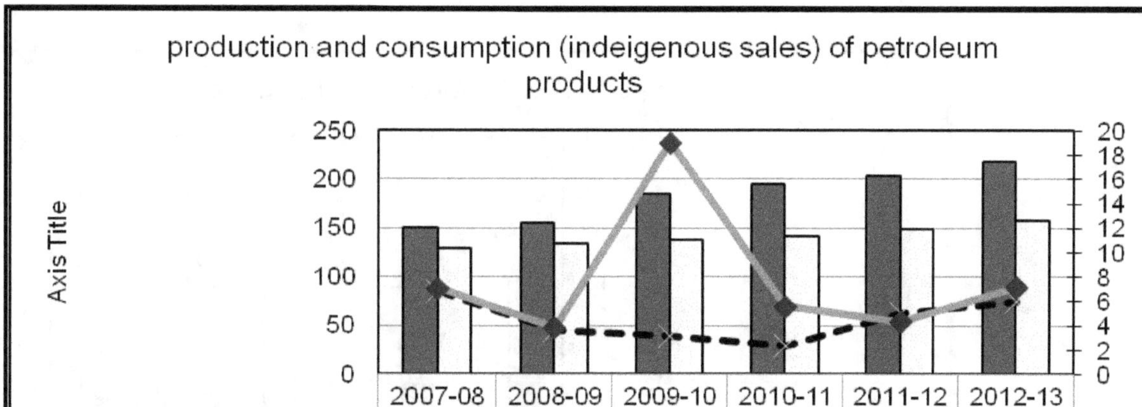

	2007-08	2008-09	2009-10	2010-11	2011-12	2012-13
production of petro products	149.472	155.148	184.608	194.821	203.202	217.736
consumption of petro products	128.946	133.599	137.808	141.4	148.132	157.057
% growth	6.79	3.61	3.15	2.35	5.03	6.02
% growth	7.02	3.8	18.99	5.53	4.3	7.15

Figure 1.10 Production and consumption of petroleum products

1.11 IMPORT AND EXPORT OF PETRO PRODUCTS

The quantity of pertroleum products improted during 2013-14 was 16.718 MMT valued at rs. 74,605 crore. During 2012-13, improts of these prodcts were 15.774 MMT valued at rs. 68,363 crore, improts of petroleum prodcuts increased by 5.98% in terms of quantity and increased by 9.13% in vlaue terms, as compared to the previous year.

During 2013-14, 13,032 MMT of LNG valued at rs. 53,307 crore, was imported, which marked decrease of 0.79% in quantity and 27.74% increase in value terms. The trend in quanity of petroluem products are given.

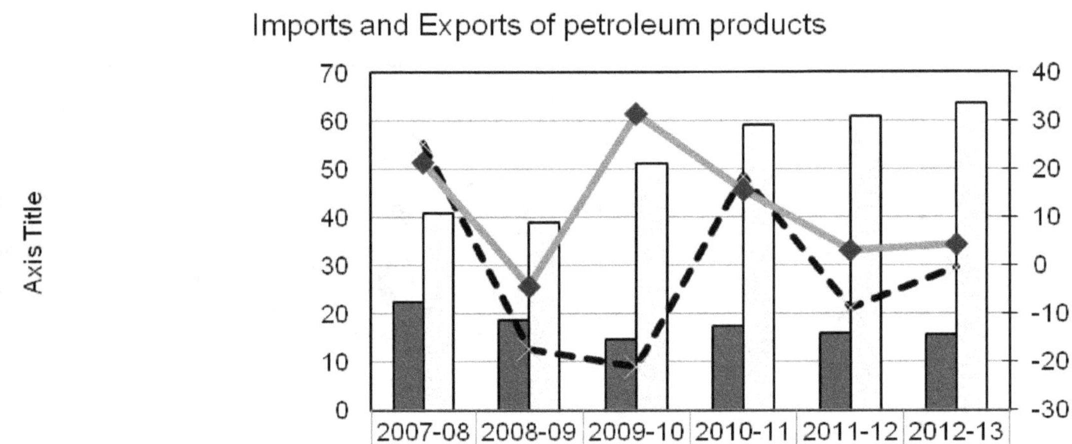

	2007-08	2008-09	2009-10	2010-11	2011-12	2012-13
imports of petroleum products	22.462	18.586	14.665	17.379	15.849	15.774
exports of petroleum products	40.779	38.944	51.155	59.077	60.837	63.408
% growth in imports of petroleum products	25.25	-17.26	-21.1	18.51	-8.8	-0.48
% growth in export of petroleum products	21.28	-4.5	31.35	15.49	2.98	4.23

Figure 1.11 imports and exports of petroleum products.

1.12 Annual growth rate of FDI in P&NG sector

The table shows movements of Foreign Direct Investment in India in context to Petroleum and Natural Gas Sector as compared to total investment in all sectors. In the year 2007-08 it was 56431 Rs.million and significantly 5.72% of the total investment. Which graduall decreased to 1.14% and 1.05% in the year 2008-09 and 2009-10 respectively. It shows some improvements in the year 2010-11 and 2011-12, by contibuting 2.61% and 6.03% in total investment, however it was the lowest in the 2012-13 i.e. 0.98%

TABLE 1.12 ANNUAL GROWTH OF FOREIGN DIRECT INVESTMENT (EQUITY)

Years	FDI inflow	P & NG Sector	% of FDI in P & NG to total FDI	Annual Growth (%)
(Amount in Rs. Million)				
2007-08	986420	56431	5.72	1331.68
2008-09	1428289	16333	1.14	-71.06
2009-10	1231196	12969	1.05	-20.6
2010-11	9730203	25431	2.61	96.09
2011-12	1651455	99551	6.03	291.45
2012-13	1219067	11925	0.98	-88.02

TABLE 1.13ESTIMATES OF CRUDE OIL PRODUCTION IN 12TH PLAN (2012-17)					
CRUDE OIL PRODUCTION (FIG. IN MMT)					
COMPANY	*2012-13	*2013-14	20147-15	2015-16	2016-17
ONGC	22561	22246	28002	26286	25456
OIL	3661	3466	4060	4160	4200
PVT/JV	11640	12076	12700	12100	11500
TOTAL	37862	37788	44762	42546	41156
*ACTUAL *(SOURCE : WORKING GROUP REPORT OF THE P&NG SECTOR (2012-17))*					

From the given table it is clear that ONGC has been increasing its crude oil production capacity along with OIL and other PVT and joint ventures. This surely contributing to the total demand of oil in the country. Due to high demand and low supply, and for growth and development, infrastructural needs it is very essential for developing company like India to increase its future outlook of production of crude.

BIBLIOGRAPHY

- Energy statistics 2014, 21st issue
- Indian Rating and Research – Fitch Group 2014 outlook
- Pratiyogita darpan july 2014 issue, vol 34
- Indicus Analytics New Delhi issue January 2009
- The Economics of Petroleum Refining Understanding the business of processing crude oil into fuels and
- Other value added products December 2013.
- Petroleum and Natural Gas statistics 2014
- Simple guide to oil refining by Exxon mobil.
- CRISIL CRB – Customized Research Bulletin June July 2012

INDEX

Sr. No	Title	Page No
2.1	Introduction	48
2.2	Oil Industry In India	48
2.3	Concept Of Profitability	48
2.4	Concept Of Liquidity	49
2.5	Literature review	49
2.6	Rationale Of The Study	53
2.7	Scope Of The Study	54
2.8	Universe Of The Study	55
2.9	Sampling design	55
2.10	Sources and collection of data	55
2.11	Sample Size	55
2.12	Objective Of The Study	56
2.13	Hypothesis	56
2.14	Analysis of data	57
2.15	Contents of study	58
2.16	Limitations of Study	59

2.1 AN INTRODUCTION TO OIL INDUSTRY IN INDIA

The origin of oil & gas industry in India can be traced back to 1867 when oil was struck at Makum near Margherita in Assam. At the time of Independence in 1947, the Oil & Gas industry was controlled by international companies. India's domestic oil production was just 250,000 tonnes per annum and the entire production was from one state - Assam.

This small amount of production made the oil experts from different countries predict the future of the oil industry as a dull one and also doubted India's ability to search for new oil reserves. But the Government of India declared the Oil industry in India as the core sector industry under the Industrial Policy Resolution bill in the year 1954, which helped the Oil Industry in India vastly.

2.2 OIL INDUSTRY IN INDIA

Oil exploration and production in India is done by companies like NOC or National Oil Corporation, ONGC or Oil and Natural Gas Corporation and OIL who are actually the oil companies in India that are owned by the government under the Industrial Policy Rule. The National Oil Corporation during the 1970s used to produce and supply more than 70 percent of the domestic need for the petroleum but by the end of this amount dropped to near about 35 percent. This was because the demand on the one hand was increasing at a good rate and the production was declining at a steady rate.

2.3 CONCEPT OF PROFITABILITY

The word 'profitability' is composed of two words, namely; profit and ability. The term profit has already been discussed at length in detail. The term ability indicates the power of a firm to earn profits. The ability of an enterprise also denotes its earning power or operating performance.Also that the business ability points towards the financial and operational ability of the business. So, on this basis profitability may be defined as —the ability of a given instrument to earn a return from its use ***Weston and Brigham defines profitability as "the net surplus of a large number of policies and decisions."*** Profit being an absolute figure fails to indicate the adequacy of income or changes in efficiency resulting from financial and operational performance of an enterprise. Much difficulty and confusion comes home while interpreting the absolute figures of profit in case of historical or inter-firm comparisons due to variation in the size of investment or volume of sales etc. Such problems are handled by relating figures of profit either with the volume of sales or with the level of investment. A quantitative relationship is thereof established either in the form of ratios or percentages. Such ratios are names as profitability ratios. Thus, profitability may be regarded as a relative term measurable in terms of profit and its relation with other elements that can directly influence the profit.

Profitability = Operating Income / Operating Assets

2.4 CONCEPT OF LIQUIDITY

By the term 'liquidity' is meant the debt-repaying capacity of an undertaking. It refers to the firm's ability to meet the claims of suppliers of goods, services and capital. According to Archer and D'Ambrosio, liquidity means cash and cash availability, and it is from current operations and previous accumulations that cash is available, to take care of the claims of both the short-term suppliers of capital and the long-term ones. It has two dimensions; the short-term and the long-term liquidity

2.5 LITERATURE REVIEW

Walker (1980) risk means (a) risk of not maintaining adequate liquidity ; (b) risk of having too much or too little inventory to maintain production and sales; (c) the risk of not granting adequate credit to support the proper level of sales. Profitability is the prime factor considered for the purpose of wealth maximization objective.

Khandelwal (1985) conducted a study on small scale industries in Jodhpur industrial estate for the period 1975-76 to 1979 -80 to highlight their working capital management policies. In this study, 40 multi group units were selected on the basis of purposive sampling from 162 small scale units. The relevant data were collected from secondary sources. The study revealed that the immediate liquidity position of the selected unit was not at all satisfactory during the period under study.

Venkatachalam and Murthy (1986) made a study to find out the working capital position and its impact on liquidity position of the medium and large public limited companies in India for the period 1973-74 to 1982-83. The data were collected from RBI monthly bulletins. The study concluded that the liquidity status of the medium and large public limited companies was not all impressive.

Misra and Khan (1990) undertook a study on working capital management of Electronic Corporation of India Ltd. (ECIL) for the period 1983-84 to 1985-86. The study exhibited that a major portion of funds was invested in current assets. It ultimately generated idle liquid funds in the hands of ECIL, which in turn produced low return in the company.

Jain (1993) undertook a study to analyze the working capital management of seven selected paper companies belonging to both public sector and private sector in India. The study showed that the current ratio of the private sector paper companies registered a declining trend during the study period, whereas this ratio was found to be highly fluctuating in the public sector paper companies.

Soenen (1993), examined the relationship between the net trade cycle as a measure of working capital and return on investment in US firms using chi – square test showed a negative relationship between the length of net trade cycle and return on assets.

Lamberson (1995) analyzed the relationship between liquidity and bankruptcy cost by applying linear regression on panel data of 223 US firms for the period 1979 to 1981. This study revealed that the liquidity ratios were positively related to the bankruptcy cost, but negatively related to financial leverage.

Reddy and Rao (1996) in their study made an attempt to examine the working capital management practices in Hindustan Cables Limited (HCL), a public enterprise on the assumption that working capital policies had a great effect on a firm's liquidity and profitability. The study was based on the data and information obtained from the annual reports of HCL form 1989-90 to 1993-94. The study demonstrated that the company maintained its current ratio and quick ratio above the conventional standard of 2:1 and 1:1 respectively.

Weinarab and Visscher (1998) examined the working capital investment and financing pattern of US industries over a period of ten years, form 1984 to 1993. The sample consisted of 15 to 33 companies from ten diverse industry groups. The study looked at to evaluate the relative relationship between the industries' aggressive and conservative working capital policies. The study concluded that the aggressive policy registered higher expectation of higher profitability but greater liquidity risk, whereas a mere conservative policy showed a greater proportion of capitl in liquid assets but at the sacrifice of profitability.

Ramesh and Patil (1999) conducted a study on Goa Urban Cooperative Bank Limited to evaluate liquidity, productivity and profitability for the period 1985-86 to 7996-97 by analyzing the necessary data and information collected from the annual reports of the bank. The study shows that the bank maintained adequate level of liquid funds to meet its short term obligation during the period of study.

Rajeshwari (2000) undertook an effort to evaluate the liquidity management of Tamilnadu Cement Corporation Ltd. For the period 1993-94 to 1997-98. The study concluded that the liquidity position of the company was highly volatile and also not at all satisfactory during the study period.

Butalal C. Ajmera (2001) has done his dissertation "interpretation and analysis of financial statement of two selected units of Birla group", in the year 2001 by using conceptual framework of financial statement, Research plan, profile of the cement industry. Birla group of companies a bird eye view, liquidity position, financial structure and suggestion, the period of 1994-95 to 1998-99. The study reveals the course of profitability.

Dr. S. J. Parmar (2001) Published a book in 2001. The book is a systematic study of the modern financial measurement techniques useful for management in planning and controlling corporate activities. With increasing participation by the general public and financial institution as present and corporate bodies have to be on their guard and manage their efficient financial efficiency in the area of globalization. This book covers topics of concept and measurement of profitability, cost & sales trend, profit margin, assets turnover, analysis of return on investment common size of value added statements.

Yadav, Jain and Rastogi (2001) in their paper assessed the effect of working capital management on liquidity of the three blue chip public sector oil companies in India. BPCL, HPCL and IOCL for the period 1987-88 to 1991-92. The data were taken from the secondary sources. The final findings of the study was that the liquidity position of BPCL was lesser satisfactory in post liberalization period as compared to the other selected companies.

Dr. Miss Kailash P. Damor (2002) has done research on "A comparative analysis of profitability trends in co-operative sugar industry of India" in the year 2002. In her research she has given clear idea about profit and profitability. Profit means; "it is an excess of Income over expenses." Profitability means "it is a capacity of earning profit." Profitability is related with two words, Profit and Ability. We discuss the word profit in many senses but the word profit is used as per its purpose, where as the ability shows the capability of earning profit from business. Profitability also shows our capacity of how much return we can give to our investors on their investment.

Deloof (2003) found significant negative relationship between gross operating income and number of days account receivables, inventories and account payables.

DR. Sanjay Bhayani (2003) Published a book in 2003 "Practical Financial Statement Analysis". The study covered 16 public limited cement companies in private sector. He made study of analysis of profitability, working capital, Capital structure and activity of Indian Cement industry. In his research he revealed various problems of Cement Industries and suggested remedied for the problem. He also suggested for the improvement of profitability and techniques of cost control.

Eljelly (2004) evaluate the relationship between profitability and liquidity measured by the current ratio and cash gap on sample of joint stock companies of Saudi Arabia, using correlation and regression analysis revealed that Cash Conversion Cycle is more important than current ratio

DR. Rasik N. Bavaria (2004) has completed his research on "A comparative analysis of profitability vis-à-vis Liquidity performance in cement industry of India" in the year 2004. He has given importance of profitability and liquidity; by the term 'Liquidity' is meant the debt- repaying capacity of an undertaking. It refers to the firm's ability to meet the claims of suppliers of goods services and capital. Study of financial statement analysis is always made objectively. Generally, the external analyst uses the information as per his requirements. Financier would like to know profitability. Management would be interested in the operational efficiency and profitability. Position of the management profitability vis-à-vis liquidity should also balance in the portfolio. But if the management likes profitability, liquidity becomes less and if the liquidity is liked more the profitability gets less, for a short period of time. In the long run both will go together.

Mukhopadhyay (2004) in his paper reviewed the working capital management of a Kolkatta based century old a heavy engineering company with special reference to its short term liquidity and solvency for the period 1993-94 to 2002-03. In this study, the interpretation of several ratios reflected that the interest of the short term creditors of the company was not at all protected by adequate liquidity.

Vishnani and Shah (2006) empirically examined the relation between liquidity and profitability in Indian Consumer Electronics Industry for a period of ten years from 1994-95 to 2004-05. For this study, 23 listed companies were selected and relevant data were collected from CMIE database. Out of 23 companies, nine companies showed negative association between liquidity and profitability whereas remaining companies registered a positive association between two variables.

DR. Harish P. Desai (2006) He has done his Ph.D. on "Financial performance appraisal of selected district dairies co-operative in Gujarat" in may 2006. Under this study he has made a modest attempt in assessing the financial health of the selected co-operative dairy units by applying accounting tools and techniques of the date of nine district co-operative dairy unions in Gujarat State. For this purpose he has used many accounting tools and techniques like common size statement, Ratio analysis, etc. He has also used some statistical techniques like, mean, Regression, F-test, T-test, Diagrammatic and graphic presentation of data.

Zakaria (2009) made an attempt to measure static and dynamic liquidity of Malaysian small and medium enterprise, this study addressed the issue of examining the relationship between earnings, cash flow and corporate liquidity; the study indicated that both earnings and cash flow had effects on corporate liquidity in small and medium business in Malaysia.

Garcia – Teruel and Martinez – Solano (2007) showed that there was an inverse relationship between working capital and firm's profitability.

DR. Shivubhai C. Vala (2011) he has done his Ph.D. on "A comparative study of profitability vis-a-vis liquidity of co-operative milk producers unions of Gujarat state." in February – 2011. Under this study he has given clear idea and importance of profitability and liquidity. By the term liquidity is meant the debt – repaying capacity of an undertaking. It refers to the firm's ability to meet the claims of suppliers of goods services and capital. For this purpose he has used many accounting tools and techniques like common size statement, Ratio analysis etc. He has also used some statistical techniques like mean, regression, F-test, T-test, Diagrammatic and graphic presentation of data

2.6 RATIONALE OF THE STUDY

As earlier mentioned in the introduction the industry is core industry and it has a very large investment of the country. So it can be said that the large investments are blocked in the refineries undertaken for the study for the research purpose, it has been many reason for the significance of the study. The significance of the study is as follows: 1) If analysis is done in various aspects like liquidity, profitability, assets utilization, the relevant information can be furnished to its various users for their decision making. 2) It is also necessary to find out some important factors which affect internal decision of industry. So this research will be useful to refinery industry itself. 3) As far as many financial and non financial institute and also government affects by its various financial aspects, its various ratios should be analyzed and the most common factors affecting refineries' financial position should be studied. So researcher feels its necessity and importance and therefore has chosen this subject for her doctoral research purpose. 4) Privatization is taking place in the oil sector. So, there should not be monopolization of any unit and competitiveness should be increased of all the unit. To create this situation, every unit should find out their financial position and various factors which affects to their financial condition. This study will help to create this type of condition. 5) A large mass of the country even from housewife to businessman has started to invest their money in the share markets. So financial analysis will be helpful to them to take proper decision to invest their money in these sectors. 6) Petroleum is a natural product and its sources are very limited. But the demand of petroleum product is increasing day by day. Oil demand grew by an average of 7.7% per year in last few years. For this, government should control his profitability and rate of oil prices. So if the data should be analyses financially. Moreover profitability and other financial aspects can be taken into the notice of this core industry. 7) Energy industry is obviously one of the most critical areas. Improving India's energy infrastructure requires a massive increase in investment in all the sub sectors. It also requires much greater level of efficiency to ensure low cost and good quality of service. So, to improve the level of efficiency analyzed data of this research will be necessary. 8) The thesis will be a guiding path for the analysis of the study of the units which are not undertaken for this research. 9) Saurashtra University M.phil. students has undertaken the research study by taking two refineries and tried to make financial analysis of relevant data. So by undertaking the 7 units for the research purpose it will be the further analysis of the industry.

2.7 SCOPE OF THE STUDY

The scope or area of the study includes the analysis of profitability vis a vis liquidity of oil refinery industry in india for the period of 2007-08 to 2012-13. The research has been focused on top seven refinery companies on the basis of paid up capital as on 31st march 2012

2.8 UNIVERSE OF THE STUDY

The universe of the study consists of all the limited oil refinery companies working in India and listed in Bombay Stock Exchange.

2.9 SAMPLING DESIGN

There are total numbers of 21 oil refinery companies working in India, out of which 17 are public sector units, 3 are private sectors and 1 is Joint Venture Company. The sample of six oil refinery were selected considering the following factors

- Listed on Bombay Stock exchange
- Paid up capital during the year as on year ended 31st march 2012
- For the period form 2007-08 to 2012-13.

2.10 SOURCES AND COLLECTION OF DATA

The main source of data was published financial reports, statistical figures, economic survey; central statistical organization survey etc, for the purpose of research secondary data will be considered.

2.11 SAMPLE SIZE

Out of the 21 oil refinery companies following six companies on the bases of their paid up capital (as on 31st March 2012) were selected for the research work.

Following companies were selected

Sr.no.	Company name	*Paid up capital (Rs.Cr)
1	ONGC	4277.76
2	RIL	3271
3	IOCL	2427.95
4	MRPL	1752.60
5	BPCL	361.54
6	HPCL	338.63

(*paid up capital as on 31-3-2012)

2.12 OBJECTIVE OF THE STUDY

Objectives of the present study are:

1. To analyze the liquidity position of selected refinery units
2. To analyze the profitability position of selected refinery units
3. To analyze liquidity vis a vis profitability position of selected refinery units
4. To establish and analyze the corelatinship among different ratios of selected refinery units

2.13 HYPOTHESIS

H0 = There is no any significant difference between profitability trends of refinery companies in india

H1 = There is significant difference between profitability of refinery companies in india

H0 = There is no any significance difference in liquidity of refinery companies in India

H1 = There is significance difference in liquidity of refinery companies in india

H0 = There is no significant relationship between profitability vis a vis liquidity ratios of refineries company in India.

H1 = There is significant relationship between profitability vis a vis liquidity ratios of refineries company in India.

2.14 ANALYSIS OF DATA

For the analysis of data, various tools techniques were taken into consideration, for analytical purpose ratio analysis was used. For checking profitability position of the company's gross profit, net profit, return on capital employed, earning per share, dividend per share, return on net worth ratios were used. Further, for verifying significance level F test was used. While to verify liquidity position of the company's current ratio, quick ratio, inventory turnover, debtors turnover, debt to equity, fixed assets turnover ratio were used, to evaluate significance level, F test was used.

Table 3.1 Analysis of variance table for one way ANOVA

Source of variation	**Sum of squares (SS)**	**Degree of freedom (d.f.)**	**Mean squares (MS)**	**F – Ratio**
Between samples or categories	$n_1 (\bar{x}_1 - \bar{\bar{x}})^2 +$ $n_k (\bar{x}_k - \bar{\bar{x}})^2$	(k-1)	$\frac{SS\ between}{(k-1)}$	$\frac{MS\ between}{MS\ within}$
Within sample or categories	$\sum(x_{1i} - \bar{x}_1)^2 +$ $\sum(x_{ki} - \bar{x}_k)^2$	(n-k)	$\frac{SS\ within}{(n-k)}$	
Total	$\sum(x_{ij} - \bar{\bar{x}})^2$ i = 1, 2, … j = 1, 2, …	(n – 1)		

(source : Research Methodology by C.R.Kothari)

While comparing profitability vis a vis liquidity position of companies, liquidity – profitability matrix was constructed, to further evaluating interrelationship multiple correlation was used. To verify interrelationship significance t test was applied.

2.15 CONTENTS OF STUDY

The researcher has divided the research work under following different chapters

Chapter-1 Overview of Oil sector

The overview of oil sector will preferably focus on refinery industry, its development in world as well as in India. Meaning of petroleum, different process like extraction, exploration and transportation of petroleum, importance, The current prospects of this sector. The researcher has provided in depth explanation about the development of oil industry in all the three segments like Extraction, Exploration and transporations.

Chapter-2 Research Methodology

Research methodology included how the research work was carried out. It also included the major parts like problem definition, objectives of study, hypothesis, data collection, period of the study, universe of the study etc.

Chapter-3 Sample profile

Under this part researcher has explained about the different refineries along with their history, production details. This part provided the complete information about the sample taken for the research work.

Chapter-4 Profitability analysis

Under this part, the researcher has considered the different tools and techniques to determine the profitability of the sample taken for research work, the researcher has also used different ratios like gross profit ratio, net profit ratio, dividend per share etc and F test was used to verify significance.

Chapter-5 Liquidity analysis

This part of research work included the liquidity analysis of the sample taken with the use different type of ratios and others techniques of research work. Different ratios like current ratio, liquidity ratio, solvency ratio, interest coverage ratio etc were considered F test was used to verify significance.

Chapter-6 Comparison of profitability and liquidity and its evaluation

This chapter dealt with the analysis of profitability vis a vis liquidity of the selected refinery industry in India. It has been done with the help of different analytical tools and statistical techniques.

Chapter-7 Summary and suggestions

This chapter provides emerging conclusion based upon the analysis carried out and point out the variations if any from the literature. It provides concrete suggestions for enhancing liquidity and profitability for financial soundness, cost control and liquidity position.

2.16 LIMITATIONS OF STUDY

The study is based upon the secondary data taken from published annual accounts and reports of selected companies

There are different methods to measure the profitability and liquidity of an industry in these context views of experts can differ from one to another.

The study is limited to period from 2007-08 to 2012-13.

BIBLIOGRAPHY

1. Deloof M. (2003). Does working capita magement affect profitability of Belgian firms? journal of business, finance and accounting, 30(3&4), April/May, 573-587.
2. Eljelly A.(2004). Liquidity- profitability tradeoff; An empirical investigation in an emerging market. International journal of commerce and management, 14(2), 48-61.
3. Garcia – Teruel, P.J., & Martinez – Solano P.(2007). Effects of working capital mangment on SME profitability. International journal of managerial finance, 3(2),164-186.
4. Jain, P.K. (1993): Management of working capital, RBSA publishers, Jaipur, India 1993.
5. Jose.M.L., Lancaster & Stevens (1996). Corporate returns and cash conversion cycle. Journal of economics and finance, 20(1),33-46.
6. Khandelwal, N.M., (1985): working capital management in small scale industries, ashish publishing house, New Delhi.
7. Lamberson, M. (1995): changes in working capital of small firms in relation to changes in economic activity, mid amreican journal of Business, vol.10, no.2, pp 45-50.
8. Lazaridis, I., & Tryfonidis, D. (2006). Relationship between working capital management and profitability of listed companies in the Athens Stock exchange. Journal of financial management and analysis, 19(1), 26-35.
9. Mishra, R.K. and Khan, N.C. (1990): Management of working capital in ECIL, journal of accounting and finance, vol 4, no.3, pp 22-28.
10. Mukhopadhay, D. (2004): working capital management in heavy engineering firms – a case study, the management accountant, vol.39, no.4, pp.317-323.
11. Rajeshwari, N. (2000): liquidity management of Tamilnadu cement corporation ltd. – a case study, the management accountant, vol.35, no.5, pp 377-378.
12. Ramesh, B. and Patil, M.R. (1999): liquidity, productivity and profitability analysis of Goa urban cooperative bank ltd – a SWOT analysis. The management accountant, march 1999,pp 176-178.
13. Reddy, P.I and Rao, K.S. (1996): Working capital management in public sector undertakings – a case study. The management accountant vol. 31, no.9, pp 643-645.
14. Soenen, L.A. (1993). Cash conversion cycle and corporate profitability. Journal of cash management,13(4),53-58.
15. Venkatachalam and Murthy, D. (1986):. Working capital trends in Indian Private corporate sector, Indian management, june 1986, pp 30-38.
16. Vishnani, S. and Shah, B.K. (2006): liquidity vs. profitability – a detailed study in perspective of Indian consumer electronics industry Pranjana, vol.9, no.2, pp. 25-30.

17. Yadav, S., Jain, P.K., and Rastogi, A.K. (2001): working capital management in oil industry in India, the management accountant, vol.36, no.7, pp 511-527.
18. Weinraub, H.J and Visscher, S.(1998): Industry practice relating to aggressive conservative working capital policies, journal of financial and strategic decisions, vol.11, no.2, pp. 11-18.
19. Walker, E.W. (1980). Towards a theory of working capital. In K.V.Smith (Ed.), reading on the mangment of working capital (pp.22-33). Mc-Grow Hill, NY, West publishing company.
20. Zakaria, N.K. (2009): Dynamic and static corporate liquidity measurement – a case of Malaysian small and medium enterprise, international journal of mangament and enterprise development, vol.6, no. 4/2009, pp 479-493.

INDEX

Sr.no.	Title	Page no.
3.1	Bharat Petroleum Corporation Ltd (BPCL)	63
3.2	Hindustan Petroleum Corporation Ltd (HPCL)	65
3.3	Indian Oil Corporation Ltd (IOCL)	67
3.4	Mangalore Refinery and Petrochemicals Limited (MRPL)	70
3.5	Oil and Natural Gas Corporation Limited (ONGC)	73
3.6	Reliance Industries Ltd (RIL)	76
3.7	Guwahati Refinery (Assam) – Indian Oil Corporation Limited (IOCL)	82
3.8	Barauni Refinery (Bihar) – Indian Oil Corporation Limited (IOCL)	82
3.9	Koyali Refinery (Gujarat) – Indian Oil Corporation Limited (IOCL)	83
3.10	Haldia Refinery (West Bengal) – Indian Oil Corporation Limited	83
3.11	Mathura Refinery (Uttar Pradesh) – Indian Oil Corporation Limited.	85
3.12	Digboi Refinery (Assam) – Indian Oil Corporation Limited. (IOCL)	85
3.13	Panipat Refinery (Haryana) – Indian Oil Corporation Limited. (IOCL)	87
3.14	Bongaigaon Refinery (Assam) – Indian Oil Corporation Limited	88
3.15	Mangalore Refinery (KARNATAKA) – Manglore Refinery and Petrochemicals Ltd. (MRPL)	89
3.16	Tatipaka Refinery (Andhar Pradesh) – Oil and Natural Gas Corporation Limited (ONGC)	90
3.17	Reliance Industries Limited (Domestic Tariff Area) (RIL- DTA) (Private Sector), JAMANAGAR (GUJARAT)	90
3.18	Reliance Industries Limited – SEZ (RIL – SEZ) (Private Sector), JAMNAGAR (GUJARAT)	90

3.1 BHARAT PETROLEUM CORPORATION LTD (BPCL)

Bharat Petroleum Corporation Ltd (BPCL) operates in the petroleum industry in India. The company operates in a single segment - Refinery and Marketing activities, which includes Downstream petroleum sector. They are also engaged in the Exploration and Production of Hydrocarbons (E&P). BPCL on a regular basis imports their LPG requirements mainly from the Middle East. Occasional there are import requirements of Gasoil, Kerosene, Gasoline and Base Oil. The company refineries consist of Mumbai Refinery, Kochi Refinery, Numaligarh Refinery and Bina Refinery. BPCL exports Fuel Oil and Naphtha and Base Oil (Group II).

Bharat Petroleum Corporation Ltd was incorporated on November 3, 1952 as a private limited company with the name Burmah Shell Refineries Ltd. The company began their work on the marshland of Trombay at Bombay. The refinery on 454 acres of land at village Mahul went on-stream on 30th January 1955, one year ahead of schedule. In January 24, 1976, Burmah Shell Group of Companies was taken over by the Government of India to form Bharat Refineries Ltd. In August 1, 1977, the company was renamed as Bharat Petroleum Corporation Ltd. The company was also the first refinery to process newly found indigenous crude (Bombay High), in the country.

During the year 2001-02, the company commissioned the Gas Turbine and Heat Recovery Steam Generator project at a cost of Rs.1750 million. Refinery Modernization Project was being implemented at a cost of Rs 18,310 million. This project besides improve distillate yield and energy efficiency of the company. The company had Allied Retail Business (ARB) also apart from the regular business, making them not only the largest non-fuel revenue generator in the oil industry, but also amongst the leading retail networks in the country, offering a basket of services ranging from C-stores, Quick Service Restaurants to financial and travel related services.

The total of 8 numbers of In & Out convenience stores made up the 'millionaire club' by clocking average sales of Rs 1 million per month. Automatic Teller Machines (ATMs) continued by the company to be a focus area in the ARB initiative under the alliance management strategy. The 222 ATMs in the network are the result of alliances with 22 banks. Given the rapid growth of the travel industry in the country and especially personal travel, the company launched 'In & Out e-Traveller', a one-stop facility for all travel and hospitality needs in during year of 2006-07. The In & Out eTraveller is an e-ticketing / e-booking facility for rail, air and bus tickets and hotel accommodation, brought through a web of alliances with best in breed travel service providers.

During the year 2009-10, the Mumbai refinery processed the Nigerian crude oil - Agbami for the first time. The company started operations at its Bina refinery in the central Indian state of Madhya Pradesh by launching their crude distillation unit, or CDU. The CDU at Bina was commissioned on June 29, 2010. Kerosene and cooking gas have been despatched to the marketing terminal. An oil refinery's CDU is the main unit where crude is separated into different petroleum products.

In August 2010, Indian Oil Corporation Ltd, Bharat Petroleum Corporation Ltd and Hindustan Petroleum Corporation Limited entered into a memorandum of understanding (MoU) with Gujarat State Petroleum Corp Ltd to form a joint venture for trunk gas pipelines. In February 2011, the company signed an initial agreement with the provincial government of Rajasthan to sell fuel products from the state's proposed refinery. The company will sell at least 75% of the volume of the products from the proposed Rajasthan refinery under the agreement.

In July 2011, the company sold a rare naphtha cargo from Haldia to Vitol at steep discounts of $63.00 a tonne to Middle East quotes on a free-on-board (FOB) basis, and the refiner may have more of such cargoes for sale.

The company plans to rise the capacity at its just commissioned Bina refinery in Madhya Pradesh to nine million tonne and is looking at the right time for a public offering of the unit. The company is planning to bid for city-gas projects in Kochi (Kerala) and Hyderabad (Andhra Pradesh) and plans to launch 600 new fuel retail outlets this fiscal, according to S Vardarajan, director, corporate finance. The company has lined up investments of Rs 50,000 crore ($11 billion) to expand their capacities in refining, retail and upstream projects over the next five years

3.2 HINDUSTAN PETROLEUM CORPORATION LTD (HPCL)

Hindustan Petroleum Corporation Ltd, a fortune 500 company, is one of the major integrated oil refining and marketing companies in India. The company is a Mega Public Sector Undertaking (PSU) with Navaratna status. The company operates in two business segments: Downstream, and exploration and production of hydrocarbons. The Downstream segment is engaged in refining and marketing of petroleum products. They operate two coastal refineries, one at Mumbai (West Coast) of 6.5 million metric tonnes per annum (MMTPA) and the other in Vishakapatnam, (East Coast) with a capacity of 8.3 MMTPA. They also hold an equity stake of 16.95% in Mangalore Refinery & Petrochemicals Ltd (MRPL), a refinery at Mangalore with a capacity of 9 MMTPA. The company owns the country's Lube Refinery with a capacity of 335,000 Metric Tonnes. The company's products and services include Refineries, aviation, bulk fuels & specialities, international trade, liquefied petroleum gas (LPG) - HP gas, Lubes - HP lubes. The company's subsidiaries include HPCL Biofuels Ltd and HPCL-Mittal Energy Ltd.

Hindustan Petroleum Corporation Ltd was incorporated in the year 1952 with the name Standard Vacuum Refining Company. Then, the name was changed to ESSO India. When ESSO and Lube India were nationalised, the company was renamed to Hindustan Petroleum Corporation Ltd in the year 1974. The Caltex undertaking was nationalized in the year 1976, which were subsequently merged with the company in the year 1978. In the year 1979, the undertakings of Kosan Gas Company, the concessionaires of HPCL in the domestic LPG market, was merged with the company.

In December 2000, the 'Guru Gobind Singh Refineries' was incorporated as a wholly owned subsidiary company. The company completed the Rs 378 crore pipeline project from Vijayawada to Secunderabad, which was commissioned on March 2002. They set up a new LPG Bottling plant with capacity of 44 TMTPA in Kota. The company implemented 15 company tank trucks in the year 2004.

During the year 2004-05, the company completed their construction of a new grassroot depot at Aonla, Bareilly inUttarpradesh with total cost of Rs 10.25 crore. Also, they completed the construction of another new grassroot depot at Ramagundam, Andhra Pradesh at a total cost of Rs 11.47 crore. Further they commissioned a total of 13100 KL additional tankage at various locations during the year. The company branded their retail outlets under the name 'CLUB HP'. They launched 'Turbojet' branded diesel and the 'Power' branded petrol in India.

During the year 2005-06, the company's Mumbai Refinery undertook mega project at an approved cost of Rs 1850 crore to meet the MS/HSD of EURO-III grade in Metro/Mega cities and Bharat stage-II grade in the rest of the country and the Visakh Refinery undertook Clean Fuel Project at an approved cost of Rs 2147.8 crore to meet the MS/HSD of Euro-III grade in Metro-Mega cities and Bharat-II grade in the rest of the country. The company commissioned 647 Retail Outlets during the year.

During the year 2008-09, the installation of facilities for production of Euro III / IV Petrol (Motor Spirit) at both the Refineries was completed. In pursuit of promoting alternate fuels, CREDA-HPCL Biofuel Ltd (CHBL) was incorporated on October 14, 2008, as a subsidiary company with equity shareholding of 74% by the company and 26% by Chhattisgarh State Renewable Energy Development Agency (CREDA). CHBL is to undertake cultivation of Jatropha plant, an energy crop used for production of bio- diesel, on 15,000 hectares of land leased by the Government of Chhattisgarh.

HPCL Refineries commissioned Clean Fuels Projects and Euro-IV MS production started prior to January 2010 as per Auto Fuels Policy. Mumbai Refinery was the First Indian PSU refinery to commence BS-IV MS production facilities and first batch of BS-IV MS was rolled out in January, 2010. In its continual effort to widen the crude basket, Mumbai Refinery processed 2 new crudes, namely Iran Mix and Ravva crude.

In April 2011, the company approved the acquisition of balance 50% shares held by other joint venture partners in Prize Petroleum Company Ltd. In November 2011, the company entered into an MoU with Greater Calcutta Gas Supply Corporation Ltd (GCGSCL) and Gas Authority of India Ltd (GAIL) to carry out Natural Gas business in the City of Kolkata and its adjoining districts.

The company is setting up a state of the art Green R&D Centre at Bangalore with an objective to become a technology leader through continuous & innovative

R&D efforts. The projects is being executed in a phase manner with a phase-I capital investment of Rs 210 crore.

Indian Oil Corporation Ltd (IndianOil) is India's flagship national oil company with business interests straddling the entire hydrocarbon value chain - from refining, pipeline transportation and marketing of petroleum products to exploration & production of crude oil & gas, marketing of natural gas and petrochemicals. The company is the leading Indian corporate in the Fortune 'Global 500' listing, ranked at the 98th position in the year 2011.

The company's operations include refineries, pipelines and marketing. Their portfolio of brands includes Indane LPGas, SERVO lubricants, XTRAPREMIUM petrol and XTRAMILE diesel and Propel Petrochemicals. In exploration and production, IndianOil's domestic portfolio includes 11 oil and gas blocks and two coal bed methane blocks while the overseas portfolio consists of 10 blocks spread across Libya, Iran, Gabon, Nigeria, Timor-Leste, Yemen and Venezuela.

3.3 INDIAN OIL CORPORATION LTD (IOCL)

Indian Oil Corporation Ltd was established in the year 1959 as Indian Oil Company Ltd. In the year 1964, Indian Refineries Ltd merged with Indian Oil Corporation Ltd. Indian Oil Blending Ltd a wholly owned subsidiary was merged with IndianOil on May 2006. The company transferred their entire equity holding in Indian Strategic Petroleum Reserves Ltd (ISPRL) to the Oil Industry Development Board, a government body functioning under the Ministry of Petroleum & Natural Gas. Consequently, ISPRL ceased to be a wholly owned subsidiary in May 2006.

The company formed one subsidiary company, namely IOC Middle East FZE, in Jebel Ali Free Trade Zone Dubai, with the objective of marketing lubricants and other petroleum products in Middle East, Africa and CIS regions. In June 2006, they incorporated a joint venture company namely, Indo-Cat Pvt Ltd with Intercat.Inc of USA for manufacture and marketing of FCC catalysts and additives.

In the year 2007, the company received plenty of awards, Oil Industry Safety Directorate Awards, 'Most Admired Retailer of the Year' award, 'CIO 100 Award 2007', SAP ACE - Awards for Customer Excellence and the only petroleum company as 'The Most Trusted Brand' in ET's Brand Equity's annual survey. The SERVO acquires prestigious MAN Global approvals, IndianOil's R&D Centre gets special recognition for Bioremediation and also SERVO secures entry into NSF White Book - H1 Category during the period. The company won Retailer of the Year - Rural Impact Award and their XtraPower won Loyalty Summit Award during the year 2008.

In January 2008, the company and Hindustan Unilever Ltd (HUL) signed an MoU for setting up Kwality Walls Kiosks at select IndianOil petrol stations across the country. Also, the company entered into an MoU with Transparency International India (TII) for implementing an Integrity Pact Programme focused on enhancing transparency in their business transactions, contracts and procurement processes. In April 2008, the company launched 'LNG at Doorstep' facility at the Pen unit of H&R Johnson, the facility, first of their kind in the country, wich are primarily aimed at catering to the needs of Liquefied Natural Gas (LNG) customers who are not located on the main natural gas pipelines. The company was conferred with the 'Maharatna' status by the Government of India which provides enhanced autonomy and larger flexibility for its operation.

During the year 2009-10, the company commissioned 238 new retail outlets and 414 Kisan Seva Kendra (KSK) outlets taking their total tally to 18,643. The company's Indane LPG brand earned the coveted status of 'Superbrand'. On the lines of KSK, the Rajiv Gandhi Grameen LPG Vitarak Yojana was launched to penetrate rural markets.

During the year, the company was granted the Petroleum Exploration License or one of the two Type-S blocks in Cambay basin for which it is the operator. Upon getting the license, exploration activities were initiated in the block. The company was awarded a project for the development, extraction, upgradation and marketing of heavy oil in Carabobo heavy oil region of Venezuela in consortium with Repsol, Petronas, ONGC Videsh Ltd. and Oil India Ltd.

During the year 2010-11, the company enrolled about 46.8 lakh new Indane LPG customers and commissioned 245 new Indane distributors taking their total to 618.3 lakh and 5,311 respectively. The LPG Bottling capacity was enhanced to 5,518 TMTPA with capacity addition of 326 TMT. In order to provide LPG to rural India, the company commissioned 145 distributors under the Rajiv Gandhi Gramin LPG

Vitaran Yojana under the auspices of Ministry of Petroleum & Natural Gas. As a part of their CSR activity, 10,052 new connections were released to BPL families.

During the year, the company formed a joint venture company was formed with Nuclear Power Corporation of India Ltd (NPCIL) for setting up Nuclear power plants. In July 2010, the company commissioned their first gas pipeline between Dadri and Panipat and thus they commenced gas supplies to Panipat Refinery. In a bid to scale up their gas infrastructure, a 5 MMTPA LNG Import & Re-gassification Terminal Project was planned at Ennore, Tamil Nadu. This LNG Terminal would be the first of its kind on the East coast of India. Furthermore, in consortium with GSPC, HPCL and BPCL, the company won gas pipeline bids for Mallavaram to Bhilwara and Vijaypur via Bhopal, Mehsana to Bhatinda and Bhatinda to Jammu and Srinagar

3.4 MANGALORE REFINERY AND PETROCHEMICALS LIMITED (MRPL)

Mangalore Refinery and Petrochemicals Limited (MRPL), a Mini Ratna company was incorporated in 7th March of the year 1988 and commenced a business in 2nd August as a joint venture oil refinery promoted by Hindustan Petroleum Corporation and Indian Rayon & Industries Limited (IRIL) & Associates (AV Birla Group), now it is a subsidiary company of ONGC. MRPL is the only refinery in India to have two CCRs producing unleaded petrol of high octane. The refinery was conceived to maximize middle distillates with the capability to process light to heavy and sour to sweet crudes with 24 to 46 API gravity.

The Company made a mega Public Issue consisting 4,31,60,000 16% Secured Redeemable Partly Convertible Debentures (PCDs) of Rs.135/- each aggregating to Rs.582.66 crores in the year 1993 and also 2,80,00,000/- 17.5% Secured Redeemable Non Convertible Debentures of Rs.200/- each (with detachable Equity Warrants) aggregating to Rs.560 crores. During the same year MRPL tied up for the process technologies with internationally reputed technology suppliers. It commissioned a 45 MW cogeneration power plant in September of the year 1995. MRPL commissioned its three million tonnes refinery towards the end of 1995-96 and it has been operating at more than 100 per cent capacity. In the year 1998, The Company had entered into an agreement with the National Securities Depository Limited (NSDL) to facilitate investors to hold the Shares in the electronic form. MRPL signed a crude-sourcing deal with the Chevron-Texaco combine in the year 1999. During the year 2000, the company and Reliance Petroleum had entered into First World markets with Petro-products like motor spirit at prices, which are not only competitive but have also contributed to the bottom lines of these companies. MRPL had enhanced its refining capacity to 12 million tonnes through a cost-effective process of debottlenecking some units. ICRA had downgraded the non-convertible debenture program in the year 2001 and also the partially convertible debenture programme of the company. The refining capacity was expanded to 9 MMT p.a from 3 MMT p.a in April of the year 2001 and commercial production started during the year.

In 2003, ONGC and MRPL had signed a Memorandum of Understanding for the supply of crude oil. As at 28th March of the year 2003, ONGC acquired the total shareholding of 37.39% held by A.V. Birla Group and further infused equity capital of Rs.600 crores consequently made MRPL a majority held subsidiary of ONGC. The Company had contributed Rs 20 crore to New Mangalore Port Trust towards construction of new jetty at the port for exclusive use of the company. Further it is participating as an equity shareholder in the 364 km long cross country multi product Mangalore-Hassan-Bangalore pipeline which will help the company in accessing wider consumption areas for its products. The Hassan-Bangalore Pipeline project of 367 KM long was operational and the first parcel of HSD was transported through this pipeline and was delivered at Bangalore on 1st August of the year 2003. The Centre for High Technology (CHT) selected the MRPL for the Jawaharlal Nehru centenary awards under energy performance of refineries for the year 2003-04. Shell made tie-up with MRPL for Petro products in the year 2004. During the year 2004-05, based on the MOU with ONGC the company purchased 3.7 MMT Mumbai High Crude on pricing formula applicable to other PSU Refineries. MRPL had signed a pact with Saudi, Iran firms for crude supply in the year 2005, also in the same year; the company had forged alliance with Ashok Leyland for retail outlets.

The Company forged alliance with Abu Dhabi firm in the year 2006 and MRPL had inked an agreement with Mauritius Company, in the identical year ICRA Ltd had assigned an Issuer Rating of IR AAA to the company. During the year 2006-07, the company took implementation of a large Refinery Upgradation and Expansion project at a cost of Rs.7943 crore. For Aromatics Project worth of Rs.4852 crore, ONGC and MRPL had incorporated a Joint Venture company under the name of ONGC Mangalore Petrochemicals Ltd (OMPL). In July of the year 2007, The Company had entered into a contract with State Trading Corporation (STC), Mauritius to supply petroleum products and also in the same year, in September, MRPL had signed a 4-year product supply agreement (extendable by another two years) with Shell India Marketing. As at January 2008, MRPL along with Shell Aviation made a landmark agreement for the purpose of entering an exclusive joint venture to market and supply aviation fuel. MRPL sold its first spot cargo to Iran in April 2008. During May of the year 2008, replacing Reliance Industries as a major supplier to the OPEC member, MRPL is all set to supply 250,000 tons of diesel to Iran over the eight months.

MRPL plans to initiate plant-scale experiments on spent caustic treatment with chlorine dioxide to treat phenols, conduct a study on ONGC-Hazira HCR samples on producing Gasoline using ONGC Hazira naphtha and MRPL reformate, and analyse the feasibility of producing US Military grade ATF-JP5. The company also plans to augment refining capacity from the present rating of 9.69 TPA to 15 TPA. Studies have been initiated to add fresh capacities to the tune of 15 TPA. Also the company plans to launch its unique branded petrol and diesel in very soon.

3.5 OIL AND NATURAL GAS CORPORATION LIMITED (ONGC)

More than half century survival in oil and gas industry is a record of work by Oil and Natural Gas Corporation Limited (ONGC). It was originated in the year of 1956 as a private sector company. Later, in the year 1993 the company was came to known as Public Sector Company. ONGC's habitual activities deals with exploration, development and production of Crude Oil, Natural Gas, LPG and some other value added petroleum products such as NGL, C2-C3, Aromatic Rich Naphtha and Kerosene. The company going along with two of its folds namely ONGC Videsh Limited (OVL) and Manglore Refinery & Petrochemicals Limited (MRPL) and ten of Joint Ventures/Associates. ONGC's Basins are totally seven in numbers, Western Offshore Basin (Mumbai & Baroda), KG Basin (Rajamundary), Cauvery Basin (Chennai), Assam & Assam-Arakan Basin (Jorhat), CBM-BPM Basin (Kolkata) and Forntier Basin (Dehradun) and ONGC has two plants situated in Uran and Hazira. The company covers five regions such as Mumbai, Baroda, Nazira, Chennai and Kolkata and also ONGC running eleven institutes for different specialisation in different locations.

During March 1999, ONGC, Indian Oil Corporation (IOC) and Gas Authority of India Limited (GAIL) both of three agreed to have cross holding in each other's stock to pave the way for Long-term strategic alliance amongst themselves for the domestic and overseas business opportunities in the energy value chain. The ONGIO International Pvt Ltd was incorporated in the year 2001 as 50:50 joint venture projects with Indian Oil Corporation Ltd with aim of providing Training, Consultancy & Services in Hydrocarbon Sector and later company has decided to wind up ONGIO due to loss. During 2001-02 the augment recovery from onshore fields of 13 projects 2 were resourcefully commissioned. By the end of the same year 2001-02 the company 's subsidiary unit ONGC Videsh Ltd commenced its commercial production of gas.

In the year of 2004 ONGC initiated Phase-I of a collaborative project on CBM in Jharia Field and successfully completed the same in 2005. During 2004-05 the company discovered its third deep-water exploration campaign 'Sagar Samriddhi' in Krishna-Godavari (KG) Basin at the location Vashistha (VA-1A) in block KG-OS-DW-IV. In the western offshore a shallow-water oil and gas was recorded in D-33, about 60 Kilometers South-West of Mumbai High, Onshore, Oil and Gas was found in Tiphuk-1 in North Assam Shelf and Oil was struck at Wamaj in Cambay Basin. Offshore, four new Platforms (2 Well Platforms, 1 Process Platforms and 1 Clamp-on) were Commissioned for enhancing production. New trunk pipelines are being laidsub-sea from Mumbai High Field to Urban Oil and Gas processing facility.

In March 2005 ONGC launched its retail marketing business with commissioning of its first autofuels outlet at Manglore under the brand 'ONGC Values' and 'Shopp'njoy' for fuel and non-fuel business respectively. The company has also received approval/license from the Government for marketing of non-subsidised LPG cooking gas, Kerosene and Aviation refueling sales. Tripura Power Development Company Pvt Ltd (TPDCL) was incorporated to set up a gas-based power-generating project in Tripura. TPDCL has been renamed as ONGC Tripura Power Company Pvt Ltd after the domination. In the same year the company has entered into various alliances in form of execution of Memorandum of Understanding with Kakinada Seaport & IL&FS with 26% equity stake for development of Port based SEZ at Kakinada, Andhra Pradesh. During the year 2006 the company was awarded 60 out of 110 exploration blocks by the Government in the five NELP rounds. Out of these 60 NELP Blocks 35 are in the form of unincorporated joint ventures and remaining blocks are company's 100% participating interest.

For the sake of its excellent concert, the company has received numerous awards every year. The highlights are NDTV Profit Business Leadership Award, Motilal Oswal CNBC TV18 Biggest Wealth Creator of India for the period of 2001-06, Golden Peacock Award 2006 for Corporate Governance in PSU category, is this award has been conferred to the company regularly. Dun & Bradstreet-American Express Corporate Awards 2006 in the oil and gas exploration sector and Greentech Gold Safety Award in petroleum sector apart from this, the company listed and ranked in Indian level also in global level by various evaluators.

ONGC entering the alternative energy segment with a Rs 1,200 crore-plus investment to generate 200 mw of wind power for captive use and the country's largest field, is all set to produce an additional 20.7 million tonnes of oil and 3.32 billion cubic metre (bcm) of gas with an investment of about Rs 5,713 crore in Mumbai High, the project envisages drilling of 86 infill wells. Five new well head platforms and six clamp-on structures are also planned. A new process platform bridge connected to the existing process complex ICP in Mumbai High South is proposed to handle the additional production. ONGC have future enhancement plans in all sector under the company, in that the production plans covers to develop Deep/Ultra Deepwater field and flow assurance issues, extraction by Twister Technology to produce about 16 TPD of condensate is conceptualized. Further, from the condensate fractionation scheme, production of about 1077 TPA of LPG and 3516 TPA of Naphtha is planned at coast of Rs.30.21 crores. Under the Drilling, formulation of polyamines enhanced High Performance Water Based Mud (HPWBM) system and integrated cementing solutions for HPHT Oil and Gas Wells and some other plans in above said categories and also under in Technology. The company being set up Rajiv Gandhi Urja Bhawan in Delhi for holistic research in Alternate Energy Sources. As on may 2008, part of the strategic alliance initiative, the ONGC proposed assignment of participating interest to BG Exploration and Production India Limited (BGEPIL), a 25 % participating interest in its Mahanadi basin deep water block, MN-DWN-2002/2.

In December 2009, the company entered into two broad enabling agreements with Iranian authorities for participation in development of gas fields and liquefaction facilities in Iran, in return for assured minimum 6 million tonne LNG per annum on long term basis. Also, ONGC Videsh entered into a non exclusive memorandum of understanding (MOU) to explore the possibilities of jointly studying and if mutually agreed, to participate in attractive oil and gas assets in Russia and third countries. In June 2010, Stealth Ventures Ltd entered into a Joint Study Agreement (JSA) with the company to evaluate emerging Unconventional Resource plays and opportunities in India. The objective of the JSA is to identify the unconventional resource plays within India, and a high priority has been given by both parties, to identify high growth profile shale gas and CBM prospects, on the basis of the large database available within ONGC. In December 2010, the company's subsidiary, ONGC Videsh Ltd signed a Framework Agreement on Cooperation in Hydrocarbon Sector in Delhi with Sistema, a public financial corporation in Russia and CIS.
The Government of India has decided to disinvest 5% paid up equity capital of ONGC out of Government shareholding.

3.6 RELIANCE INDUSTRIES LTD (RIL)

Reliance Industries Ltd is an India-based company. The company is India's largest private sector company on all major financial parameters. They are the first private sector company from India to feature in the Fortune Global 500 list of 'World's Largest Corporations' and ranks 117th amongst the world's Top 200 companies in terms of profits. The company operates world-class manufacturing facilities across the country at Allahabad, Barabanki, Dahej, Hazira, Hoshiarpur, Jamnagar, Nagothane, Nagpur, Naroda, Patalganga, Silvassa and Vadodara.

The company operates in three business segments: petrochemicals, refining, and oil and gas. The petrochemicals segment includes production and marketing operations of petrochemical products. The refining segment includes production and marketing operations of the petroleum products. The oil and gas segment includes exploration, development and production of crude oil and natural gas. The other segment of the company includes textile, retail business and special economic zone (SEZ) development.

In the year 1966 the RIL was founded by Shri Dhirubhai H.Ambani, it was started as a small textile manufacturer unit. In May 8, 1973 RIL was incorporated and conformed their name as RIL in the year 1985. Over the years, the company has transformed their business from manufacturing of textiles products into a petrochemical major.

The company has set up a texturising / twisting facilities in 1979, RIL has also set up plants for Polyester Staple Fiber (PSF) in 1986 and for Linear Alkyl Benzene (LAB) & Purified Terephthalic Acid (PTA) in 1988. RIL has setup a petrochemical facility to produce HDPE and PVC at Hazira, Gujarat in technical collaboration with DuPont and BF Goodich respectively. The Hazira petrochemical plant was commissioned in 1991-92.

In the year 1995-96, the company entered the telecom industry through a joint venture with NYNEX, USA and promoted Reliance Telecom Private Limited in India. Reliance became the first corporate in Asia to issue bonds in the U.S at the year of 1996-97. The company commissioned an 80,000 tonne bottle grade PET chip plant at Hazira manufacturing complex. Reliance's PET chips has been accepted internationally due to their high quality during the year 1997-98 and in the same year Reliance Industries Planned to invest around Rs. 5000 crores (USD 1,250 million) in building two world-scale plants at the site of the Jamnagar refinery in Gujarat. In 1998-99, RIL introduced packaged LPG in 15 kg cylinders under the brand name Reliance Gas. In 1999-2000, RIL commissioned the world's largest 1.4 million tonnes per annum Paraxylene (PX) plant at its new integrated petrochemicals complex at Jamnagar which was planned at 1997-98. Reliance Petroleum Limited (RPL) was amalgamated with Reliance Industries Ltd in the year 2002-03.

In 2004-05, RIL acquired the polyester major, Trevira GmbH, headquartered in Frankfurt, Germany which has the capacity of 130,000 tonnes per annum of polyester staple fibers, polyester filament yarns and polyester chips. In the year 2006, the company set up a new export-oriented refinery through its subsidiary, Reliance Petroleum Limited (RPL).

In the year 2007, Indian Petrochemicals Corporation Limited (IPCL) merged with the company. Also, Reliance Retail entered the organised retail market in India with the launch of its convenience store format under the brand name of 'Reliance Fresh'. During the year, the company commissioned their largest expansion project. The company expanded its polypropylene (PP) capacity by 280 KTA at Jamnagar that increased the combined capacity to 1,710 KTA.

During the year 2007-08, the company signed an agreement to certain polyester (capacity) assets of Hualon, Malaysia. It took over the majority control of Gulf Africa Petroleum Corporation (GAPCO) and started shipping products to the East African markets. Also, the company signed MoU with GAIL (India) Ltd to explore opportunities of setting up petrochemical plants in feedstock rich countries outside India. In April 2008, the company signed gas sales and purchase agreement (GSPA) with the customers in power sector for supply of natural gas to be produced from the KG-D6 block.

During the year, Reliance Commercial Associates Ltd, Reliance Neutraceuticals Pvt Ltd, Reliance Pharmaceuticals (India) Pvt Ltd, Reliance Petroinvestments Ltd, Gull Africa Petroleum Corporation (Mauritius), Gapco

Tanzania Ltd, Gapoil Tanzania Ltd, Gapco Kenya Ltd, Gapco Uganda Ltd, Gapco Rwanda SARL, Gapoil Zanzibar Ltd, Transenergy Kenya Ltd, Recron (Malaysia) SDH BHD, Peninsula Land Kenya Ltd, Reliance International Exploration and Production INC, Wavely Investments Ltd, Reliance Digital Retail Ltd, Reliance Lifestyle Holdings Ltd, Reliance Universal Ventures Ltd, Reliance Home Store Ltd, Reliance Autozone Ltd, Reliance Trade Services Centre Ltd, Reliance Integrated Agri Solutions Ltd, Reliance Agri Products Distribution Ltd, Reliance Food Processing Solutions Ltd, Reliance Supply Chain Solutions Ltd, Reliance Digital Media Ltd, Strategic Manpower Solutions Ltd, Reliance Gems and Jewels Ltd, Reliance Leisures Ltd, Reliance Loyalty & Analytics Ltd, Reliance Retail Securities and Broking Company Ltd, Delight Proteins Ltd, Reliance F&B Services Ltd, Reliance Hypermart Ltd, Reliance Financial Distribution and Advisory Services Ltd, Reliance Retail Travel & Forex Services Ltd, Reliance Trends Ltd, Reliance Wellness Ltd, Reliance Brands Ltd, Reliance Footprint Ltd, Abcus Retail Pvt Ltd, Bigdeal Retail Pvt Ltd, Advantage Retail Pvt Ltd and RIL (Australia) PTY Ltd became subsidiaries of the company.

During the year 2008-09, Reliance People Serve Ltd, Reliance Infrastructure Management Services Ltd, Reliance Global Business, BV, Reliance Gas Corporation Ltd, Reliance Globalenergy Services Ltd, Reliance One Enterprises Ltd, Reliance Personal Electronics Ltd, Reliance Global Energy Services (Singapore) Pte Ltd, Reliance Polymers (India) Pvt Ltd, Reliance Polyolefins Pvt Ltd, Reliance Aromatics and Petrochemicals Pvt Ltd, Reliance Energy and Project Development Pvt Ltd, Reliance Chemicals Pvt Ltd, Reliance Universal Enterprises Pvt Ltd, International Oil Trading Ltd, Reliance Nutritional Food Processors Pvt Ltd, Reliance Review Cinema Pvt Ltd, Reliance Replay Gaming Pvt Ltd, RIL USA Inc. Reliance Commercial Land Infrastructure Pvt Ltd, Reliance Corporate IT Park Ltd, Reliance Eminent Trading & Commercial Pvt Ltd, Reliance Progressive Traders Pvt Ltd, Reliance Prolific Traders Pvt Ltd, Reliance Universal Traders Pvt Ltd, Reliance Prolific Commercial Pvt Ltd, Reliance Comtrade Pvt Ltd, Reliance Ambit Trade Pvt Ltd, Reliance Petro Marketing Pvt Ltd, LPG Infrastructure (India) Pvt Ltd and Reliance Infosolution Pvt Ltd beaome subsidiaries of the company. Also, Abcus Retail Pvt Ltd ceased to be a subsidiary of the company.

During the year, Reliance Petroleum Ltd (RPL) merged with the company with effect from April 1, 2008. From April 2, 2009, the company commenced production of hydrocarbons in its KGD6 block in the Krishna Godavari basin with the production of sweet crude of 420 API. In November 2009, the company discovered first oil exploration in the on land exploratory block CB-ONN-2003/1 (CB 10 A&B) awarded under the NELP-V round of exploration bidding. In December 2009, the company discovered gas in the exploration block KG-DWN-2003/1 (KG-V-D3) of NELP-V. The deepwater block KG-DWN-2003/1 is located in the Krishna basin, about 45 kilometers off the coast in the Bay of Bengal.

In April 2010, the company commissioned a 1 MW solar Photo Voltaic power plant at Thyagaraj stadium in New Delhi. The power plant is expected to generate around 1.4 million units of electricity a year. It would cater to the power requirements of the stadium and the surplus would be fed to the grid at 11 KV. In addition, the company's subsidiary Reliance Marcellus LLC executed definitive agreements to enter into a joint venture with United States based Atlas Energy, Inc, of Pittsburgh, Pennsylvania under which Reliance will acquire a 40% interest in Atlas' core Marcellus Shale acreage position.

In June 2010, the company entered into an agreement to acquire asubstantial stake in Infotel Broadband Services (P) Ltd, which emerged as asuccessful bidder in all the 22 circles of the auction for Broadband Wireless Access (BWA) Spectrum conducted by the DOT. The company sees the broadband opportunity as a new frontier of knowledge economy in which it can take a leadership position and provide India with an opportunity to bein forefront among the countries providing world-class 4G network and services.

In August 2010, the company through their subsidiary, Reliance Industries Investment and Holding Pvt Ltd acquired the equity shares of EIH Ltd representing 14.12% from Oberoi Hotels Pvt Ltd and certain other promoters at a total cost of Rs 1,021 crore.

In December 2010, the company entered into a joint venture agreement with Russian petrochemical company SIBUR for the production of butyl rubber in India. The joint venture facility will have an initial capacity of 100,000 tonnes of butyl rubber at the company's integrated refining cum petrochemical site in Jamnagar and is expected to be commissioned by 2013.

In January 2011, the company's wholly owned subsidiary, Reliance Ventures Ltd entered into an agreement with Infrastructure Leasing and Financial Services Ltd, whereby IL&FS will become a strategic partner and co-promoter of a project which intends to develop a model economic township and other infrastructure facilities at Jhajjar in Haryana.

In February 2011, the company entered into a strategic partnership with BP which comprises BP taking a 30% stake in 23 oil and gas production sharing contracts that the company operates in India for a consideration of USD 7.20 billion and the formation of a 50:50 joing venture between the two companies for the sourcing and marketing of gas in India. The joint venture will also endeavour to accelerate the creation of infrastructure for receiving, transporting and marketing of natural gas in India.

In March 2011, the company and D E Shaw Group agreed to establish a joint venture to build a leading financial services business in India. This joint venture will incorporate the D E Shaw Group's investment and technology expertise with the company's operational knowledge and extensive presence across India to offer a comprehensive array of financial services to the Indian marketplace.

In June 10, 2011, the company and their associate, Reliance Industrial Infrastructure Ltd entered into an agreement with Bharti Enterprises for acquiring Bharti's shareholding of 74% in Bharti Axa Life Insurance Co Ltd and Bharti Axa General Insurance Co Ltd. On completion of the proposed transaction, the company and Reliance Industrial Infrastructure Ltd would effectively own 57% and 17% respectively in both insurance companies and would become Axa's joint ventures partners in India.

In September 2011, Reliance Security Solutions Ltd, a subsidiary of the company Siemens Ltd signed an MoU to jointly develop Homeland Security Solutions for Highways in India. In November 2011, the company and BP incorporated India Gas Solutions Pvt Ltd, a 50:50 joint venture company which will focus on global sourcing and marketing of natural gas in India. The joint venture company will also develop infrastructure to accelerate transportation and marketing of natural gas within the country. India Gas Solutions Pvt Ltd will be funded with equal equity from BP and RIL.

In November 2011, AXA SA, Bharti, Reliance Industries Limited (RIL) and its associate Reliance Industrial Infrastructure Limited (RIIL) announced that they have mutually agreed to terminate their negotiations on the proposed acquisition by RIL and RIIL of Bharti's shareholding of 74% in Bharti AXA Life Insurance Co. Ltd and Bharti AXA General Insurance Co. Ltd.

In February 2012, the company and SIBUR have agreed to form a joint venture named Reliance Sibur Elastomers Pvt Ltd to produce 100,000 tons of butyl rubber per year in Jamnagar, India. The joint venture will be the first manufacturer of butyl rubber in India and the fourth largest supplier of butyl rubber in the world

3.7 GUWAHATI REFINERY (ASSAM) – INDIAN OIL CORPORATION LIMITED (IOCL)

Guwahati refinery, the first in public sector, was set up in collaboration with Romania at a cost of Rs.17.29 crore and commissioned on 1st January, 1962 with design capacity of 0.75 MMTPA. The present capacity of the Refinery is 1.00 MMTPA. Hydrotreater Unit along with Hydrogen Generation unit for improving the quality of diesel has been installed and commissioned in 2002. The refinery has also installed Indmax unit, a novel technology developed by IOCL R&D centre for upgrading heavy ends to LPG, motor spirit and diesel oil in 2003.

Under the Motor Sprit Quality Upgradation project, Guwahati Refinery commissioned Naptha Hydrotreater, Isomerization and allied facilities in December 2010 for meeting present Motor spirit quality requirements.

3.8 BARAUNI REFINERY (BIHAR) – INDIAN OIL CORPORATION LIMITED (IOCL)

Barauni Refinery in eastern India was build in collaboration with the Soviet Union at a cost of Rs. 49.4 crore and was commissioned in July, 1964. By 1969, capacity was expanded to 3.3 MMTPA and further increased to 4.2 MMTPA in 2000. A Catalytic Reformer Unit (CRU) was also added to the refinery in 1997 for production of unleaded motor spirit. The refining capacity was further increased to 6 MMTPA in 2002 with the implementation of Barauni Refinery Expansion Project, which also included Residue Fluidized Catalytic Cracking Unit (RFCCU) and Diesel Hydrotreating Unit along with Hydrogen generation unit.

3.9 KOYALI REFINERY (GUJARAT) – INDIAN OIL CORPORATION LIMITED (IOCL)

The Koyali Refinery was built with Soviet assistance at a cost of Rs. 26 crore and was commissioned in October, 1965. The refinery had an initial capacity of 2 MMTPA and was designed to process crude from Ankleshvar, Kalol and Nawagam oil fields of Oil and Natural Gas Commission in Gujarat. In September, 1967, the capacity of the refinery was expanded to 3 MMTPA. The capacity of the refinery was further increased to 4.3 MMPTA through debottlenecking measures and to 7.3 MMTPA in October, 1978 by implementing an expansion project of Rs. 56.07 crore, with the implementation of additional processing facilities, the refinery could achieve capacity of 9.5 MMTPA in 1989.

To match secondary processing capacity in line with crude processing capacity, Hydrocracking unit (HCU) was commissioned in December 1993. The refining capacity was further expanded to 12.5 MMTPA CDU in September, 1999. For meeting diesel quality norms, DHDS unit was installed and commissioned in June 1999. The present refining capacity is 13.7 MMTPA.

A Linear Alkyl Benzene (LAB) plant was commission in August 2004 for conversion of kerosene to high value products. In order to meet Motor spirit quality requirements, CCRU plant was commissioned in October 2006.

3.10 HALDIA REFINERY (WEST BENGAL) – INDIAN OIL CORPORATION LIMITED

The Haldia Refinery for processing 2.5 MMTPA of middle East crude was commissioned in January, 1975 with two sectors –one for producing fuel products and other for lube oil base stocks. The fuel sector was built with French collaboration and the Lube sector with Romanian collaboration. The fuel sector includes Catalytic Reforming unit and Kero Hydrodesulphurization units which were commissioned in January, 1975.

The refining capacity of the Refinery was increased to 3.16 MMTPA in May 1988 and further to 3.5 MMTPA in May 1996 through debottlenecking measures. The refining capacity was further expanded to 4.4 MMTPA with the commissioning of new crude distillation unit of 1.0 MMTPA in March, 1997. The capacity of the second crude distillation unit was augmented to 2.4 MMTPA in June 1999 and further to 4.1 MMTPA in Jan 2010. The present refining capacity of this refinery is 7.5 MMTPA. Hydrogen Generation Unit and Diesel Hydro-desulphurization (DHDS) units were commissioned for meeting diesel quality in Aug'1999 and Sept' 1999 resepecitvely. Catalytic De-waxing unit was commissioned in March 2003 which can produce API group – II Lube base stock and first of its kind in India. Residue Fluidized Catalytic Cracker Unit (RFCCU) was commissioned in Sept'2001 as additional secondary processing unit.

3.11 MATHURA REFINERY (UTTAR PRADESH) – INDIAN OIL CORPORATION LIMITED.

The Mathura Refinery with a capacity of 6.00 MMTPA was set up at a cost of Rs. 253.92 crore. The refinery was commissioned in January, 1982 excluding Fluidized Catalytic cracking unit (FCCU) and Sulphur Recovery Units (SRU) which were commissioned in Jan, 1983. The major secondary processing units provided were Fludised Catalytic Cracking Unit (FCCU), Visbreaker unit (VBU) and Bitumen Blowing Unit (BBU). While CDU, VBU and BBU units were designed by USSR (RUSSIA), the technology for FCCU and VBU were obtained from U.S.A. For production of unleaded gasoline, Continuous Catalytic Reforming Unit (CCRU) was commissioned in 1998 with technology from France.

The refining capacity of this units was expanded to 7.5 MMTPA in 1989 by debottlenecking and revamping. A DHDS unit was commissioned in 1999 for production of HSD with low sulphur content of 0.25% wt. (max.). once through Hydrocracker (OHCU) project was commissioned in July' 2000 as additional secondary processing unit.

For meeting diesel and Motor Spirit quality, Diesel Hydro – Treater (DHDT) and Penex units were commissioned in May'2005 and June'2005 respectively. MS quality up gradation project for treatment of FCCU gasoline was implemented in February'2010 for meeting the quality requirement of BS – III and BS – IV Motor Spirit. The current refining capacity of this refinery is 8.00 MMTPA.

3.12 DIGBOI REFINERY (ASSAM) – INDIAN OIL CORPORATION LIMITED. (IOCL)

The refining was set up at Digboi in 1901 by Assam Oil Company Limited. The Indian Oil Corporation Ltd. Took over the Refinery and marketing management of Assam Oil Company Ltd. With effect from 14th October 1981 and created a separate division. This division had both Refinery and Marketing operations. The refinery at Digboi had an installed capacity of 0.50 MMTPA. The refining capacity of the refinery was increased to 0.65 MMTPA by modernization of refinery in July, 1996. A new Delayed Coking Unit of 1,70,000 TPA capacity was commissioned in

1999. A new Solvent Dewaxing Unit for maximizing production of micro – crystalline was installed and commissioned in 2003.

The refinery has also installed Hydrotreater and Hydrogen plant in 2003 to improve the quality of diesel. Naptha Hydrotreater and Isomerization units were commissioned in December' 2010 under the Motor Spirit Quality Up gradation project aimed at meeting the current Motor Spirit quality requirement.

3.13 PANIPAT REFINERY (HARYANA) – INDIAN OIL CORPORATION LIMITED. (IOCL)

The refinery was set up in 1998 at Baholi Village in District Panipat, Haryana at a cost of Rs. 3868 crore with a refining capacity of 6.0 MMTPA. Refining capacity was expanded from 6 MMTPA to 12 MMTPA in Augsut'2006. Major secondary units in the extended facilities include Hydro – cracking unit, Delayed Coking unit, Diesel Hydro – treating Unit etc. Country's largest Purified Terepthalic Acid (PTA) plant was commissioned in June' 2006.

MS Quality Up gradation project for treatment of FCCU gasoline was implemented in January' 2010 for meeting the quality requirement of BS III and BS IV Motor Spirit.

The refining capacity of Panipat Refinery was enhanced from 12.0 MMTPA to 15.0 MMTPA after the revamp of its Crude Distillation Unit in November' 2010. Capacity augmentation of Delayed Coking unit and once through Hydro – cracking unit were also carried out in 2010. Heralding Indian Oil's entry into plastic industry, Panipat Naphtha Cracker Unit, Mono ethylene Glycol (MEG) unit, Poly propylene (PP) unit, Linear Low density Poly Ethylene (LLDPE) and High density Poly ethylene (HDPE) units etc., were commissioned progressively between March 2010 to May 2010.

3.14 BONGAIGAON REFINERY (ASSAM) – INDIAN OIL CORPORATION LIMITED.

Bongaigaon Refinery & Petrochemicals Ltd. (BRPL) was incorporated on 20th February 1974 as a Govt. company fully owned by the central government with the objective of installation of the refinery having a crude processing capacity of 1.0 MMTPA and a petrochemical complex consisting of Xylene, Di – Methly Terepthalate (DMT) and Polyester Staple Fibre (PSF) units. The initial authorized capital of the company was rs. 50 crores.

The complex was built and commissioned in phases. The capacity of Crude Distillation Unit – I which was commissioned in 1979, was increased to 1.35 MMTPA from April, 1987 by de bottlenecking. Delayed coking unit – I and coke calcinations units were commissioned in 1981. Catalytic Reforming unit was commissioned in 1984. The crude processing capacity of the refinery has been increased to 2.35 MMTPA in june, 1995 by installing Crude distillation unit – II of 1 MMTPA capacity. Delayed coking unit – II was commissioned in 1996.

The authorized capital of the company was increased to rs.200 crores by December' 1983 and the paid up capital was increased to rs. 199.82 crores. The Government of India was holding the entire paid up capital of the company till 1990-91. Government disinvested 25.54% of its share holding in BRPL to UTI (Unit Trust of India) and other financial institutions and employees of the company during 1991-92 to 1993-94. The last disinvestment of 74.46% was made in favor of Indian Oil Corporation Ltd. Bongaigaon Refinery and Petrochemical Limited has been amalgamated with the holding company, Indian Oil Corporation Limited effective from March 25, 2009.

Diesel Hydrotreater and Light Naphtha isomerisation and Hydrogen Generation unit have been commissioned in 2011 for meeting Diesel and motor spirit quality.

3.15 MANGALORE REFINERY (KARNATAKA) – MANGLORE REFINERY AND PETROCHEMICALS LTD. (MRPL)

Mangalore Refinery and Petrochemicals Limited (MRPL) operates a grass root refinery with a capacity of 15 MMTPA, at Maglore, on the west coast in the ever green Dakshina Kannada District, about 350 kms, from Bangaluru. The refinery's first phase of 3.69 MMTPA was commissioned in March 1996. In second phase, the capacity was increased to 11.82 MMTPA and in the third phase, the company has increased its refining capacity to 15 MMTPA in 2012.

MRPL was originally set up as a Joint Venture refinery, promoted by Hindustan Petroleum Corporation Ltd. (HPCL) and the Aditya Birla Group of Companies, pursuant to an MOU entered into amongst Govt. of India, HPCL and Indian Rayon (Aditya Birala Group of Companies). On 28th March, 2003 ONGC acquired the total share holding of Birla Group and further infused equity capital of rs.600 crores thus making MRPL a majority held subsidiary of ONGC. The lenders also agreed to the Debt Restructuring Package (DRP) proposed by ONGC, which included inter alia, conversion up to 365 crore of their loans into equity. Subsequently, ONGC has acquired equity allotted to the lenders pursuant to DRP raising ONGC's holding in MRPL to 71.62%

The refinery has got a versatile design with high flexibility to process Crudes with 24 to 46 API gravity and has high degree of automation. MRPL is the only refinery in India to have 2 Hydrocrackers producing premium diesel. It is also the only Refinery in India to have 2 CCRs producing unleaded petrol of high octane.

MRPL has high standards in refining and environment protection matched by its commitments to society. MRPL has also developed a Green Belt around the entire refinery with plant species specially selected to blend with local flora.

3.16 TATIPAKA REFINERY (ANDHAR PRADESH) – OIL AND NATURAL GAS CORPORATION LIMITED (ONGC)

A mini refinery (Phase – I) of ONGC with capacity of 0.066 MMTPA with an aporoved cost of rs. 27 crore was commissioned in September, 2001 at Tatipaka in East Godavari Districts of Andhra Pradesh. Under Phase – II, an additional refinery of same capacity of 0.0066 MMTPA is under construction with an approved cost of rs.43.85 crore.

3.17 RELIANCE INDUSTRIES LIMITED (DOMESTIC TARIFF AREA) (RIL-DTA) (PRIVATE SECTOR), JAMANAGAR (GUJARAT)

Reliance Industries Limited (RIL) has two refineries. The present capacity of the first refinery (RIL – DTA) is 33 MMTPA. RIL – DTA is the World's biggest grassroots refinery having petrochemical plant for the production of 1,550 KTPA Paraxylene, a polymer plant for the production of 1,000 KTPA Polypropylene and a Captive Power Plant with an installed capacity of 450 MW power through Gas Turbines & steam Turbines.

3.18 RELIANCE INDUSTRIES LIMITED – SEZ (RIL – SEZ) (PRIVATE SECTOR), JAMNAGAR (GUJARAT)

Post amalgamation of Reliance Petroleum Limited with RIL, RPL refinery (a unit in Jamanagar SEZ) has become the second refinery of RIL. The Scheme of amalgamation is effective from 11th September 2009 with an appointed date being 1st april 2008. The capacity of the second refinery (RIL – SEZ) is 27 MMTPA. The SEZ refinery has a unique design and path breaking configuration with 'Clean Fuels' process plant. It is designed with high level of flexibility to change grades based on economy and to capture margins based on market dynamics. The new SEZ refinery is the first refinery in India to produce Euro – IV grades of gasoline and diesel.

BIBLIOGRAPHY

- Oil and gas background paper

Websites

- http://www.capitaline.com
- http://www.bharatpetroleum.in
- http://www.hindustanpetroleum.com
- http://www.indianoilcoproration.com
- http://www.relianceindustrylimited.com
- http://www.ongc.nic.in
- http://www.mospi.gov.in

INDEX

SR.NO.	TITLE	PAGE NO.
4.1	INTRODUCTION	93
4.2	MEANING OF ACCONTING PROFIT	93
	2.1 GROSS PROFIT AND NET PROFIT	93
	2.2 NORMAL PROFIT, SUPERNORMAL PROFIT	93
	2.3 ACCOUNTING PROFIT V/S ECONOMIC PROFIT	94
	2.4 RELATIONSHIP BETWEEN COST TO PROFIT	94
	2.5 PROFIT AND PROFITABILITY	94
	2.6 SOCIAL PROFITABILITY	95
	2.7 VALUE ADDED PROFITABILITY	96
4.3	TOOLS FOR FINANCIAL ANALYSIS	96
4.4	MEANING OF RATIOS	98
	4.1 DU PONT ANALYSIS	101
	4.2 USERS OF RATIO	102
	4.3 OBJECTIVES OF RATIO	102
	4.4 ADVANTAGES OF RATIO	103
	4.5 LIMITATIONS OF RATIO	104
5	ANALYSIS OF PROFITABILITY	107
6	CONCLUSION	127
7	BIBLIOGRAPHY	128

"Profitability comes from loyalty, productivity, and having a character base from which to work."

Zig Ziglar (an American author)

1 Introduction

The prime motive of any business is to earn profit. Profit can be used as a yardstick to measure the performance of business. In layman's language it is an excess of income over expenditure. Higher amount of profit can be considered as an achievement for a business. **According to Lord Keynes, "profit is the engine that drives the business enterprise."**

2 Meaning of accounting profit

In accordance to accounting, profit is an excess of total revenue over total cost. There is also difference in profit due to methods of accounting. Cash profit differs from mercantile profit. Saving is also a different term from profit. Non accounting person sometime consider saving as a profit, but as far as accounting profit is considered it is a very complex in nature and also differed from stakeholders to shareholders as well as managers to employees and from government to general public. For all share holders profit is EBIT or Earnings before interest and Tax or operating profit, but specifically for equity share holders it is EBIT less preference share dividend. So according to need of users term profit is manipulated as well as interpreted.

In general terms, to study profit one should consider two parameters i.e. cost and revenue. Increase in profit is due to either increase in revenue or decrease in cost. In today's highly competitive and price sensitive market one can not increase revenue by increasing price of the product or service, so it is better to reduce cost and for that one should clearly understand the relationship between cost and profit.

2.1Gross profit and Net profit

People generally believe that profit is a residual to all income – an income left after payment to all the hired factors have been made. Actually, this is a gross profit. Gross profit also contains interest on the owner's own capital, rent due to his own land used in business, the wages of his non entrepreneurial labour work. The earnings of these self used factors and services which he thus loses, (i.e., implicit cost) must also be added to his paid out or explicit cost to arrive at the total cost. ***Gross profit = Total Receipts – Total explicit cost, Net profit = Gross profit – Implicit cost.***

2.2 Normal profit and Supernormal profit

When an entrepreneur enters in a particular field of productions, he expects some minimum return for his function as an entrepreneur. So long as he gets that minimum expected return, he stays in business, else he quits. ***The minimum return that is necessary to keep the produced in present field of production is called his normal profit. If his earnings exceed the normal profit, then these earnings which are in addition to normal profit are known as supernormal profit.*** Actual profit = Normal profit – Supernormal profit.

2.3 Accounting profit and Economic profit

Profit, in the accounting sense, is the excess of revenue receipts over the cost incurred in producing this revenue. But this concept of profit differs form that used by the economist, precisely because for the accountant, the cost of business is only the paid out of cost while for an economist; the costs are opportunity cost also. Thus the ***economist's profit equals to accountant's profit minus imputed costs.***

2.4 Relationship of cost to profit

Cost can be broadly classified into two types, fixed cost and variable cost. Semi variable cost includes characteristics of both types of cost. Variable cost is directly related to output, it increases as output increases and vice versa. Fixed cost is fixed up to level of production capacity. It does not change with the increase or decrease in production units. It doesn't vary or change according to level of output, therefore by producing more in quantity one can reduce fixed cost per unit up to some extent and take advantage of economies of large scale of production.

2.5 Profit and Profitability

Profit and Profitability are different terms together, most of times used interchangeably. The term profit as we have already discussed earlier is an absolute term, where as profitability is a relative term. We can understand the term better by comparing it with production and productivity, as the production is related to total quantity produced, while productivity means quantity produced per unit of factor of production, by increasing input one can raise production if productivity is good, where as production concept does not signify this. So productivity is an appropriate concept than production. In same manner profit is raw figure doesn't justify the earning capacity of an enterprise one has to study profitability to get better idea about enterprise's earning capacity. Profitability is made up of two terms i.e. profit and ability, ability means power to earn profit for enterprise.

According to Howard and Miller. "profitability means ability of given instrument to earn profit.

According to Weston and Brigham. " It is a net surplus of a large number of policies and decisions.

Profit and profitability are not substitute terms, but they are complimentary or inter dependent to each other. Profit is a residual part of income, remained after deducting all types of expenses, whereas profitability is a firm's ability to earn profit, therefore a wise businessmen should always look for a better profitability then profit as a sole purpose, because in short run company may not earn good amount of profit due to societal or customer oriented policy, but as the company is maintaining its prestige and doing what is good only may positively lead towards greater profitability.

According to Goodman. "The accounting concept of profit measures what have been accumulated, the analytical concept of profitability is concerned with future accumulation of wealth.

Therefore, profit is a residual, dead or past data, where as profitability is a futuristic and relative terms.

According to Hermanson, Edward and Salmanson , " profitability is the relationship of income to some balance sheet measure which indicates the relative ability to earn income on assets employed.

The firm is said to be successful if its profitability exceeds the weighted average cost of capital to the firm. The profitability acts as a yardstick to measure the operating efficiency of the enterprise. The greater the profitability the more will be the efficiency and vice-versa. It also indicates public acceptance of the goods produced or service rendered by the enterprise and shows the combined effect of liquidity, assets management and debt management on operating results. It reflects the ultimate impact of various policy decisions adopted by the enterprises on its business operations. The profitable investment of excess cash, minimization of inventories, speedy collection of receivables and avoidance of unnecessary and costly short-term financing all contribute to the maximization of profitability. Thus profitability is the basic measure of overall success of the firm. It is the necessary condition for the growth and survival stability of the enterprise. The profitability of the enterprise is popularly measured with the help of financial ratios conveying quantitative relationship between two variables considered for the purpose.

2.6 Social Profitability

Profit should not be prime motive for business. There must be some societal objectives. As we need society to do business, we need business for welfare and development of society. There are various social objectives that a business can fulfil under corporate social responsibility, besides providing good quality of goods and services, it should also create better working environment. It should also provide better hygiene and healthy environment to work. As per Earnest Dale, "it appears to urge the executive to assume an infinitely broad gauge burden of responsibilities to all various public with whom he deals." Besides social responsibility a business should also consider environmental responsibility while doing business. Social responsibility accounting and Environmental accounting are other developing concept in modern accountancy. Profit should be altogether with sustainable development does not necessarily earn through unfair means which in return damage the environment in long run. Profit should be reasonable and justifiable to maintain environment and also developing the same. ***C.Mean Cardiner has rightly said, "The darkness of avarice has been dispelled by the light of new kind of social responsibility".***

2.7 Value added profitability

Value added profitability is having broader acceptance than the term profit, in india it not compulsory to prepare value added statement. Value additions mean wealth generation. It was rightly said by D.C. Jain (C.A.), " An enterprise may survive without making profit but would cease to do so without adding value, the enterprise not making profit, is bound to become sick but not adding value may cause its death over a period of time. In simple terms value addition is an edge on income or revenue over cost of goods sold or services rendered. The cost of production includes cost of material purchase, wages , carriage etc. Income or revenue should be considered after deducting any rebates or discounts, in short value addition is not profit but charge to be levied for significant improvement by the producer or provider (in case of service) for providing goods or rendering services.

3 Tools for financial Analysis:

Financial statements contain absolute figure of assets, liabilities, revenues, expenses and profit or loss of an enterprise. They do not reveal the earning capacity, liquidity and financial soundness of the enterprise. They are not readily understandable to their users. Hence they are analysed to present them in simple and understandable form. Various tools or devices employed for analysing the financial statements are as follows

1) **Comparative Statements**: When financial statements figures for two or more years are placed side by side to facilitate comparison, these are called 'Comparative financial statements', in such a statement figures of production, sales, expenses, profits etc. are put side by side to draw conclusions about the profitability and financial health of the business. It also indicates the trend of change as well as the strong points and weak points of the enterprise.

2) **Common size statements**: In these statements, various figures are converted into percentages to some common base, in profit and loss account, sales figure is taken at 100 and all other figures are expressed as percentage of sales. Similarly

in balance sheet total assets are taken at 100 and all assets are expressed as percentage of the total assets.

3) **Trend analysis**: It is one of the most useful form of horizontal analysis in making comparative study of the financial statements for a number of years. For calculating trend percentages any year is selected as the 'base year'. Each item of the base year is assumed to be equal to 100 and on that basis the percentage of each item of each year is calculated. The trend percentage is helpful in revealing the trend increase or decrease in various items.

4) **Cash flow statement**: It shows the inflows and outflows of cash and cash equivalents during a particular period and analyses the reasons for changes in balance of cash between the two balance sheet dates. A firm may earn huge profits yet it may have paucity of cash or when it suffered a loss it may still have plenty of cash. The reasons for this deviation can be analysed and understood by preparing cash flow statements.

5) **Funds flow statement**: A fund flow statement is designed to show changes in assets, liabilities, capital of the firm between the dates of two balance sheets. It indicates the causes of changes in the working capital of an enterprise during the year. It also discloses the sources form which funds were obtained by the enterprise and the specific uses to which such funds were applied.

6) **Break Even analysis**: Break even point is the point where total costs are exactly equal to the total sales. At this point, there is neither any profit nor any loss. It can also be termed as 'No profit – No loss' point.

7) **Accounting ratios:** Absolute figures expressed in monetary terms in financial statements by themselves are meaningless. These figures often do not convey much meaning unless expressed in relation to other figures. For e.g. Mr. Ajay earns a profit of Rs.1,50,000, whereas another trader Mr. Anil earns a profit of Rs. 1,80,000. Which one of them is more efficient? Generally we can say that Anil is more efficient as he is earning more profits. But in order to given the correct answer, we must find out, how much the capital is employed by each of them. Suppose, Ajay has employed a capital of Rs.10,00,000 and Anil has employed Rs.15,00,000, we can now calculate the percentage of profit earned by each of them on capital employed.

Ajay = 1,50,000/10,00,000 X 100 = 15%

Anil = 1,80,000/15,00,000 X 100 = 12%

This shows that Ajay has earned Rs.15 for every Rs.100 of capital, whereas Anil has earned Rs.12 for every Rs.100 of capital. As such, Ajay is using his capital more efficiently.

The above example shows that figures assume significance only when expressed in relation to other figures. Just as in the example given above, the absolute figure of profit was meaningless but when the figure of profit was expressed in relation to capital, it gains importance.

4 Meaning of Ratio

Relationship between two figures, expressed in arithmetical terms is called a 'ratio'. In the words of **R.N.Anthony : "A ratio is simply one number expressed in terms of another. It is found by dividing one number into another."**

Ratios can be expressed in the following four ways:

1) ***'Proportion' or Pure Ratio or Simple Ratio***: It is expressed by the simple division of one number by another number. For example, if the current assets of a business are Rs.2,00,000 and its current liabilities are Rs.1,00,000, the ratio of 'current assets to current liabilities' will be 2:1.

2) ***'Rate' or 'So Many Times'*** : In this type, it is calculated how many times a figure is, in comparison to another figure. For example, if a firm's credit sales during the year are Rs.2,00,000 and its debtors at the end of the year are Rs. 40,000, its Debtors Turnover ratio is 5 times. It shows the credit sales are 5 times in comparison to debtors.

3) ***Percentage*** : In this type, the relation between two figures is expressed in hundredth. For example, if a firm's capital is Rs.10,00,000 and its profit is Rs.2,00,000, the ratio of profit to capital in terms of percentage is 20%.

4) ***Fraction*** : for example net profit is $1/5^{th}$ of the capital.

While calculating a ratio, it should be understood that it is desirable to divide "more favorable figures" by the "less favorable figures".

CROSS SECTIONAL AND TIME SERIES ANALYSIS

The ratio analysis involves comparison for a useful interpretation of financial statements. A single ratio in itself does not indicate favorable or unfavorable position. It should be compared with that of some other firm in the same industry or with that of past ratios of the same firm.

a) Cross Sectional Analysis

It involves the comparison of firm's ratios with that of some selected firms in the same industry or industry average at the same point of time. Such a comparison is helpful in assessing the relative financial position and performance of the firm. Cross sectional ratio analysis is also used to provide conclusive evidence of the existence of a problem and which, in turn, will help to initiate corrective actions. However, care has to be taken in the selection of other firms. The other firms selected for comparison must have a common variable of similarity. The similarity may be raw material consumption, production process or end product. A can firm can easily resort to cross sectional analysis, as it is not difficult to get difficult to get published financial statements of the similar firms.

b) Time Series Analysis

Another way of comparison is to compare a firm's present ratios with its past ratios. When ratios of the same firm over a period of time are compared, it is known as the time series analysis. Such an analysis gives an indication of direction of change or developing trends and reflects whether the firm's financial performance has improved, deteriorated or remained constant over a period time. However, in order to derive meaningful conclusion from time series analysis, we need similar data quality over period of time. Care must be taken regarding change in accounting policy, technological development and competition over the period of analysis. For example, a firm may have changed the method of providing depreciation from straight line to written down value. The effect of such a change has to be ironed out to make time series analysis meaningful.

c) *Pro forma Analysis*

Sometimes future ratios are used as the standard of comparison. Future ratios can be developed from the projected or pro forma, financial statements. The comparison of current or past ratios with future ratios shows the firm's relative strengths and weaknesses in the past and the future. If the future ratios indicate weak position, corrective actions should be initiated.

d) *Industry Analysis*

To determine the financial condition and performance of a firm, its ratios may be compared with average a ratio of the industry of which firm is a member. This sort of analysis, known as industry analysis, helps to ascertain the financial standing and capability of the firm vis a vis other firms in the industry. Industry ratios are important standards in view of the fact that each industry has its characteristics which influence the financial and operating relationships.

Here, using cross sectional, time series and industry analysis have been taken to evaluate and justify the research purpose.

Benchmarks

As stated earlier, a single ratio in itself cannot be said to be good or bad. In order to comment on the quality of a ratio it has to be compared with some standard benchmark. These benchmark could be :

1) ***Past ratio*** : A ratio could be compared or benchmarked with the last year's ratio. It is also known as time series analysis.

2) ***Ratios of similar firms or industry average*** : A ratio could be compared with the ratios of similar firms in the same industry or by industry average at the same point of time.

3) ***Rule of thumb*** : Certain 'Rule of thumb' based upon well proven conversations have evolved over period of time. For example, rule of thumb for current ratio is 2:1, meaning thereby the current assets should be at least twice the current liabilities.

4.1 DU PONT ANALYSIS

The DuPont model is a technique that can be used to analyze the profitability of a company using traditional management tools. To enable this, the DuPont model integrates elements of the Income Statement with those of the balance sheet.

DU PONT CHART

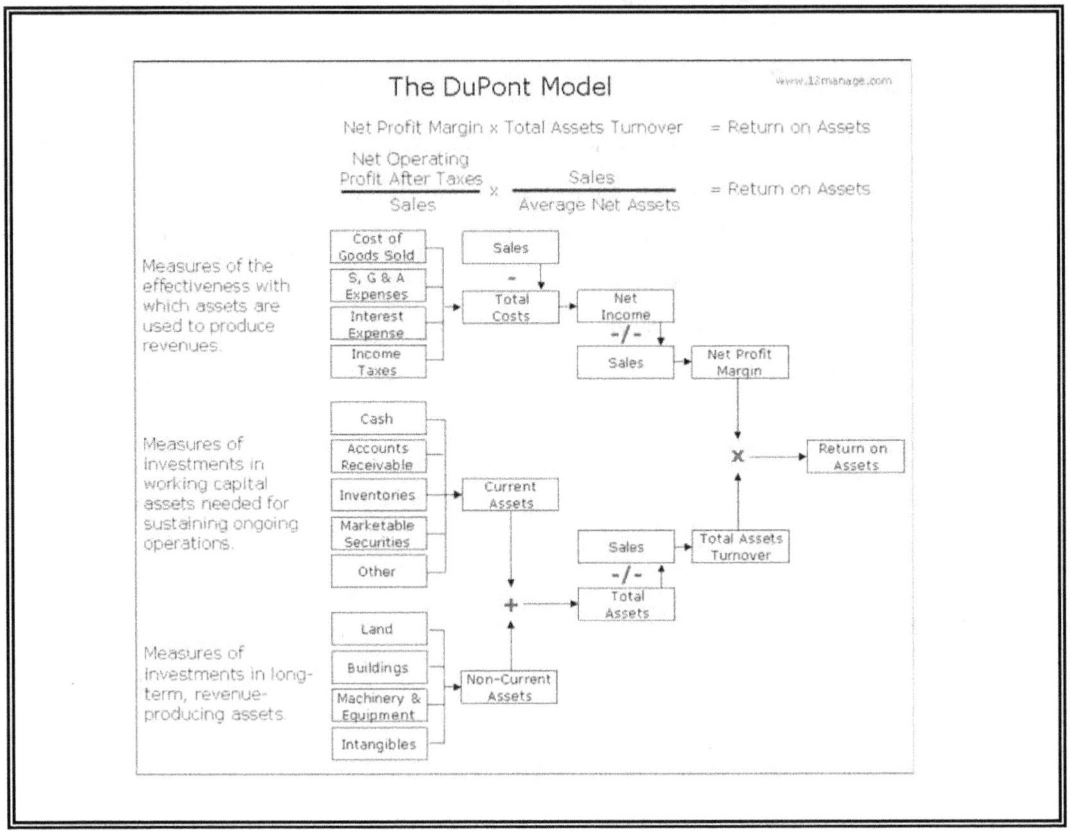

(image source : www.12manage.com)

The DuPont model of financial analysis was made by F.Donaldson Brown, an electrical engineer who joined the DuPont (a giant chemical company) in 1914, after few years, DuPont purchased 23% stake in General Motors Corp. and Brown was provided task to clean up the company's complex finances matters. Brown recognized a mathematical relationship that existed between two commonly computed ratios, viz. net profit margin and total assets turnover ratio. It was the relationship between efficiency ratio and profitability ratio. These two are the basic parameters to analyze company's financial assets. The product of the net profit margin and total asset turnover equals to Return on Assets (ROA). At this point of time maximizing return on assets was a common corporate goal. Return on Assets was impacted by both profitability and efficiency led to the development of a system of planning and control for all operating decisions within a firm, and this has become the dominant form of financial analysis until 1970s. In 1970s the generally accepted goal of financial management became 'maximizing wealth of firms' owners' and focus was shifted from ROA to ROE (return on Equity). This led to the first major modification of the original DuPont model. In addition to profitability and efficiency the way in a firm financed its activities i.e. its use of 'leverage' became a third area of attention for financial managers. The new ratio of interest was called the equity multiplier (total assets / equity). Thus ratio analysis as a tool provides a wealth of information that is useful in this regard and one type of analysis in particular, the DuPont technique can be used to enhance decisions making with an eye on improving return. It is a also good tool to control as in the words of ***Dun & Bradstreet, "A poor financial practices is second only to economic conditions as a cause of business failures."***

4.2 Users of Ratio analysis

a) ***Trade creditors*** are interested in firm's ability to meet their claims over a very short period of time. Their analysis will, therefore, confine or restricted to the evaluation of the firm's liquidity position

b) ***Suppliers*** of long term debt on the other hand, are concerned with the firm's long term solvency and survival. They analyze the firm's profitability over time, its ability to generate cash to be able to pay interest and repay principal and the relationship between various sources of funds.

c) ***Investors*** who have invested their money in the firm's shares, are most concerned about firm's earnings, they restore more confidence in those firms that show steady growth in earnings.

d) ***Management*** of the firm would be interested in every aspect of the financial analysis, it is their overall responsibility to see that the resources of the firm are used most efficiently and effectively.

e) ***Government*** on behalf of the society as a whole looks for environmental policy, corporate social responsibility, transparency in accounting policies, human resources etc. for the development and well being of the society.

4.3 Objectives of Ratio Analysis

1) To locate the weak spots of business which need more attention.

2) To provide deeper analysis of the liquidity, solvency, activity and profitability of the business.

3) To provide information for making cross – sectional analysis, i.e. for making comparison with that of some selected firms in the same industry.

4) To provide information for making time series analysis, i.e. for making comparison of a firm's present ratios with past ratios.

5) To provide information useful for making estimates and preparing plans for the future.

4.4 Advantages of ratio analysis

Financial statements, i.e., Profit and Loss account and Balance sheet prepared at the end of the year do not always convey to the reader the real profitability and financial health of business. They contain various facts and figures and it is for the reader to conclude, whether these facts indicate a good or bad managerial performance. Ratio analysis is the most important tool of analyzing these financial statements. ***It helps the reader in giving tongue to the mute heaps of figures*** given in financial statements. The figures cans speak of liquidity, solvency, profitability etc. of the business enterprise. Some important advantages derived by a firm by the use of accounting ratios are :-

1) Helpful in analysis of financial statements
2) Simplification of accounting data
3) Helpful in comparative study
4) Helpful in locating the weak spots of the business
5) Helpful in forecasting
6) Estimate about the trend of business
7) Fixation of ideal standards
8) Effective control
9) Study of financial soundness

4.5 Limitations of Accounting ratios

1) False accounting data gives false ratios
2) Comparison is not possible if different firms adopt different accounting policies.
3) Ratio analysis becomes less effective due to price level changes
4) Ratios may be misleading in the absence of absolute data
5) Limited use of single ratio
6) Window dressing
7) Lack of proper standards
8) Ratios alone are not adequate for proper conclusions
9) Effect of personal ability and bias of the analyst.

4.6 Classification of Ratios

Ratios may be classified into the four categories as follows :

a) ***Liquidity ratios*** : "liquidity" refers to the ability of the firm to meet its current liabilities. The liquidity ratios, therefore, are also called 'short term solvency ratios'. These ratios are used assess the short term financial position of the enterprise.

   According to **Saloman J. Flink, "Liquidity is the ability of the firm to meet its current obligations as they fall due."**
   In the words of **Herbert B. Mayo, "Liquidity is the ease with which assets can be converted into cash without loss."**
   Short term creditors of the firm are primarily interested in the liquidity ratios of the firm as they want to know how promptly or readily the firm can meet its current liabilities. It has been discussed broadly in next chapter.

b) ***Solvency ratios*** : This ratios are calculated to assess the ability of the firm to meet its long term liabilities as and when they become due. These ratios reveal as to how much amount has been raised from outside sources.

Solvency ratios disclose the firms' ability to meet the interest cost regularly and long term indebtedness at maturity. Some important solvency ratios are :

a. Debt equity ratio
b. Total assets to debt ratio
c. Proprietary ratio

c) ***Activity or turnover ratios*** : These ratios are calculated on the basis of 'cost of sales' or 'sales', therefore, these ratios are also known as 'Turnover ratios'. Turnover indicates the speed or number of times the capital employed has been rotated in the process of doing business. In other words, these ratios indicate how efficiently the working capital and stock is being used to obtain sales. Higher turnover ratios indicate the better use of capital or resources and in turn led to higher profitability. Some important turnover ratios are

a. Stock turnover or inventory turnover ratio
b. Debtors turnover or receivable turnover ratio
c. Creditors or payable turnover ratio
d. Working capital turnover ratio
e. Fixed assets turnover ratio

d) ***Profitability ratios or income ratios*** : one of the most important and the main object of all the business concerns is to earn profit. Profit is the measurement of the efficiency of the business. Profitability ratios measure the various aspects of the profitability of a company, such as 1*) what is the rate of profit on sales? 2) Whether the profit are increasing or decreasing, and if decreasing, then the cause of their decrease.* Some important profitability ratios are :

a. Gross profit ratio
b. Operating ratio

c. Net profit ratio

d. Return on Net capital employed

e. Earnings Per Share

f. Dividend Per share

Gross profit margin ratio

This ratio indicates the relationship between gross profit and sales. It reflects how well cost of goods sold, a major expense item, is being controlled. It shows the profit made on sales before taking account of overheads. Thus the gross profit margin highlights the production efficiency of a concern. It is always preferred to express this ratio in terms of percentage. The gross profit margin is computed by deducting cost of goods sold from the amount of sales as shown under;

Gross profit margin ratio = sales – cost of goods sold/ sales X 100

= gross profit / sales X 100

While interpreting the gross profit margin ratio, it is important to observe any trend, but in making comparisons between companies it is vital to appreciate that gross profit margin vary considerably from industry to industry. However, gross profit margin must be sufficient to meet administrative and distribution expenses, dividend and accumulation of reserves. The ratio is compared with earlier year's ratio and important conclusions are drawn from such comparisons to the previous year, it may be concluded that:-

a) Price of material purchased, freight, wages and other direct charges may have gone up but selling price may not have gone up in proportion to the increase in cost.
b) The selling prices may have fallen but the prices of materials, freight, wages and other direct charges may not have fallen relatively.
c) There may be misappropriation, theft or pilferage of stocks during the year.
d) There is fall in the sale of more profitable varieties of goods.
e) There is fall in the prices of unsold goods, thereby reducing the value of closing stock.

TABLE NO. 4.1 GROSS PROFIT RATIO OF THE SELECTED REFINERY INDUSTRY UNDER THE STUDY FOR THE PERIOD OF (2007-08 TO 2012-13)

	2012-13	2011-12	2010-11	2009-10	2008-09	2007-08	AVG	SD	COV(%)
BPCL	1.74	0.93	1.24	1.86	2.58	1.86	1.70	0.57	30.71
HPCL	1.1	1.3	1.43	2	1.84	0.95	1.44	0.41	43.37
IOCL	1.9	3.09	2.43	4.4	3.46	3.47	3.13	0.88	25.26
MRPL	-0.46	2.19	4.12	4.39	6.21	5.14	3.60	2.39	46.49
ONGC	30.34	50.22	47.58	53.87	43.58	42.99	44.76	8.16	18.99
RIL	5.91	6.8	9.76	10.13	13.35	13.14	9.85	3.10	23.58
AVG	6.76	10.76	11.09	12.78	11.84	11.26	10.75	16.06	142.65

Source: Compiled and computed from ' Capitalline Corporate Database' of Capital market Publishers (I) Ltd., Mumbai

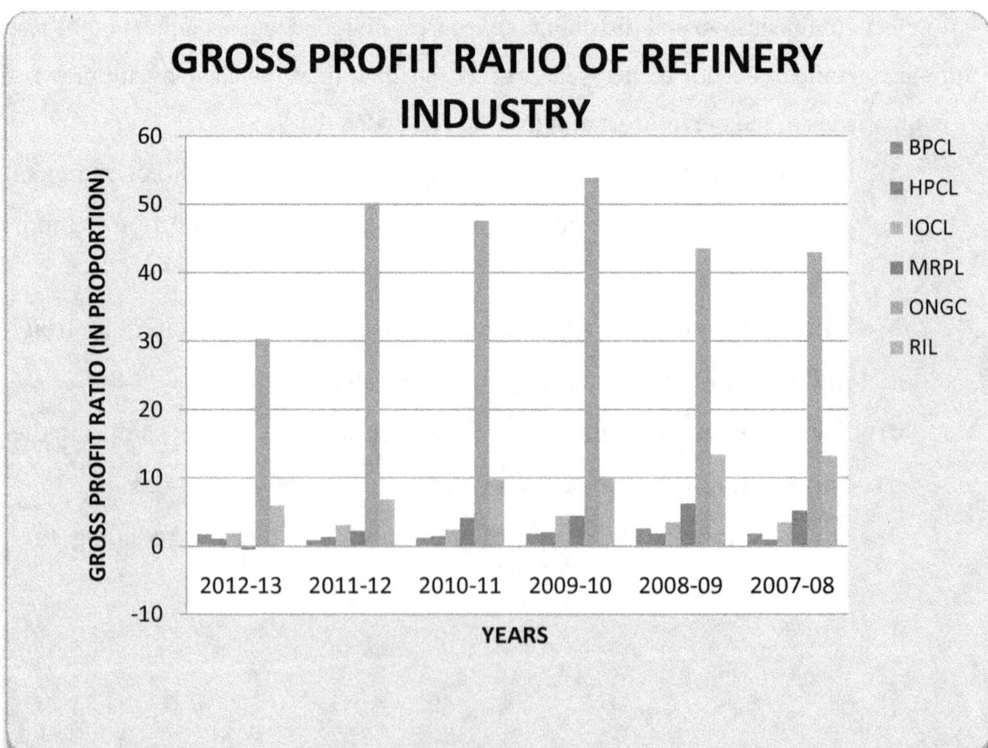

The above table no. 4.1 shows gross profit ratio of refinery industries taken under sample.During study period BPCL has maintained average gross profit margin of 1.70%, which was very low compare to industry average of 10.75%, the margin was ranged between 2.58% in 2008-09 to 0.93% in 2011-12, the standard deviation was 0.57 as compared to industry average of 16.06 which means there was a less fluctuation in gross profit margin during period of research. Overall the company has shown satisfactory gross profit margin.

Gross profit margin of HPCL varied between 2% in 2009-10 to 1.1% in 2012-13. Average gross profit margin was 1.44% which was also the lowest among the average of other companies' as well as industry average of 16.06%. Overall it was clear that company has maintained very poor gross profit margin on sales due to high cost of production and direct expenses.

During period of study gross profit margin of IOCL was showing mix trend, ranged between 3.47% in 2007-08 to 1.9% in 2012-13. The company has maintained average gross profit margin of 3.13% which was less than the industry average of 16.06%. Overall the company has maintained satisfactory gross profit margin.

MRPL was the only exception showing negative return of gross profit on sales. Although company has maintained average return of 3.60%, during last year it was negative. Highest return was in 2008-09 which was 6.21%. Due to heavy cost of production company couldn't maintain positive return on sales.

ONGC has shown very sound profitability position. It has shown average of 44.76% which was more than the industry average of 10.75%. Gross profit margin was ranged between 53.87% in 2009-10 to 30.34% in 2012-13. Standard deviation of 8.16% compared to industry average of 16.06% which means there was a less fluctuations in gross profit margin during period of research.

RIL has shown downtrend in gross profit during research period, ranged between 13.35% in 2008-09 to 5.91% in 2011-12, during last four years of study, there was a continuous decrease in gross profit margin, which shows negative future profitability position. The company has managed average 9.85% return on gross profit which was also less than the industry average.

ANOVA TEST ON GROSS PROFIT RATIO

Null Hypothesis: - There is no significant difference in gross profit ratio of selected refinery Industries during study period

Alternative Hypothesis: - There is significant difference in gross profit ratio of selected refinery Industries during the study period.

Level of significance: 5% Level

TABLE NO. 4.2 ANOVA TABLE ON GROSS PROFIT RATIO:-

ANOVA					
Source of Variation	SS	df	MS	F	F crit
SS between companies	8613.7	5	1722.74	150.39	2.60
SS between years	129.7	5	25.94	2.26	2.60
Error	286.4	25	11.45		
Total	9029.8	35			

Calculated F value: 150.39

Table F value: 2.6

Result: Significant

The analysis showed the significant result. It can be seen from the table, that the calculated value of F was found as 150.39, while the table value of F was 2.6, AT 5% level of significance. The calculated value of F, being more than the table value of F, the alternate Hypothesis stood accepted and the null hypothesis got rejected at 5% level of significance. So it proves that the differences among the average of this group were much significant and the average profitability of the groups of the refinery Industries differ much.

Net profit margin ratio

It monitors the net profit made in relation to sales. This ratio, also known as net operating margin, is calculated by dividing the net profit after tax by the amount of sales. While interpreting the net profit margin ratio it is important to bear in mind that such ratios vary considerably from firm to firm. Firms engaged in retailing are likely to have quite rapid turnover and to operate on low margins allied to high volume, while those firms engaged in selling a few large items must make a high profit in relation to the sales value of each one. The net profit margin ratio provides a relatively clear picture of how efficiently the firm maintains control over its total expenses. In addition, the analyst may wish to calculate the relationship between each expense item and sales to determine the extent to which specific expenses are under control or are tending to move out of control. For this purpose, expense ratio is also used. **According to Hingorani, Ramanathan and Grewal**. " Net profit margin indicates the net margin earned on sales of rs.100." **According to Van Home**. " it tells us the relative efficiency of the firm after taking into account all expenses and income – taxes, but not extraordinarary charges. It also describes managerial efficiency in the form of administrative, financing and selling. Again the difference between gross profit and net profit shows the proportion of these expenses into total cost.

Net profit ratio (NP ratio) = net profit after tax/net sales x 100

Net profit after tax (profit after tax) = net profit before tax – provision for tax

Net sales = total sales – sales return

Normally, this ratio is expressed in percentage.

This ratio indicates the total profitability of an enterprise. By means of NP ratio, the amount and rate of total profit earned by an enterprise from its all activities including trading activity can be known. The higher ratio exhibits the better profitability.

According to M.Y.Khan and P.K.Jain. " A high net profit margin would ensure adequate return to the owners as well as enable to a firm to withstand adverse economic conditions when the price is declining, cost production is rising and demand for the product is falling."

TABLE NO. 4.3 NET PROFIT RATIO OF THE SELECTED REFINERY INDUSTRY UNDER THE STUDY FOR THE PERIOD OF (2007-08 TO 2012-13)

	2012-13	2011-12	2010-11	2009-10	2008-09	2007-08	AVG	SD	COV(%)
BPCL	1.09	0.61	1	1.26	0.54	1.42	0.99	0.35	24.69
HPCL	0.43	0.5	1.14	1.2	0.45	1.08	0.80	0.38	34.73
IOCL	1.11	0.98	2.22	3.74	0.95	2.78	1.96	1.15	41.36
MRPL	-1.15	1.67	3	3.45	3.1	3.89	2.33	1.86	47.78
ONGC	23.66	31.02	26.37	26.35	23.5	25.93	26.14	2.72	10.5
RIL	5.7	5.99	8.08	8.35	10.65	14.45	8.87	3.27	22.65
AVG	5.14	6.80	6.97	7.39	6.53	8.26	6.85	9.36	113.34

Source: Compiled and computed from ' Capitalline Corporate Database' of Capital market Publishers (I) Ltd., Mumbai

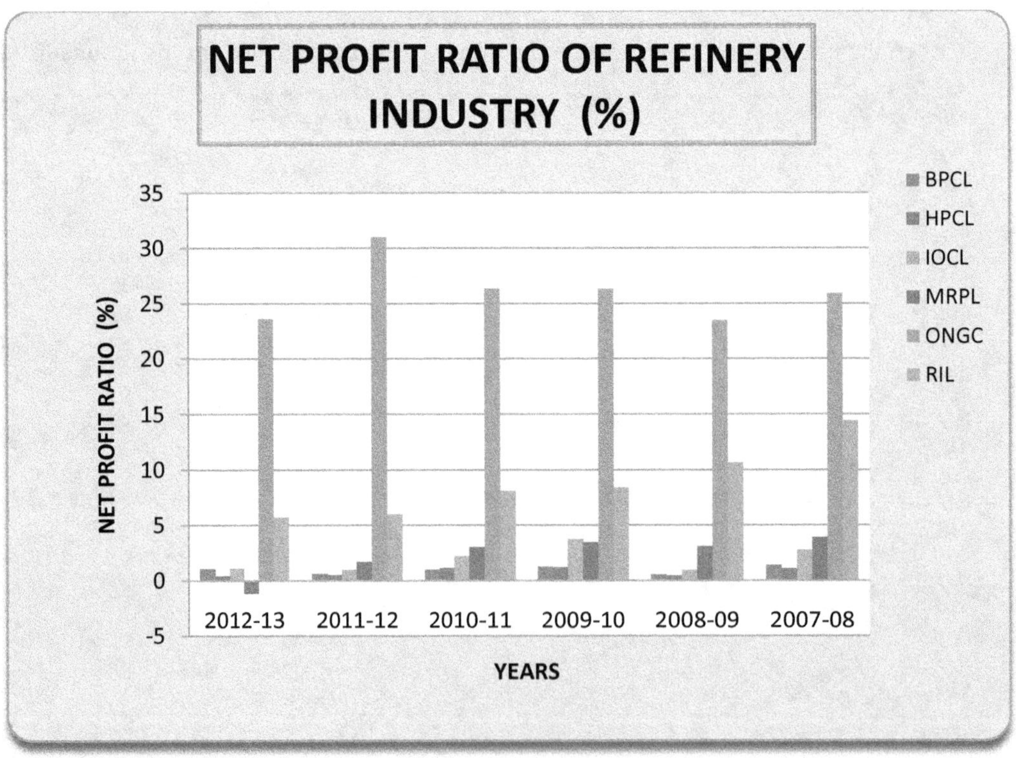

The above table no. 4.2 shows net profit ratio of refinery industries taken under sample Above table shows net profit margin of BPCL. The company has maintained average 0.99% net profit margin which was less than industry average of 6.85%. The margin was ranged between 1.26% in 2009-10 to 0.54% in 2008-09. It was fluctuating during research period. Standard deviation was 0.35% which was less than the industry average of 9.36%. Overall it shows very low net profit margin as compared to other industry players of research sample.

HPCL had the lowest average of net profit margin among other companies, i.e. 0.80% whereas average industry net profit margin was 6.85%, the margin was ranged between 1.2% in 2009-10 to 0.43% in 2012-13. During research period, the net profit margin has shown mix trend. In short the company had maintained poor net profit margin during research period.

During study period, net profit margin of IOCL was ranged between 3.74% in 2009-10 to 0.95% in 2008-09. Average net profit margin was 1.96% which was below industry average of 6.85%. Overall it shows satisfactory net profit margin.

MRPL had shown good net profit margin during the first three years of research, ranged between 3.89% in 2007-08 to 3% in 2010-11, but during last two years of study there was a downtrend in net profit margin, moreover it was negative 1.15% in 2012-13. Due to high cost of production company couldn't maintain net profit margin.

ONGC has shown better net profit margin during research period. The company was having the highest average of net profit margin i.e. 26.14% far better than the industry average of just 6.85%, margin was ranged between 31.02% in 2011-12 to 23.5% in 2008-09. The company is having very strong profitability prospectus.

RIL had maintained average 8.67% net profit margin slightly more than industry average of 6.85%, the margin was ranged between 14.45% in 2007-08 to 5.7% in 2012-13. The company was having very sound profitability position, except the constraint that negative trend of net profit margin will lead to adverse profitability condition in future.

ANOVA TEST ON NET PROFIT RATIO

Null Hypothesis: - There is no significant difference in net profit ratio of selected refinery Industries during study period

Alternative Hypothesis: - There is significant difference in net profit ratio of selected refinery Industries during the study period.

Level of significance: 5% Level

TABLE NO. 4.4 ANOVA TABLE ON NET PROFIT RATIO

ANOVA					
Source of Variation	SS	df	MS	F	F crit
SS between companies	2948.650	5	589.73	175.71	2.60
SS between years	31.920	5	6.38	1.90	2.60
Error	83.910	25	3.35		
Total	3064.470	35			

Calculated F value: 175.71

Table F value: 2.6

Result: Significant

The analysis showed the significant result. It can be seen from the table, that the calculated value of F was found as 175.71, while the table value of F was 2.6, AT 5% level of significance. The calculated value of F, being more than the table value of F, the alternate Hypothesis stood accepted and the null hypothesis got rejected at 5% level of significance. So it proves that the differences among the average of this group were much significant and the average profitability of the groups of the refinery Industries differ much.

Return on capital employed

One of the most widely used ratios is the return on assets. Since assets are used to generate income, the higher the income, the more productive assets were during the period. In computing the return on assets, the analyst must bear in mind that both borrowed as well as owned funds are used by the business for the acquisition of assets, therefore, the return on assets should be computed before accounting for the interest on borrowed funds/ capital. At the same time, income tax too is not considered while calculating this ratio because taxes are calculated on income after interest deductions. Consequently, earnings before interest and tax (EBIT) is usually used to measure return on capital employed.

The term assets is also somewhat complex to understand, in simple terms the funds used net current assets are considered as capital employed, where net current assets is a difference between current assets and current liabilities. While there are some debatable points which require clarification.

Valuation of fixed assets: there are mainly three methods for the valuation of fixed assets i.e gross value, book value and replacement value or market value. Gross value is the historical cost of an assets, whereas book value is a value of assets after deducting depreciation. Replacement value can be found out with the help of index numbers or market price.

Intangible assets: Intangible assets like goodwill, copyright, patent, franchise etc. should be considered at their realizable value unless they should be written off as soon as possible.

Non performing Assets: Non performing assets are also known as idle assets. As return on capital employed is a test of efficiency, one should not consider the assets which doesn't generate any income or do not contribute towards profitability of an enterprise.

Fictitious assets: Preliminary expenses, Underwriting commission, advertisement suspense, misc. expenditure not written off etc. are not assets at all. Fictitious assets are those items of balance sheet which pretended to be assets, but actually they are expenses not written off and therefore shouldn't be considered while calculating capital employed.

Return on capital employed (ROCE) = EBIT/ capital employed x 100

It is normally expressed as a percentage

It indicates the rate of return earned by an enterprise form its total capital employed in the business. It is also an indicator of the profit earning capacity of an enterprise. A higher return reveals a better profitability on the total capital employed in the business.

Earning Before Interst and Tax = net profit ascertained after comparing all the revenue incomes with all the revenue expenses except interest on loan and provision for income tax.

Capital employed = propritors'fund+ long terms fund

Propertiors' fund = share capital + reserve and surplus – fictitious assets

TABLE NO. 4.5 RETURN ON CAPITAL EMPLOYED OF THE SELECTED REFINERY INDUSTRY UNDER THE STUDY FOR THE PERIOD OF (2007-08 TO 2012-13)

	2012-13	2011-12	2010-11	2009-10	2008-09	2007-08	AVG	SD	COV(%)
BPCL	14.57	10.18	11.5	11.11	14.88	11.37	12.27	1.96	0.16
HPCL	7.31	8.27	7.93	9.91	9.48	6.23	8.19	1.36	0.17
IOCL	8.64	13.08	10.32	15.83	14.64	14.06	12.76	2.75	0.22
MRPL	-1.43	11.76	21.86	23.07	38.15	29.91	20.55	13.90	0.68
ONGC	24.6	28.56	28.38	34.54	34.29	36.3	31.11	4.59	0.15
RIL	12.5	12.18	12.6	11.35	10.96	15.68	12.55	1.67	0.13
AVG	11.03	14.01	15.43	17.64	20.40	18.93	16.24	9.6	0.59

Source: Compiled and computed from ' Capitalline Corporate Database' of Capital market Publishers (I) Ltd., Mumbai

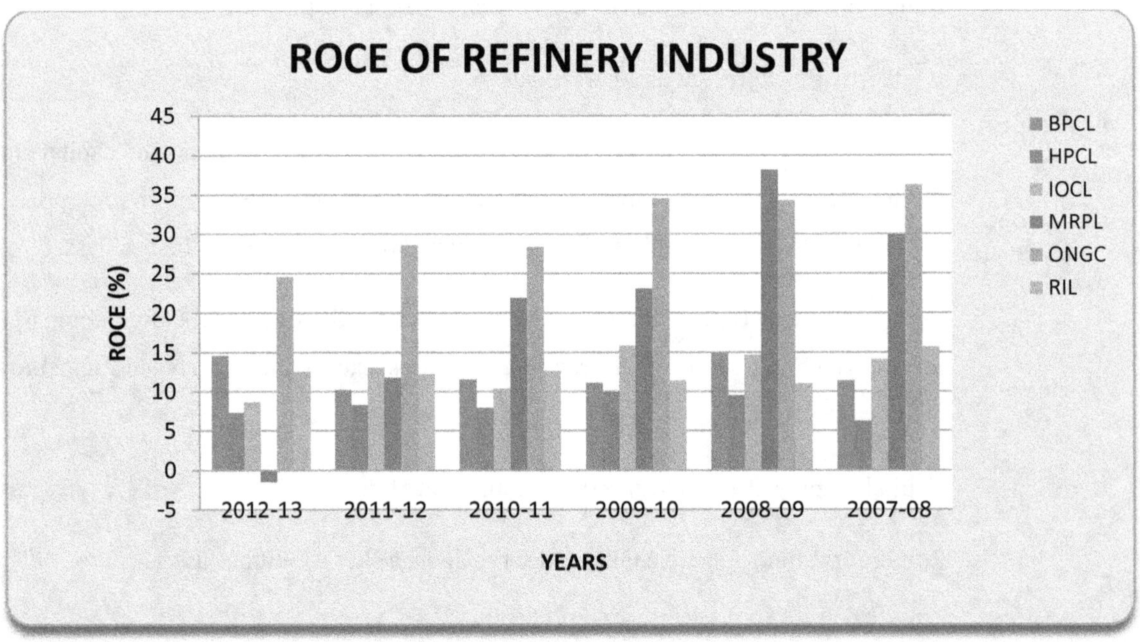

The above table no. 4.3 shows Return on Capital Employed of refinery industries taken under sample The above table shows return on capital employed of BPCL average return was 12.27% which was less than industry average of 16.24%. Standard deviation of 1.96 means there was a less fluctuations during research period of study. The average was between 14.86% in 2008-09 to 10.18% in 2011-12.

Return on capital employed of HPCL was satisfactory at an average of 8.19% with industry average of 16.24% almost half of the industry average, which shows poor return on capital employed as compare to other companies, ratio was ranged between 9.91% in 2009-10 to 6.23% in 2007-08. Standard deviation of 1.36, less than the industry average means less fluctuation in return on capital employed during study period.

Ratio of return on capital employed of IOCL was ranged between 15.83% in 2009-10 to 8.64% in 2012-13. The ratio has shown mixed trend. The average return was 12.76% which was also less than industry average of 16.24%. Overall the company has maintained satisfactory return on capital employed.

MRPL was the only company which had given negative return to capital employed due to heavy loss after tax and high expenses to revenue. In 2012-13, it has shown negative return of 1.43%, however company could maintain average ratio of 20.55% which was unexpectedly higher than the industry average of 16.24%.

ONGC has given the highest average return on capital employed i.e. 31.11%, ranged between 36.3% in 2007-08 to 24.6% in 2012-13. Standard deviation was 4.59 which was also less than the industry average of 9.6 which means there was less uncertainty in return on capital employed during study period. Overall the company is having good prospects in return on capital employed.

RIL has maintained 12.55% average return on capital employed. The ratio was ranged between 15.68% in 2007-08 to 10.96% in 2008-09, however during last two years of research period, company has maintained upward trend in return on capital employed. Standard deviation was 1.67 compared to industry average of 9.6 means less deviation in return on capital employed.

ANOVA TEST ON RETURN ON CAPTIAL EMPLOYED

Null Hypothesis: - There is no significant difference in return on capital employed of selected refinery Industries during study period

Alternative Hypothesis: - There is significant difference in return on capital employed of selected refinery Industries during the study period.

Level of significance: 5% Level

TABLE NO. 4.6 ANOVA TABLE ON RETURN ON CAPITAL EMPLOYED

ANOVA					
Source of Variation	SS	df	MS	F	F crit
SS between companies	2076.76	5	415.35	13.05	2.60
SS between years	355.42	5	71.08	2.23	2.60
Error	795.67	25	31.83		
Total	3227.85	35			

RETURN ON CAPTIAL EMPLOYED:-

Calculated F value: 13.05

Table F value: 2.6

Result: Significant

The analysis showed the significant result. It can be seen from the table, that the calculated value of F was found as 13.05, while the table value of F was 2.6, AT 5% level of significance. The calculated value of F, being more than the table value of F, the alternate Hypothesis stood accepted and the null hypothesis got rejected at 5% level of significance. So it proves that the differences among the average of this group were much significant and the average profitability of the groups of the refinery Industries differs much.

Return on share holders' fund or net worth

Return on net worth = net profit after interest and tax / net worth x 100

It is normally expressed in percentage

It indicates the rate of return earned by an enterprise on the capital invested by its owners. This is an indicator of the rate of return on the share holders' fund invested in the business. A high rate of return shows the efficiency of management in employment of owners' funds in an effective way, whereas low rate of return shows misappropriate handling of owners' fund. It also indicates low profitability or over investment in fixed assets. **According to Clifton. " the return on equity relates net to stockholders' equity."**

TABLE NO. 4.7 RETURN ON NET WORTH OF THE SELECTED REFINERY INDUSTRY UNDER THE STUDY FOR THE PERIOD OF (2007-08 TO 2012-13)

	2012-13	2011-12	2010-11	2009-10	2008-09	2007-08	AVG	SD	COV(%)
BPCL	15.88	8.79	11	11.74	6.06	13.53	11.17	3.46	30.99
HPCL	6.59	6.94	12.26	11.25	5.35	10.74	8.86	2.90	32.72
IOCL	8.18	6.83	13.45	20.22	6.71	16.99	12.06	5.72	47.45
MRPL	-11.7	12.57	18.04	19.9	25.26	33.71	16.30	15.47	94.95
ONGC	16.81	22.24	19.4	19.39	20.65	23.87	20.39	2.47	12.09
RIL	11.66	12.29	13.88	12.64	13.36	24.66	14.75	4.92	33.35
AVG	7.90	11.61	14.67	15.86	12.90	20.58	13.92	7.79	55.96

Source: Compiled and computed from ' Capitalline Corporate Database' of Capital market Publishers (I) Ltd., Mumbai

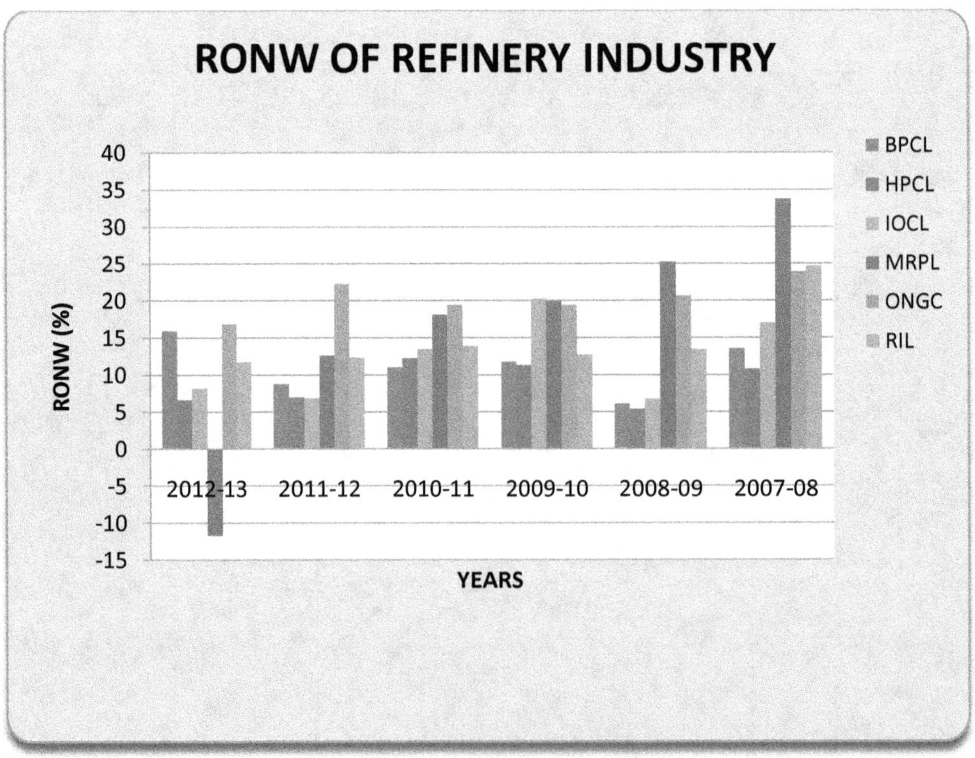

The above table no. 4.4 shows Return on Net Worth of refinery industries taken under sample. The above table shows ratio of return on net worth of BPCL. The ratio showed mix trend during research period. The average was 11.17% which was little less than industry average of 13.92%. The ratio was ranged between 15.88% in 2012-13 to 6.06% in 2008-09. The standard deviation was 3.46 which also less than the industry average of 7.79 showing less fluctuation in return on net worth of company. In short the company has maintained good ratio of return on net worth.

The ratio of return on net worth of HPCL shows fluctuating trend. The company had given average return of 8.86% as compared to industry average of 13.92%, which was the lowest return compare to other companies included in research study. The ratio was ranged between 12.26% in 2010-11 to 5.35% in 2008-09. Overall the company has given satisfactory return on net worth during period of study.

The ratio of return on net worth of IOCL has also shown mix trend, ranged between 20.22% in 2009-10 to 6.71% in 2008-09. Overall the company has maintained average return of 12.06% which was little less than industry average of 13.92. overall the company could maintain satisfactory return on net worth during period of study.

The ratio of return on net worth of MRPL has shown exceptionally negative return in 2012-13 i.e. 11.7% due to negative profit after tax. However the company has managed average return of 16.30% on net worth which was more than the industry average of 13.92%, but as far as company is showing negative trend it was adverse for future profitability.

ONGC has given the highest return on net worth at an average of 20.39% compared to industry average of 13.92%, ratio was ranged between 22.24% in 2011-12 to 16.81% in 2012-13. Standard deviation was mere 2.47 which mean less fluctuation in return. Overall the company has performed well and given good returns to shareholders.

RIL has maintained return on net worth with an average of 14.75% which was better than industry average of 13.92%, although the ratio has shown decreasing trend during last three years of study period. The ratio was ranged between 24.66% in 2007-08 to 11.66% in 2012-13. Overall the company has given satisfactory return to their shareholders.

ANOVA TEST ON RETURN ON NET WORTH

Null Hypothesis: - There is no significant difference in return on net worth ratio of selected refinery Industries during study period

Alternative Hypothesis: - There is significant difference in return on net worth of selected refinery Industries during the study period.

Level of significance: 5% Level

The higher return reveals better profitability position to the shareholders of the company.

Net worth = Propertiors' fund = share capital + reserve and surplus – fictitious assets

TABLE NO. 4.8 ANOVA TABLE ON RETURN ON NET WORTH

ANOVA					
Source of Variation	SS	df	MS	F	F crit
SS between companies	509.530	5	101.91	2.39	2.60
SS between years	547.780	5	109.56	2.57	2.60
Error	1066.560	25	42.66		
Total	2123.860	35			

Calculated F value: 2.39

Table F value: 2.6

Result: Insignificant

The analysis showed the insignificant result. It can be seen from the table, that the calculated value of F was found as 2.39, while the table value of F was 2.6, AT 5% level of significance. The calculated value of F, being less than the table value of F, the alternate Hypothesis will be rejected and the null hypothesis stood accepted at 5% level of significance. So it proves that the differences among the average of this group were not much significant and the average profitability of the groups of the refinery Industries does not differ much.

DIVIDEND PER SHARE

Dividend policy of the firm greatly determines the dividend payment and retained earning ratio of enterprise. Company may adopt conservative, liberal or stable dividend policy. It should be selected carefully as it may affect the market value of a firm. **According to Weston and Brigham, "when dividend of a firm is widely fluctuating, the shareholders can never say what they get in any particular year from their holding in such a company. Investment in the shares of such company becomes a sort of speculation which only a few can afford."** Dividend per share are the amount of dividend that public or listed company pays per share of common stock, over their reporting period, that they have issued. The remainder of company's net income, which is not paid out as dividends, is retained by the company for growth and is known as retained earnings.

The proportion of earning used to pay out as dividend to investors by the company is called dividend payout ratio.

DPS = Dividend paid / number of equity shares outstanding (withheld with public)

TABLE NO. 4.9 DIVIDEND PER SHARE OF THE SELECTED REFINERY INDUSTRY UNDER THE STUDY FOR THE PERIOD OF (2007-08 TO 2012-13)

	2012-13	2011-12	2010-11	2009-10	2008-09	2007-08	AVERAGE	STD DEV	COV(%)
BPCL	11	11	14	14	7	4	10.17	3.97	39.04
HPCL	8.5	8.5	14	12	5.25	3	8.54	4.08	47.8
IOCL	6.2	5	9.5	13	7.5	5.5	7.78	3.02	38.86
MRPL	0	1	1.2	1.2	1.2	1.2	0.97	0.48	49.51
ONGC	9.5	9.75	8.75	33	32	32	20.83	12.61	60.52
RIL	9	8.5	8	7	13	13	9.75	2.60	26.7
AVG	7.37	7.29	9.24	13.37	10.99	9.78	9.67	8.05	83.25

Source: Compiled and computed from ' Capitalline Corporate Database' of Capital market Publishers (I) Ltd., Mumbai

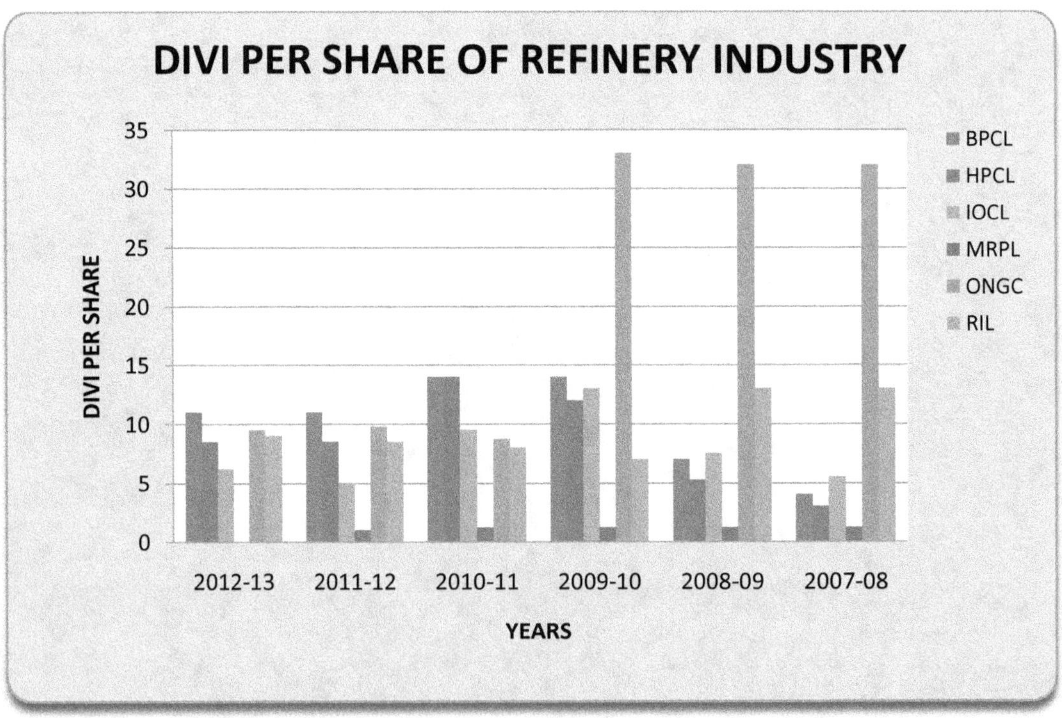

The above table no. 4.5 shows Dividend Per Share of refinery industries taken under sample The Dividend Per Share of BPCL has shown increasing trend during firs four years of study period, whereas during last two years company could maintain DPS of rs.11 per share. Average DPS of BPCL was 10.17 rs. Per share, which was little more than the industry average of Rs.9.67 per share. Overall it shows positive and satisfactory dividend per share.

HPCL, has maintained increasing trend of DPS during first four years, whereas during last two years, company had shown constant DPS of rs. 8.5 per share. The average DPS was rs. 8.54, which was less than the industry average of rs.9.67 per share. Standard deviation of 4.08 shows less fluctuations in dividend per share of a company.

During study period, IOCL has maintained the average DPS of rs. 7.78 per share, ranged between 13 in 2009-10 to rs. 5 per share in 2011-12. Standard deviation was 3.02 which is less than industry average of 8.05 which means less changes in dividend payment during research period.

MRPL has shown average DPS of 0.97 per share, which was far below than the industry average of rs.9.67 per share. During first four years of research company had constant DPS of rs. 1.2, gradually it decreased to 1 re. per share and nil. Due to negative earnings after tax , company couldn't maintain proper dividend policy.

ONGC has shown the highest average of rs. 20.83 per share, as compared to industry average of rs. 9.67 per share, it was ranged between 33 rs. Per share in 2009-10 to 8.75 per share in 2010-11. But dividend during last two years of study were near to industry average. Moreover the standard deviation is 12.61 which is also more than the industry average of 8.05, which means inconsistency in payment of dividend during study period.

During period of study, Dividend Per Share of RIL was ranged between rs.13 per share in 2007-08 to rs.8 per share in 2010-11. Company has maintained average DPS of 9.75, which was also more than the industry average of rs.9.67 per share. Standard deviation was 2.60, less than the industry average of 8.05, which means less changes in dividend payment during study period. Overall the company has maintained satisfactory dividend payment policy.

ANOVA TEST ON DIVDEND PER SHARE

Null Hypothesis: - There is no significant difference in dividend per share of selected refinery Industries during study period

Alternative Hypothesis: - There is significant difference in dividend per share of selected refinery Industries during the study period.

Level of significance: 5% Level

TABLE NO. 4.10 ANOVA TABLE ON DIVIDEND PER SHARE

ANOVA					
Source of Variation	SS	df	MS	F	F crit
SS between companies	1232.72	5	246.54	7.01	2.60
SS between years	159.42	5	31.88	0.91	2.60
Error	878.16	25	35.12		
Total	2270.30	35			

Calculated F value: 7.01

Table F value: 2.6

Result: Significant

The analysis showed the significant result. It can be seen from the table, that the calculated value of F was found as 7.01, while the table value of F was 2.6, AT 5% level of significance. The calculated value of F, being more than the table value of F, the alternate Hypothesis stood accepted and the null hypothesis got rejected at 5% level of significance. So it proves that the differences among the average of this group were much significant and the average profitability of the groups of the refinery Industries differ much.

Earnings per share (EPS)

EPS = Net profit after tax & preference dividend /number of equity shares

The ratio is an indicator of the amount of revenue profit of the concern that goes to each share. It indicates the quantum of earning of the company that is received by each equity share. Along with return on investment, shareholders are also interested in knowing EPS. **According to Herald and Alien, "The earning per share simply shows the profitability of the firm on per share basis, it does not reflect how much is paid as dividend and how much is retained by the business."**

Sometimes when denomination of shares is different, EPS is calculated on the basis of percentage instead of per share. It measures the profit to equity share holders on per share basis.

TABLE NO. 4.11 EARNING PER SHARE OF THE SELECTED REFINERY INDUSTRY UNDER THE STUDY FOR THE PERIOD OF (2007-08 TO 2012-13)

	2012-13	2011-12	2010-11	2009-10	2008-09	2007-08	AVERAGE	STD DEV	COV (%)
BPCL	65.05	36.27	42.78	42.53	20.35	43.72	41.78	14.40	34.46
HPCL	26.72	26.92	45.45	38.43	16.98	33.51	31.34	10.01	31.95
IOCL	20.61	16.29	30.67	42.1	24.74	58.39	32.13	15.68	48.8
MRPL	-4.32	5.18	6.71	6.35	6.8	7.26	4.66	4.46	95.57
ONGC	24.46	29.36	22.12	78.39	75.4	78.09	51.30	28.59	55.72
RIL	65.05	61.26	61.97	49.64	97.28	133.86	78.18	31.63	40.45
AVG	32.93	29.21	34.95	42.91	40.26	59.14	39.90	29.18	73.13

Source:* *Compiled and computed from ' Capitalline Corporate Database' of Capital market Publishers (I) Ltd., Mumbai

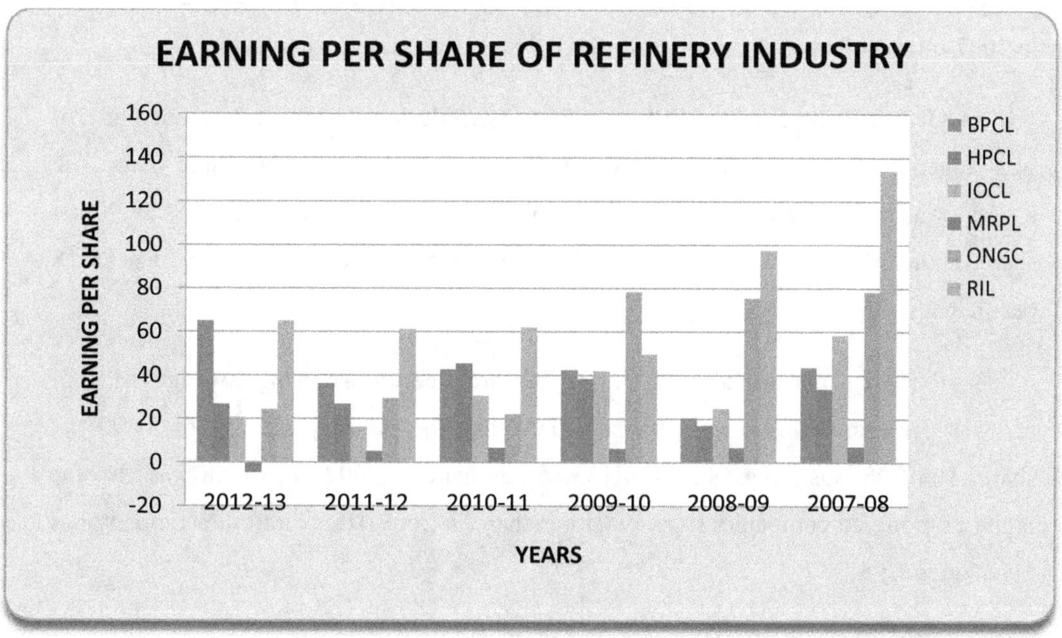

The above table no. 4.6 shows Earning Per Share of refinery industries taken under sample. The above table shows fluctuating trend in EPS of BPCL with an average of rs. 41.78 per share, which was more than the industry average of rs. 39.90 per share. EPS was ranged between rs. 65.05 per share in 2012-13 to 36.27 rs. Per share in 2011-12, standard deviation is 14.40 which was also less than the industry average of 29.18. Overall EPS of company was satisfactory.

HPCL has shown average EPS of rs. 31.34 per share, which was less than industry average of rs.39.90 per share. The highest EPS was rs.45.45 in 2010-11, where as it was minimum in 2008-09 i.e. rs.16.98. standard deviation was 10.01, less than the industry average showing less changes in EPS.

IOCL has shown average EPS of 32.13, which was lower than the industry average of rs.39.90 per share. EPS was ranged between 58.39 in 2007-08 to 16.29 in 2011-12. Standard deviation of 15.68, below the industry average shows consistency in EPS.

MRPL has shown negative EPS in the year 2012-13 i.e. -4.32 rs. Per share. Moreover, the company has shown the lowest average of rs.4.66 per share which was far below than the industry average of rs.39.90. EPS was ranged between 7.26 per share in 2007-08 to -4.32 per share in 2012-13. Overall it was very dissatisfactory.

ONGC has maintained EPS of rs.78 to rs.75 during first three years then after it was ranged between rs.22.12 per share to rs.29.36 per share during last three years. The average was rs.51.30 per share which was more than the industry average of rs.39.90 per share. Standard deviation was 28.59 slightly less than the industry average of rs.29.18 per share.

RIL, has performed well during research period showing average EPS of rs.78.18 per share, which was almost double than the industry average of 39.90 per share. The EPS was ranged between 133.86 per share in 2007-08, which was also the highest among all companies to rs.49.64 per share in 2009-10, overall the company has given good EPS.

ANOVA TEST ON EARNING PER SHARE

Null Hypothesis: - There is no significant difference in EPS of selected refinery Industries during study period

Alternative Hypothesis: - There is significant difference in EPS of selected refinery Industries during the study period.

Level of significance: 5% Level

TABLE NO. 4.12 ANOVA TABLE ON EARNING PER SHARE

ANOVA					
Source of Variation	SS	df	MS	F	F crit
SS between companies	17843.9	5	3568.79	10.43	2.60
SS between years	3399.6	5	679.91	1.99	2.60
Error	8553.3	25	342.13		
Total	29796.8	35			

Calculated F value: 10.43

Table F value: 2.6

Result: Significant

The analysis showed the significant result. It can be seen from the table, that the calculated value of F was found as 10.43, while the table value of F was 2.6, AT 5% level of significance. The calculated value of F, being more than the table value of F, the alternate Hypothesis stood accepted and the null hypothesis got rejected at 5% level of significance. So it proves that the differences among the average of this group were much significant and the average profitability of the groups of the refinery Industries differs much.

BIBLIOGRAPHY

1. Mallick, A.K., Sur, D. and Rakshit, D. (2005): "Working Capital and Profitability: A study On Their Relationship With Reference To Selected Companies in Indian Pharmaceutical Industry", GITAM Journal of Management, Vol.3, No.2, July to December, pp-51-62.
2. Mukherjee, A.K. (1988): "Management of Working Capital in Public Enterprises", Vohra Publishers& Distributers, Allahabad, India.
3. Parashar, S. P. (1986): "Liquidity Management-Principles and practice of Managing Cash Flow", Vision Books Pvt. Ltd, New Delhi, pp-9-31
4. Rao, K.V. (1990): "Management of Working Capital in Public Enterprises", Deep & Deep Publications, New Delhi, pp-269-275.
5. Sur, D., Biswas, J., and Ganguly, P. (2001): " Liquidity Management in Indian Private Sector Enterprises: A Case Study of Indian Primary Aluminium Producing Industry ", Indian Journal of Accounting, IAA, Ajmer, June, pp. 8-14.
6. Sur, D. (2000): "Liquidity Management: An overview of Four Companies in Indian Electric Industry", The Management Accountant, June, pp-407-412.
7. Van Horne, J.C. (1993): "Financial Management and Policy", Prentice-Hall of India Pvt. Ltd., New Delhi, pp-374-376.
8. VijayaKumar, A. & Venkatachalam, A. (1995): "Working Capital and Profitability-An Empirical Analysis", The Management Accountant, ICWAI, June, pp-748-750.
9. N.R. Parasuram (2006), "Synchronous movement of Key Parameters with Profitability-An Explanatory study on the Two Wheeler and Three wheeler sector", GIM Journal of Management. Vol.I., No.1, pp.26-28.
10. Singh. K.P., "Capital Structure and Returns" (1981), The management Accountant, Vol. 16. No.8., pp.375-376.

INDEX

Sr. No.	Particular	Page no.
5.1	Introduction	130
5.2	Cash and liquidity	131
5.3	Meaning of liquidity	131
5.4	Significance of liquidity management	132
5.5	Factors affecting liquidity management	133
5.6	Monitoring and control of liquidity	138

"When the music stops in terms of liquidity, things will get complicated. But as long as the music is playing, you've got to get up and dance. We're still dancing. "

- Chuck Prince, Citigroup

1.Introduction

Cash is the important current asset for the operations of the business. Cash is the basic input needed to keep the business running on a continuous basis; it is also the ultimate output expected to be realised by selling the service or product manufactured by the firm. The firm should keep sufficient cash, neither more nor less. Cash shortage will disrupt the firm's manufacturing operation while excessive cash will supply remain idle, without contributing anything towards the firm's profitability. Thus a major function of the financial manager is to maintain sound cash position.

According to S.E.Balton "Cash has been described as the oil to lubricate the ever turning wheels of business; without the process grinds to a stop."

Cash is the money which a firm can disburse immediately without any restriction. The term cash includes coins, currency and cheques held by the firm, and balances in its bank accounts. Sometimes near – cash items, such as marketable securities or bank time deposits, are also included in cash. The basic characteristic of near cash assets is that they can readily be converted into cash. Generally, when a firm has excess cash, it invests it in marketable securities. This kind of investment contributes some profit to the firm.

Cash management concerned with the managing of : i) cash flows into and out of the firm, ii) cash flows within the firm, and iii) cash balances held by the firm at a point of time by financing deficit or investing surplus cash.

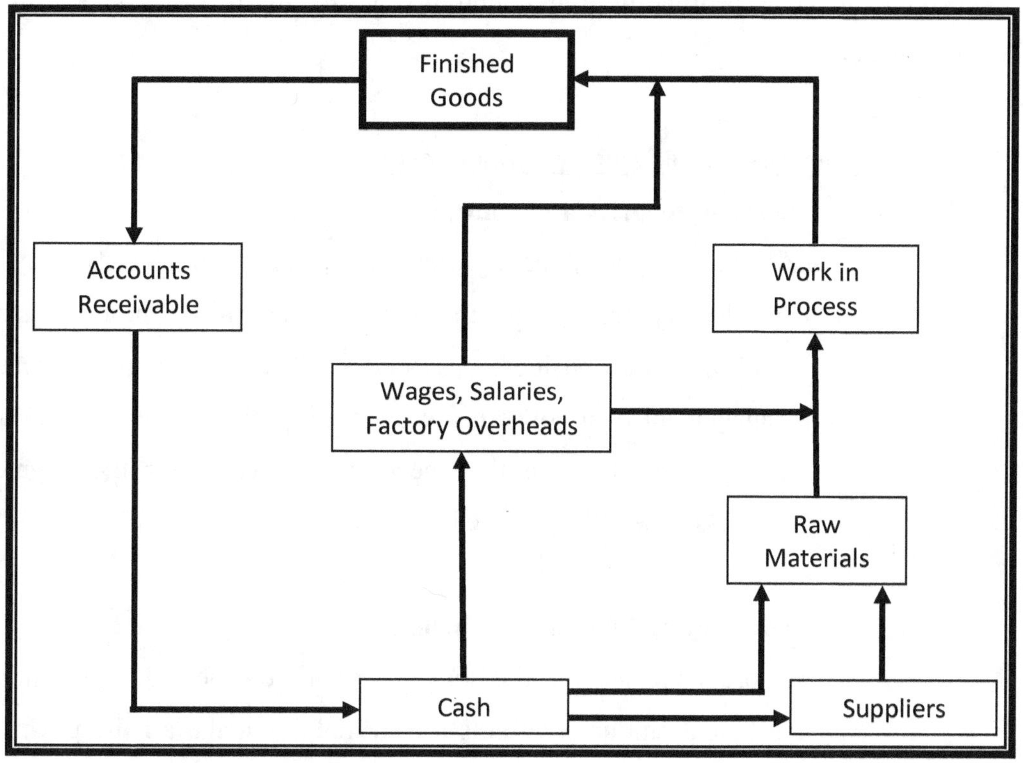

2. Cash and liquidity

Cash and liquidity are two different term and sometimes mistaken interchangeably. For individual it doesn't make any difference but for a businessman it needs to get separated. Cash is a part of liquidity management along with other variables like inventory, accounts receivable, accrued income, outstanding expenses etc. cash is a vital ingredient to study the recipe of liquidity management. Cash is also an essential element as all other variables for measuring liquidity at last get converted into cash. Although cash is an important element of liquidity management but one cant study only cash, otherwise it will not provide clear picture about liquidity. Business can not be done only though cash, it also requires money to be invested in the form inventory, receivables etc. so together with all these variables one has to study concept of liquidity.

3.Meaning of Liquidity

Liquidity of a firm mean the ability of the firm to meet its short term current obligation or liabilities as and when they become due for payment. In fact, liquidity is a pre requisite for the very survival of a firm. The short term creditors of the firm are interested in sort term liquidity of a firm. But liquidity also implies keeping in view profitability, and liquidity is required for efficient financial management.

4. Significance of liquidity management

1 **Sense of security and confidence**

Adequate liquidity management creates sense of security, confidence and loyalty throughout the business and also among customers, creditors and business associates. The proprietor officials or management of a concern are carefree. If they have proper liquidity arrangements because they need not to worry for the payment of business expenditure or creditors.

2 **Solvency and continuous production**

In order to maintain the solvency of the business, it is essential that sufficient amount of funds are available t make all the payments in time as and when they are due. In the absence of liquidity management, production will suffer, particularly in the present era of cut throat competition. A business can never flourish in the absence of adequate liquidity.

3 **Sound goodwill and debt capacity**

Promptness of payment in the business creates goodwill and increase the debt capacity of the business. If investors and borrowers are confident that they will get their due interest and payment of principal in time, a firm can raise funds from the market, purchase the goods on credit and borrow short term funds from banks etc.

4 **Distribution of dividends**

Short of liquidity, a company can not distribute dividend to its shareholders in spite of sufficient profits. To make up for the deficiency of liquidity profits are to be retained in the business. On the other hand, ample dividends can be declared and distributed. It increases market value of share.

5 **Exploitation of good opportunity**

Good opportunities can be exploited in case of adequacy of capital in a concern, for e.g. a company may take off seasonal purchases resulting in substantial savings or it can fetch big supply orders resulting in good profits.

6 **Increase in efficiency of fixed assets**

Due to proper maintenance of adequate liquidity increases the efficiency of the fixed assets of the business. Without proper liquidity, fixed assets are like a gun which can not be shoot as there is no cartidges. It has been rightly said ***"the fate of large scale investment in fixed capital is often determined by a relatively small amount of current assets."***

7 **Increased in production efficiency**

A continuous supply of raw materials, research programmes, innovations and technical developments and expansion programmes, employees training can successfully be carried out if adequate capital is maintained in the business. It increases the production capacity which increases the efficiency and morale of the employees as well.

5. Factors affecting liquidity management

1 **Nature of business**

The working capital requirement of a firm is closely related to the nature of its business. A service frim, like an electircity undertaking or transport corportion, which has a short operating cycle and which sells predominantly on cash basis, has a modest working capital requirement and deficiency of liquidity. On the other hand, a manufacturing concern like a machine tools unit, which has a long operating cycle and which sells largely on credit, has a very substantial working capital requirement, following table shows relative proportions of investment in current assets and fixed assets for certain industries.

Proportions of current assets and fixed assets		
Current assets (%)	**Fixed assets (%)**	**Industries**
10-20	80-90	Hotel and restaurants
20-30	70-80	Electricity generation and distribution
30-40	60-70	Aluminium, shipping
40-50	50-60	Iron and steel, basic industrial chemical
50-60	40-50	Tea plantation
60-70	30-40	Cotton textile, sugar
70-80	20-30	Edible oils, tobacco
80-90	10-20	Trading, construction

(Source : Prasanna Chandra 'fundametals of financial management')

2 **Seasonality of operations**

Firms which have marked seasonality in their operations usually have highly fluctuating working capital requirements. For e.g., a firm manufacturing A.Cs. the sale of A.Cs. reach a peak during the summer months and drops sharply during the winter period. The need of liqudity of such a firm is likely to increase considerably in summer months and decrease significantly during the winter period. On the other hand, a firm manufacturing a product like lamps, which have fairly even sales around the year, tends to have stable liqudity in the business.

3 **Production policy**

A firm marked by pronounced seasonal fluctuations in its sales may pursue a productin policy which may reduce the sharp variations in liqudity management. For e.g., a manufacturer of A.Cs may maintain a steady production thoroughout theyear rather than intensify the production activity during peak business season. Such a production policy may reduce the requirement of liquidity in business up to a great extent.

4 **Market conditions**

The degree of competition prevailing in the market place has an important bearing on liquidity needs. When competiton is keen, a larger inventory of finished goods is required to promplty serve cutomers who may not be inclined to wait because othe manufacturers are ready to meet their needs. Further, generous credit terms may have to be offered to attract customers in a highly competitive market. Thus, working capital needs tend to be high because of greater investment in finished goods inventory and acconts recievable. On the other hand market is strong and competition is weak, a firm can manage with smaller inventory of finished goods because customers can be served with delay. Futher, in such situation the firm can insist on cash payment and avoid lock up of funds in accounts receivable and even can ask for advance payment, partial or total.

5 **Conditions of supply**

The inventory of raw materials, spares and stores depends on the conditons of supply. If the supply is prompt and adequate, the firm can manage with small inventory. However, if the supply is unpredictable and scant then the firm, to ensure continuity of production, would have to acquire stocks as and when they are avabilable and carry larger inventory on an average. A similar policy may have to be followed when the raw material is avialible only seasonally and production operations are carried out round the year.

Financing liquidity requirements

1 **Accruals**

The major accrual items are wages and taxes. Theser simply what the firm owes to its employees and to the govenrment. Wages are usually paid on a weekly, fortnighlty or monthly basis – between payments, the amount owed but not yet paid is shown as accrued wages on the balance sheet. Income taxes are payable quaterly and other taxes may be payable half yearly or annually. Accruals vary with the level of activity of the firm. When the activity level expands, accruals increae and vice versa. Since no interest is paid by the firm on accurals, ***they are often regard as a 'free' source of financing.*** While accrurals are free souce of financing, they are typically not amenable to contrl by management. The payment period of employees is determined by the practice in industry and provisions of law.

2 **Trade credit**

Trade credit represents the crdit extended by the suppliers of goods and services. It is spontaneous soucre of finance in the sense that it arises in the normal transactions of the firm without specific negotiations, provided the firm is considered creditworthy by its suppliers. It is an important source of finance.

3 **Working capital advance by commerical banks**

Working capital advance by commercial banks play imortant role in liquidity management. They may be provided in the forms of cash credits, overdrafts, short term loans, rediscounting of bills. In addition to these fomrs of direct finance, commercial banks help their customers in obtaining credit from other sources through the letter of credit arragement.

4 **Public deposits**

Many firms, large and small, have resorted to unsecured deposits from the public in recent years, mainly to finance their short term requirements. It is easy to take as no security is offered against it, hence the mortgageable assets of the firm are conserved, but there are some legal procedures to be followed like credit rating of company, restrictions on fund raising and it could not be more than 25% of company shares and reserves.

5 **Inter – corproate deposits**

A deposti made by one company with another, normally for a period up to six months is referred as an inter corporate deposit. Such deposits are ususally of three types : call deposit, three months deposit, six months deposit. Traditionally some prosperous companies in the fold of big business houses such as Birlas and Goenkas carried substantial liquid funds meant primarily to exploit investment opportunities in the form of corporate acquistions and takeovers. Until such opportunity arose, the liquid funds were deposited with other companies with an understanding that they would be withdrawn at short notice.

6 **Short term loans from financial institutions**

The Life Insurance Corporation of India, the General Insurance Corporation, and the Unit Trust of India provide short term loans to manuafacturing companies with an excellent trade record. But there are some eligiblity criteira in the form of company's debt equity ratio, dividend payment history as interest coverage ratios etc.

7 **Rights debentures for working capital**

Public limited companies can issue "Right" debentures to their shareholders with an object of augmenting the long term resources of the company for working capital requirments.

8 **Commerical paper**

Commercial paper represents short term unsecured promissary notes issued by fimrs which enjoy a farirly high credit rating. Generally, large firms with considerable financial strength are able to issue commerical paper.

9 **Factoring**

A factor is a financial arragment which offers services relating to mangment and financing of debts arising from credit sales, while factoring is well established in Western contries, only two factors, the SBI Factoring and Commercial Services Limited and Canbank

Factoring Ltd., which have been mandated by the Reserve Bank of India to operate in the western region and the southern regions respectively, have been set up recently in India. The factor selects the accounts of the client that would be handled by it and establishes, along with client, the credit limit applicable to the selected accounts.

6. Monitoring and control of liquidity

The liquidity management in a business require continuous monitoring and review. The manager can adopt different tools and techniques in monitoring, evaluating, reviewing and controlling the liquidity. Some of them are as follows:

1 **Monitoring the Operating cycle**

The total liquidity need depend upon the length of the operating cycle, lengthier the operating cycle, the greater would be the working capital needs and vice versa. The operating cycles of the firm consist of different cycles for different elements of the working capital. In order to have an effective control over liquidity, the finance manager must monitor duration of all these individual operating cycles of different elements.

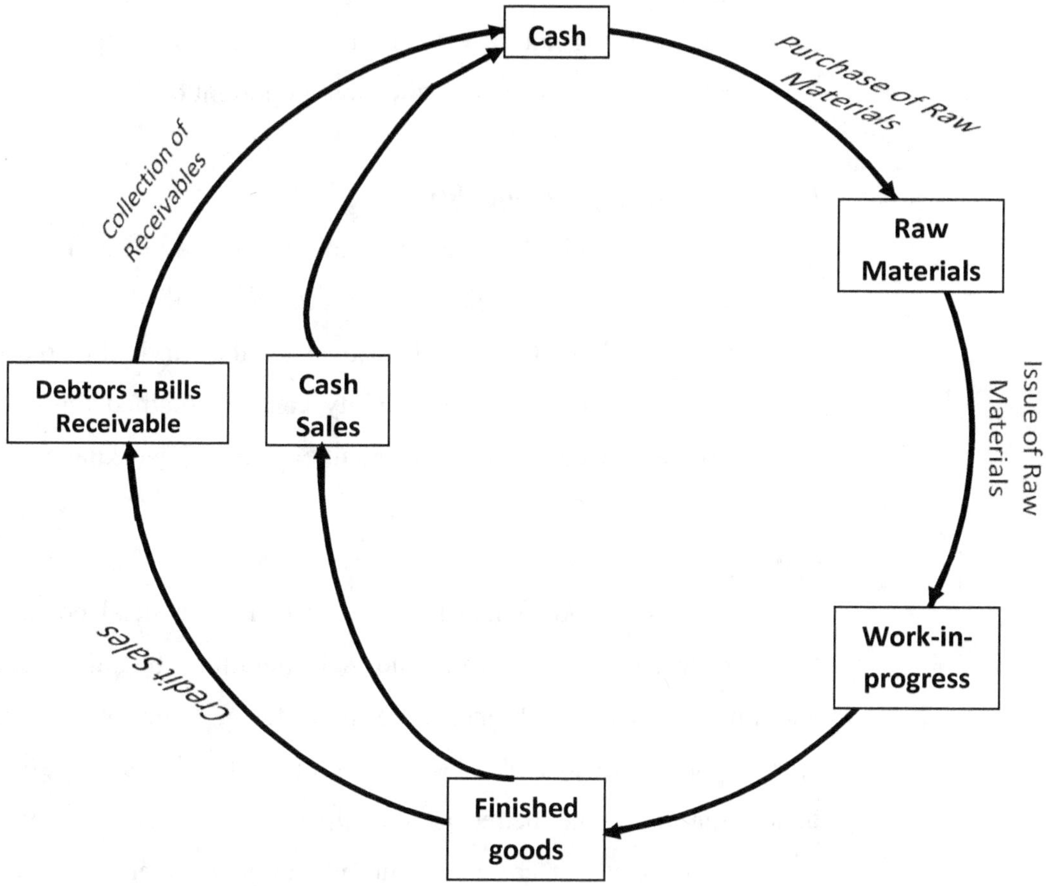

Diagram 1: Operating Cycle of Manufacturing Concern

The actual operating cycle period should be ascertained for each element i.e., raw materials, the work in progress, finished goods etc., over a period of time and it should be compared with standard operating cycle period set for the same firm or for the industry as a whole. There should always an effort to reduce the length of operating cycle not only for each element but also for whole. This would help the firm have comfortable liquidity.

2 Liquidity ratios

Another analytical tool that is adopted in order to monitor the liquidity is accounting ratios. The various liquidity measurement ratios are:

Current ratios

Liquidity ratios

Stock turnover ratios

Debtors turnover ratios etc,

These ratios are used to find out the number of years to attain the emerging liquidity position of the firm. Among the above ratios, the current ratio is the most important one.

3 **Monitoring the liquidity**

Even though in the long run, profitability and selection of good investment are crucial to the prosperity of the firm. It is however liquidity which is critical for the survival of the firm in short run. Sufficient liquidity can be obtained through an efficient management of different elements of working capital.

<u>Current ratio</u>

This is a fundamental measure of firms' financial position in the short run, its ability to meet normal operating obligations during one financial year. A higher ratio indicates a large proportion of current assets are available to meet current liabilities. Usually the higher the ratio, the better is a company's financial position and normally the better it can meet current obligations, but at the same time, a higher current ratio would also mean that the company may have an excessive investment in current assets that does not produce sufficient return. On the other hand, a low current ratio would indicate that the sufficient cash is not available to pay current liabilities. A frequently used standard current ratio is 2:1 or 2. However there seems to be very little justification for such a standard. For some business, these may be an adequate current ratio, for others it may be a too high or too low. It highly depends upon the nature of business.

This ratio indicates whether an enterprise possesses sufficient current assets to pay off its current liabilities. This ratio is an indicator of short –term solvency or liquidity position of an enterprise. Conventional standard or ideal ratio is 2:1, i.e. the enterprise should have twice the current assets than the current liabilities, to exhibit ideal short-term solvency position. The ratio is used to assess the firm's ability to meet its short term liabilities on times. The standard ratio 2:1 means that current assets of a business should, at least be twice of its current liabilities. The higher the ratio, the better it is, because the firm will be able to pay its current liabilities more easily. The reason for assuming 2:1 as the ideal ratio is that the current assets include such assets as stock, debtors etc., from which full amount cannot be realised in case of need. Hence, even if half the amount is realised from the current assets on time, the firm can still meet its current liabilities in full.

If the current ratio is less than 2:1, it indicates lack of liquidity and shortage of working capital. But a much higher ratio, even though it is beneficial to the short term creditors, is not necessarily good for the company. A much higher ratio than 2:1 may indicate the poor investment policies of the management. A much higher ratio may also be considered to be adverse under following reasons:

a) A much higher ratio indicates that sock might be pilling up because of poor sales.
b) Large amount is locked up in debtors due to inefficient collection policy.
c) The cash or bank balances might be lying idle because of no proper investment opportunity are available.

It is therefore, dangerous to use ratio alone as n index of measuring the short term financial position of a concern.

Current ratio = Current Assets / Current liabilities

As CAs – CLs = WC. This ratio is also called working capital ratio and it indicates the quantum of the working capital of an enterprise.

Current assets = stock + debtors + cash at bank + cash in hand + prepaid expenses + accrued incomes etc.

Current liabilities = creditors + bills payable + outstanding expense + pre received income + bank overdraft etc.

Following point should be carefully considered wile calculating the current ratio:

a) Only those assets, which are expected to be realised within a year, should be included in current assets.
b) Only those liabilities, which are expected to be paid within a year, should be included in current liabilities. Those long term loans and

debentures, which will be due for payment within one year, are also included in current liabilities.

c) The term 'investment' is used for fixed assets. Trade investments are treated as fixed assets. But 'short term investment' and 'marketable security' should be included in current assets.

d) Loose tools, patents, goodwill and trade marks are not included in current assets.

e) Fictitious assets such as preliminary expenses, share issue expenses etc., appearing on the assets side of the balance sheet should not be included in current assets.

f) 'Bank overdraft' should be included in current liabilities.

g) 'Loan', 'Loan on Mortgage', and 'Bank loan', are treated as long term liabilities, therefore should not be included in current liabilities.

TABLE 5.1 CURRNET RATIO OF THE SELECTED REFINERY INDUSTRY UNDER THE STUDY FOR THE PERIOD OF (2007-08 TO 2012-13)

Source: Compiled and computed from ' Capitalline Corporate Database' of Capital market Publishers (I) Ltd., Mumbai

	2012-13	2011-12	2010-11	2009-10	2008-09	2007-08	AVERAGE	STD DEV	COVAR (%)
BPCL	0.78	0.76	0.65	0.72	0.5	0.74	0.69	0.10	15.04
HPCL	0.68	0.66	0.77	0.74	0.93	1.03	0.80	0.15	18.36
IOCL	0.83	0.83	0.8	0.76	0.61	0.84	0.78	0.09	11.24
MRPL	0.92	1	0.94	1.01	1.36	1.15	1.06	0.17	15.63
ONGC	2.37	1.13	1.17	1.39	1.45	1.56	1.51	0.45	29.88
RIL	1.43	1.44	1.16	1.04	1.06	0.98	1.19	0.20	17.06
AVG	1.17	0.97	0.92	0.94	0.99	1.05	1.01	0.36	35.52

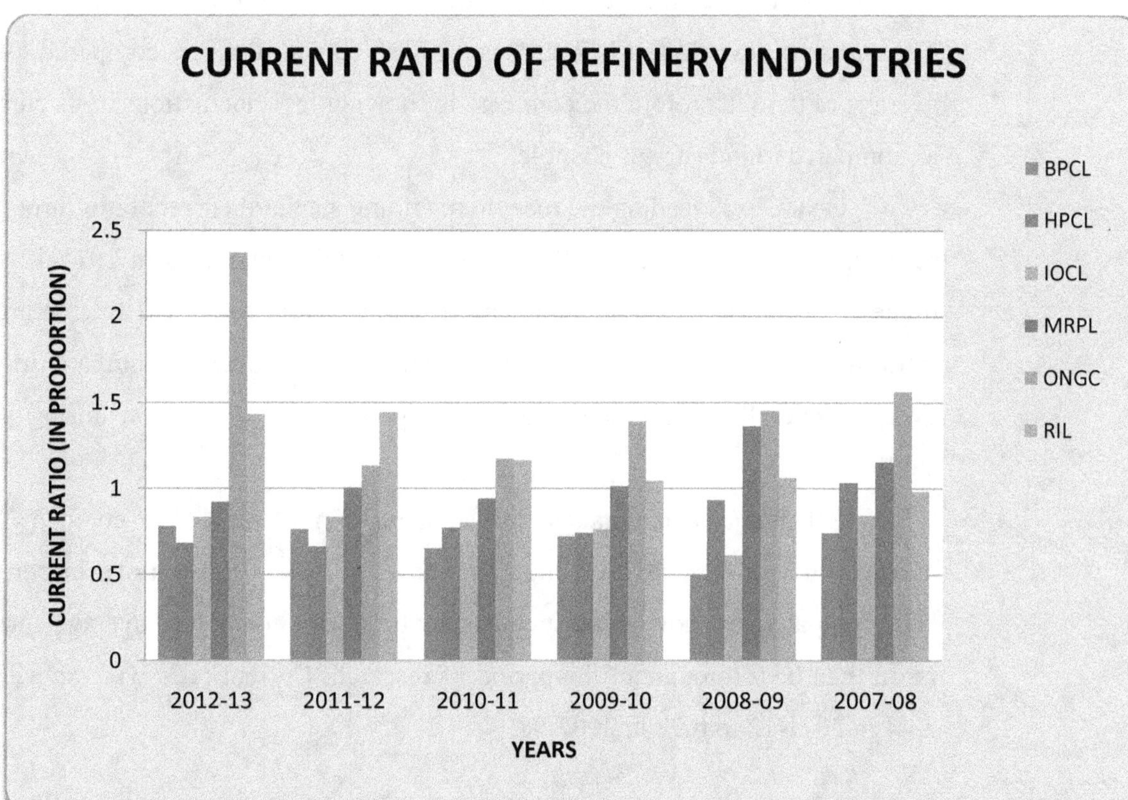

The above table no. 5.1 shows current ratio of refinery industries taken under sample. During research period, current ratio of BPCL was ranged between 0.78 in 2012-13 to 0.5 in 2008-09. The ratio shows fluctuating trend. The average ratio during the period was 0.69 which was the lowest one compare to other industry average. Company couldn't maintain the ideal current ratio during the study period, hence not able to pay its current liabilities in time.

During period of study current ratio of HPCL was between 1.03 in 2007-08 to 0.68 in 2012-13, with an average of 0.80 which was near to ideal current ratio, but below to industry average of 1.01. During most of the years company was not able pay its current liabilities as ratio was less than 1.

The above table shows the current ratio of IOCL, which was the highest 0.84 in 2007-08 and the lowest in 2008-09 i.e. 0.61, trend shows very little fluctuations with an industry average of 0.78. liquidity position was good, but exact standard ratio couldn't be maintained.

While, MRPL shows ideal current ratio during most of the period, the ratio was ranged between 1.36 in 2008-09 to 0.92 in 2012-13. The company has also maintained average current ratio of 1.06 which was more than the industry average. The standard deviation of MRPL was 0.17 which was also less compared to industry average of 0.36. therefore the company is showing less fluctuations in its current ratio as compared to industry as a whole.

ONGC was leading the race, maintaining standard current ratio throughout the research period, maximum 2.37 in 2012-13, to minimum 1.13 in 2011-12, with the highest average of 1.51. the company has shown mix trend and fluctuating current ratio with standard deviation of 0.45 which was moderate compare to industry average. overall the company has shown good liquidity position during period of study.

RIL has also maintained the standard current ratio. The company has kept average current ratio at 1.19. the data shows very less fluctuations in current ratio .The company has shown almost consistent trend and maintained average current ratio more than 0.90 throughout the period of research. Current ratio was ranged between 1.44 in 2011-12 to 0.98 in 2007-08.

ANOVA TEST ON CURRENT RATIO

Null Hypothesis: - There is no significant difference in current ratio of selected refinery Industries during study period

Alternative Hypothesis: - There is significant difference in current ratio of selected refinery Industries during the study period.

Level of significance: 5% Level

Table 5.2 ANOVA TEST ON CURRENT RATIO

ANOVA					
Source of Variation	*SS*	*df*	*MS*	*F*	*F crit*
SS between companies	2.9	5	0.58	11.07	2.6
SS between years	0.25	5	0.05	0.97	2.6
Error	1.31	25	0.05		
Total	4.46	35			

CURRENT RATIO :-

Calculated F value: 11.07

Table F value: 2.6

Result: Significant

The analysis showed the significant result. It can be seen from the table, that the calculated value of F was found as 11.07, while the table value of F was 2.6, AT 5% level of significance. The calculated value of F, being more than the table value of F, the alternate Hypothesis stood accepted and the null hypothesis got rejected at 5% level of significance. So it proves that the differences among the average of this group were much significant and the average liquidity of the groups of the refinery Industries differed much.

<u>Stock turnover ratio or stock velocity ratio</u>

The liquidity of inventories is measured by the number of times per year that inventory is converted into cost of goods sold. Hence it is a device to measure the efficiency of the inventory management, however, in its zeal to show a high ratio, inventories are not allowed to drop down below the danger level.

Inventory turnover rates vary tremendously by the nature of the business. It is usually desirable to compare a firm's inventory turnover with the turnover experience by comparable companies. It is not unusual for retailers of perishable goods to experience a higher inventory turnover than those retailers who deal in durable goods. At the other hand, retailers of jewellery frequently reflect a low inventory turnover. This ratio indicates the movement of stock during a particular period, in other words, it indicates how fast goods are sold out from the stock of those goods, higher ratio indicates a faster movement of stock.

Stock turnover ratio/stock velocity ratio = cost of goods sold/average stock

Cost of goods sold = sales – gross profit

Average stock = opening stock + closing stock /2

Where the cost of goods sold cannot be ascertained, it may be replaced by sales i.e. in the absence of adequate information regarding cost of goods sold, the ratio may be taken as sales / average stock.

A low stock turnover ratio indicates that stock does not sell quickly and remains lying in the godown for quite a long time. This results in increased storage costs, blocking of funds and losses on account of goods becoming obsolete or unsalable. This ratio can be used for comparing the efficiency of sales policies of two firms doing same type of business. The stock policy of the management of that firm, whose stock turnover ratio is higher, will be treated as more efficient. Similarly, by comparing the stock turnover ratio of current year with the previous year, the management can assess whether stock has been more efficiently used or not.

TABLE 5.3 STOCK TURNOVER RATIO OF THE SELECTED REFINERY INDUSTRY UNDER THE STUDY FOR THE PERIOD OF (2007-08 TO 2012-13)

	2012-13	2011-12	2010-11	2009-10	2008-09	2007-08	AVERAGE	SD	COV(%)
BPCL	14.39	13.29	9.86	11.09	21.91	11.64	13.70	4.33	31.63
HPCL	13.13	9.68	8.68	9.28	15.31	9.47	10.93	2.66	24.39
IOCL	7.85	8.15	7.56	8.37	13.98	9.09	9.17	2.41	26.34
MRPL	9.78	7.32	11.01	12.03	23.6	10.53	12.38	5.72	46.22
ONGC	14.55	14.81	16.59	87.82	111.98	122.77	61.42	51.76	84.27
RIL	8.69	10.42	9.59	8.29	12.92	10.57	10.08	1.66	16.48
AVERAGE	11.40	10.61	10.55	22.81	33.28	29.01	19.61	27.46	140.03

Source: Compiled and computed from ' Capitalline Corporate Database' of Capital market Publishers (I) Ltd., Mumbai

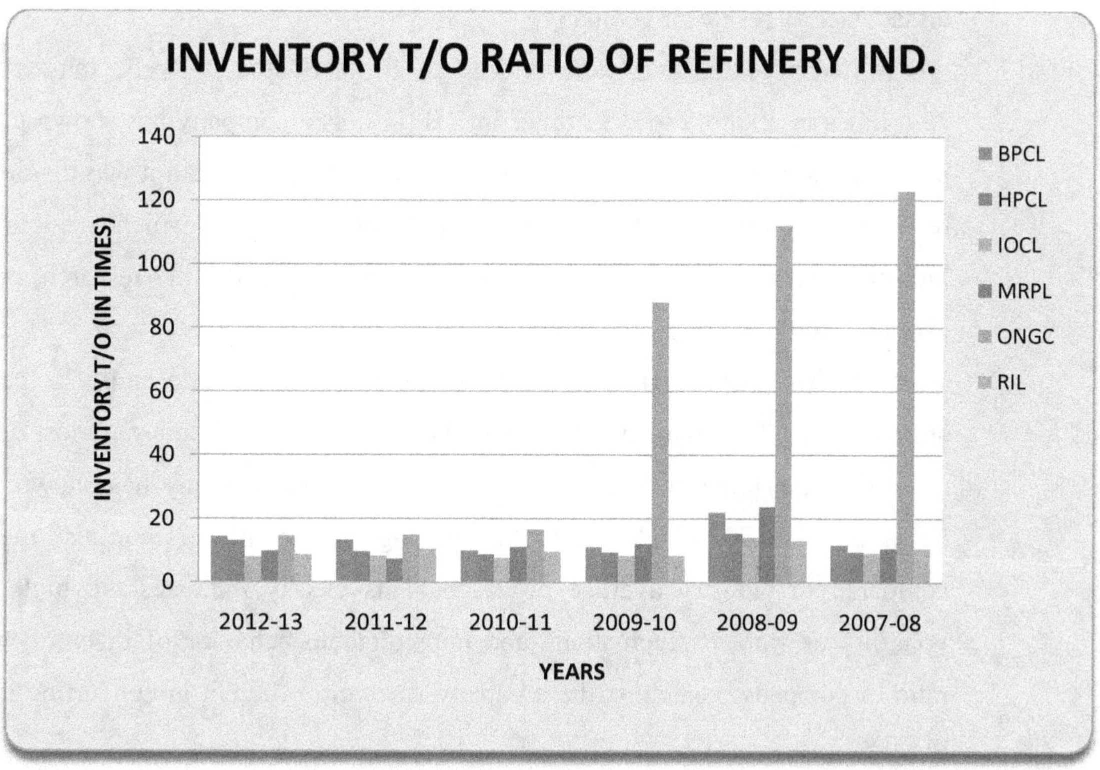

The above table no. 5.2 shows inventory turnover ratio of refinery industries taken under sample. The above table shows inventory turnover ratio of BPCL, the data shows fluctuating trend in ratio. It was 11.64 times in 2007-08, then the highest 21.91 times in 2008-09, and further declined to 11.09 times and lowest 9.86 times in the 2009-10 and 2010-11 respectively. The company has maintained average turnover at 13.70 times which was below to industry average of 19.61 times. Overall the company has maintained satisfactory turnover ratio.

The inventory turnover ratio of HPCL has also shown mix trend. The turnover was ranged between 15.31 times in 2008-09 to 8.68 times in 2010-11. During study period, company has maintained average turnover at 10.93 times less than the industry average of 19.61 times. Overall the company has kept moderate inventory turnover ratio.

Where as IOCL was having the lowest average of 9.17 times of inventory turnover. IOCL was struggling to move inventory faster as compare to other companies of sample study. The company has figured out the lowest turnover ratio of 7.56 times in 2010-11, and highest was 13.98 times in 2008-09. Overall it was dissatisfactory result for company.

Inventory turnover ratio of MRPL shows fluctuating trend ranged between 23.6 times in 2008-09 to 7.32 times in 2011-12. The company has shown the lowest inventory turnover ratio to other companies under study. Overall it was dissatisfactory result of company. The standard deviation of MRPL was 5.72 which was less than the industry average of 27.46, showing less fluctuation during research period in inventory turnover ratio of company.

ONGC has shown tremendous inventory turnover ratio and also the highest among others. The company has shown the average of 61.42 times, almost 3.20 times more than the industry average of 19.61 times. The company has shown standard deviation of 51.76, which was highest among industry players and also the highest compared to industry average of 27.46. This clearly indicates the high level of volatility as well as fluctuations and unpredictable behavior of inventory turnover ratio of company. somehow the company was very efficient in converting inventory to sales.

During study period RIL has shown mix trend ranged between 12.92 times in 2008-09 to 8.29 times in 2009-10. The company could maintain 10.57 times inventory turnover during period of research which was less than industry average of 19.61

times. Standard deviation of RIL was the lowest one suggesting low fluctuations in ratio, it was the lowest in industry i.e. 1.66.

ANOVA TEST ON INVENTORY TURNOVER RATIO

Null Hypothesis: - There is no significant difference in inventory turnover ratio of selected refinery Industries during study period

Alternative Hypothesis: - There is significant difference in inventory turnover ratio of selected refinery Industries during the study period.

Level of significance: 5% Level

Table 5.4 ANOVA TEST ON INVENTORY TURNOVER RATIO:-

ANOVA					
Source of Variation	*SS*	*df*	*MS*	*F*	*F crit*
SS between companies	12663.92	5	2532.784	5.95	2.6
SS between years	3096.77	5	619.35	1.46	2.6
Error	10635.33	25	425.41		
Total	26396.02	35			

Calculated F value: 5.95

Table F value: 2.6

Result: Significant

The analysis showed the significant result. It can be seen from the table, that the calculated value of F was found as 5.95, while the table value of F was 2.6, AT 5% level of significance. The calculated value of F, being more than the table value of F, the alternate Hypothesis stood accepted and the null hypothesis got rejected at 5% level of significance. So it proves that the differences among the average of this group were much significant and the average liquidity of the groups of the refinery Industries differs much.

DEBTORS TURNOVER RATIO

By the analysis of debtors turnover ratio we know the information about liquidity of a company. The ratio shows the efficiency of credit and collection policy implemented by the company. The liquidity position depends upon the quantity of debtors of a company to a great extent. It measures the rapidity or slowness of their collectability. The higher the ratio the shorter will be time lag between credit sales and cash collection. A low ratio on the other hand means that the debts are not being collected rapidly.

Debtors Turnover ratio = Net credit sales / average debtors + average bills receivables
Where average debtors include bills receivalbes
Average debtors = opening debtors B/R + closing debtors + B/R / 2

This ratio indicates the speed with which the amount is collected from debtors. The higher the ratio, the better it is. Since it indicates that amount from debtors is being collected more quickly. The more quickly the debtors pay, the less the risk from bad debts, and so the lower the expenses of collection and increase in the liquidity of the firm, on other hand lower debtors turnover ratio will indicate the inefficient credit sales policy of the management. The more quickly debtors pay, the less risk from bad debts. It is difficult to set up for this ratio. It depends upon the policy of management and the nature of the industry. Moreover it is also difficult to maintain one type of policy for every customer, it should be tailor made according to customers' personal profile.

TABLE 5.5 DEBTORS TURNOVER RATIO OF THE SELECTED REFINERY INDUSTRY UNDER THE STUDY FOR THE PERIOD OF (2007-08 TO 2012-13)

	2012-13	2011-12	2010-11	2009-10	2008-09	2007-08	AVG	SD	COV(%)
BPCL	46.16	47.58	58.38	58.81	88.37	70.48	61.63	15.80	25.64
HPCL	48.7	57.48	52.33	45.87	63.23	63.44	55.18	7.42	13.44
IOCL	37.2	36.01	45.15	45.91	48.15	36.5	41.49	5.49	13.23
MRPL	17.68	17.97	18.63	21.65	21.93	19.16	19.50	1.85	9.47
ONGC	12.71	15.02	19.38	16.87	15.16	16.87	16.00	2.26	14.09
RIL	23.78	18.4	17.05	23.67	26.29	26.87	22.68	4.07	17.94
AVG	31.04	32.08	35.15	35.46	43.86	38.89	36.08	19.44	53.88

Source:* *Compiled and computed from ' Capitalline Corporate Database' of Capital market Publishers (I) Ltd., Mumbai

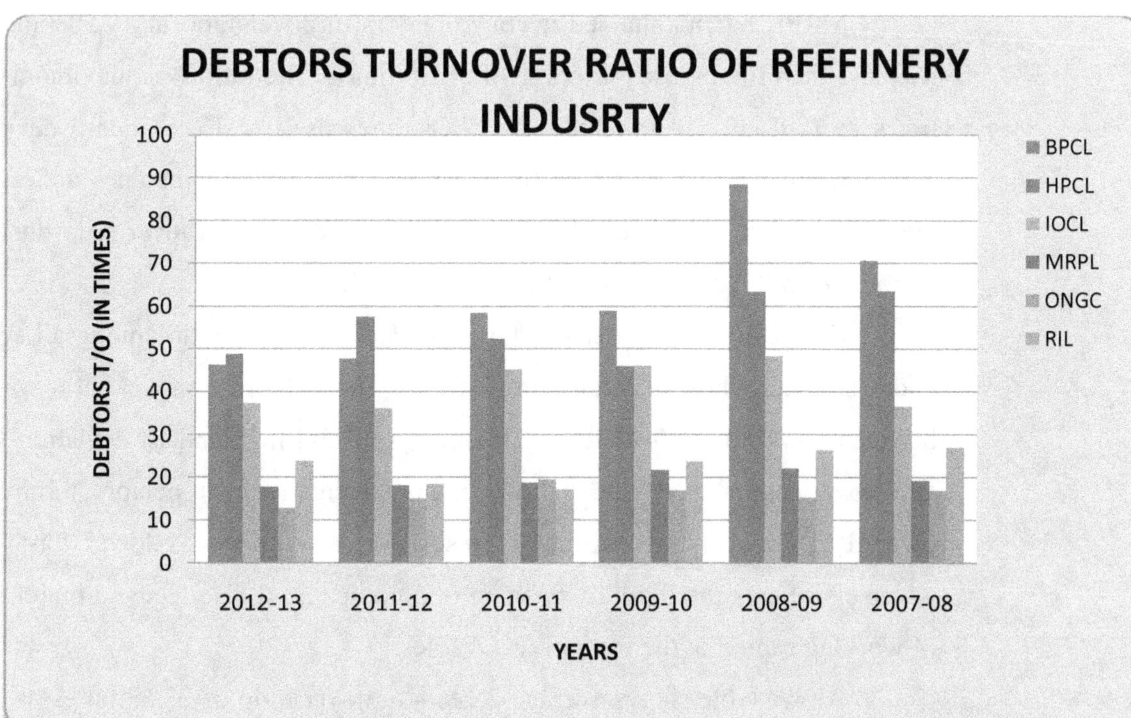

The above table no. 5.3 shows Debtors Turnover ratio of refinery industries taken under sample. Above table shows debtors turnover ratio of BPCL. Average ratio was of 61.63 times more than the industry average of 36.08 times. Company's average debtor's turnover ratio was higher among all companies under study. The turnover was ranged between 88.37 times in 2008-09 to 46.16 times in 2012-13. Standard deviation was 15.80 and co variance was 25.64% shows greater fluctuations in debtors turnover ratio during study period. BPCL was quick to convert credit sales into cash and has implemented good collection policy.

HPCL was next to BPCL in context to average debtors turnover ratio during study period. It was 55.18 times, more than the industry average of 36.08. the ratio was ranged between 63.44 times in 2007-08 to 48.7 in 2012-13. Standard deviation of 7.42 and co variance of 13.44% show fewer fluctuations in debtors turnover ratio. Overall the company has maintained good credit collection policy.

The average debtors turnover ratio of IOCL was 41.49 times. It was also more than the industry average of 36.08 times. The turnover ratio was less fluctuating as standard deviation was 5.49 and co variance was 13.23%. Debtors turnover ratio was ranged between 48.15 times in 2008-09 to 36.01 times in 2011-12.Overall the company has maintained satisfactory collection policy.

MRPL has maintained average debtors turnover ratio at 19.50 times, which was less than the industry average of 36.08 times. The ratio was maximum of 21.93 times in 2008-09 and minimum of 17.68 times in 2012-13. Standard deviations of 1.85 and co variance of 9.47% were the least among all companies under study. It means that there was a very little fluctuations in debtors turnover ratio during study period. Overall it shows moderate collection policy.

ONGC has exceptionally shows the least turnover ratio among all companies under study. It shows average of 16 times. The debtors turnover ratio was ranged between 19.38 in 2010-11 to 12.71 times in 2012-13. Standard deviation was 2.26 and covariance was 14.09% shows major fluctuations in debtors turnover ratio. Overall it was very dissatisfactory result for a company as lower turnover ratio adversely affects the liquidity position of a company. It also leads to major blockage of working capital in the form of receivables.

Above table shows average debtors turnover ratio of 22.68 times of RIL. The ratio was more than the industry average of 36.08 times. It was ranged between 26.87 in 2007-08 to 18.4 times in 2011-12. Standard deviation was 4.07 whereas covariance of 17.94% shows fewer fluctuations in debtors turnover ratio during period of study. Overall it shows good collection policy.

ANOVA TEST ON DEBTOR TURNOVER RATIO

Null Hypothesis: - There is no significant difference in debtors turnover ratio of selected refinery Industries during study period

Alternative Hypothesis: - There is significant difference in debtors turnover ratio of selected refinery Industries during the study period.

Level of significance: 5% Level

Table 5.6 ANOVA TEST ON DEBTOR TURNOVER RATIO

ANOVA					
Source of Variation	*SS*	*df*	*MS*	*F*	*F crit*
SS between companies	11425.37	5	2285.07	50.4	2.6
SS between years	666.07	5	133.22	2.94	2.6
Error	1133.52	25	45.34		
Total	13224.96	35			

Calculated F value: 50.4

Table F value: 2.6

Result: Significant

The analysis showed the significant result. It can be seen from the table, that the calculated value of F was found as 50.4, while the table value of F was 2.6, AT 5% level of significance. The calculated value of F, being more than the table value of F, the alternate Hypothesis stood accepted and the null hypothesis got rejected at 5% level of significance. So it proves that the differences among the average of this group were much significant and the average liquidity of the groups of the refinery Industries differ much.

Liquid/quick/acid test ratio

Quick ratio indicates whether the firm is in a position to pay its current liabilities within a month or immediately. As such, the quick ratio is calculated by dividing liquid assets by liquid liabilities. It provides even more critical look at the ability of the company to meet its day to day obligations. It signifies a very short term liquidity of a business concern and is, therefore called 'liquid ratio'. If it is desired to apply a still stiffer and rigorous test for evaluating a firm's financial position in short period, the application of acid test ratio is recommended.

$$\text{Liquid / quick / acid test ratio} = \frac{\text{liquid / quick assets}}{\text{Liquid / quick liabilities}}$$

Liquid assets = current assets – stock

Liquid liabilities = current liabilities – bank overdraft

This ratio indicates whether an enterprise possesses sufficient liquid/quick assets to pay off its liquid/quick liabilities. This ratio is an indicator of the liquidity position of an enterprise.

Liquid or quick assets mean the asset which is receivable within a financial year during which it comes into existence and more easily convertible into cash, liquid assets = current assets – stock.

Liquid or quick liability means the liability which is payable within financial year and more quickly payable in cash, liquid liabilities = current liabilities – bank overdraft.

Ideal ratio is at least 1:1, i.e., an enterprise should have at least an equal amount of liquid to pay off its liquid/quick liabilities. It is considered to be better. The idea is that for every rupee of liquid liabilities, there should at least be one rupee of liquid assets. The ratio is better test of short – term financial position of the company than the current ratio, as it considers only those assets which can be easily and readily converted into cash. Stocks and similar items are excluded from current assets which are already in liquid form, or may be easily converted into cash by discounting or factoring. The acid test ratio assumes that stock may not be realized immediately and therefore, it was excluded. Some experts advocate that the bank overdraft should also be excluded, because bank overdraft is a permanent way of financing no hurry to pay it back. Quick ratio removes the shortcomings of current ratio by excluding stock and bank overdraft to show better liquidity position.

TABLE 5.7 QUICK RATIO OF THE SELECTED REFINERY INDUSTRY UNDER THE STUDY FOR THE PERIOD OF (2007-08 TO 2012-13)

	2012-13	2011-12	2010-11	2009-10	2008-09	2007-08	AVG	SD	COV(%)
BPCL	0.71	0.71	0.45	0.68	0.67	0.61	0.64	0.10	15.55
HPCL	0.71	0.52	0.44	0.43	0.53	0.51	0.52	0.10	19.25
IOCL	0.5	0.74	0.51	0.45	0.47	0.54	0.54	0.11	19.67
MRPL	0.5	0.54	0.54	0.71	0.98	0.57	0.64	0.18	28.38
ONGC	2.26	1.22	1.08	1.22	1.27	1.39	1.41	0.43	30.55
RIL	1.12	1.17	0.94	0.69	0.87	0.89	0.95	0.18	18.59
AVG	0.97	0.82	0.66	0.70	0.80	0.75	0.78	0.37	47.94

Source: Compiled and computed from ' Capitalline Corporate Database' of Capital market Publishers (I) Ltd., Mumbai

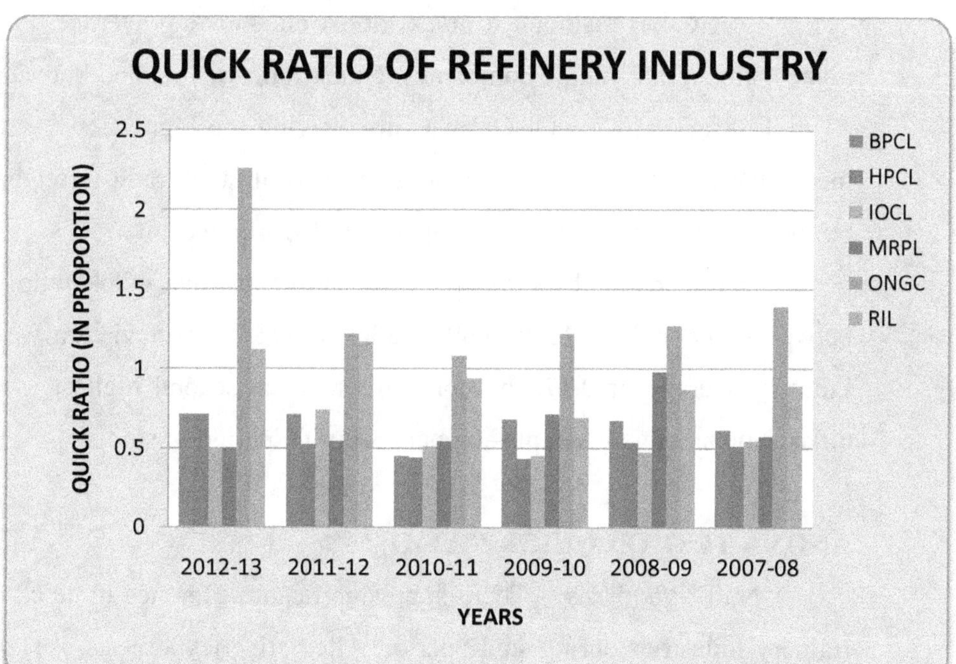

The above table no. 5.4 shows Quick ratio of refinery industries taken under sample. BPCL has shown average quick ratio of 0.64 during research period, which was less than the industry average of 0.93. the ratio was mostly consistent during research period except the lowest one 0.45 in 2010-11. During last two years it was consistent as well as maximum i.e. 0.71. the company has also shown the lowest variation of 15.55% from average.

HPCL had lowest average of quick ratio i.e. 0.52 among other companies. Moreover the company has shown the fluctuating trend in quick ratio, ranged between 0.52 in 2011-12 to 0.71 in 2012-13. The standard deviation was 0.10 which was also less than industry average of 0.37, means less inconsistency in ratio.

IOCL has maintained mix trend of quick ratio during period of study showing average of 0.54 at a covariance of 19.67%, the company couldn't maintain ideal quick ratio. The ratio was ranged between 0.74 in 2011-12 to 0.45 in 2009-10.

MRPL had quick ratio ranged between 0.98 in 2008-09 to 0.5 in 2012-13. The company has maintained average of 0.64 which was less than industry average of 0.78. Standard deviation of 0.18 compared to industry average of 0.78 shows less fluctuations in quick ratio during study period.

ONGC has maintained quick ratio well, showing average quick ratio of 1.41 highest among all sample companies. Quick ratio was ranged between 2.26 in 2012-13 to 1.08 in 2010-11. ONGC was also having the highest co variance of 30.55% means there were greater fluctuations in trend of quick ratio throughout the research period. Overall it was a good management of working capital.

During research period RIL has shown average quick ratio of 0.95, ranged between 1.17 in 2011-12 to 0.69 in 2009-10. Standard deviation was 0.18 less than industry average of 0.37. the company was the second highest in maintenance of quick ratio among all sample companies during period of study.

ANOVA TEST ON QUICK RATIO

Null Hypothesis: - There is no significant difference in quick ratio of selected refinery Industries during study period Alternative Hypothesis: - There is significant difference in quick ratio of selected refinery Industries during the study period.

Level of significance: 5% Level

Table 5.8 ANOVA TEST ON QUICK RATIO:-

ANOVA					
Source of Variation	*SS*	*df*	*MS*	*F*	*F crit*
SS between companies	3.52	5	0.7	16.79	2.6
SS between years	0.35	5	0.07	1.68	2.6
Error	1.05	25	0.04		
Total	4.92	35			

Calculated F value: 16.79

Table F value: 2.6

Result: Significant

The analysis showed the significant result. It can be seen from the table, that the calculated value of F was found as 16.79, while the table value of F was 2.6, AT 5% level of significance. The calculated value of F, being more than the table value of F, the alternate Hypothesis stood accepted and the null hypothesis got rejected at 5% level of significance. So it proves that the differences among the average of this group were much significant and the average liquidity of the groups of the refinery Industries differ much.

Debt – equity ratio

It develops the relationship between owned funds and the borrowed funds. This reflects the extent to which borrowed capital is used in place of equity capital. Business firms acquire assets both with owners and creditors' funds. The larger the portion of funds provided by owners, the less risk is assumed by creditors. The debt – equity ratio is worked out as:

Debt – equity ratio = Total debts/ total owner's equity

The ratio represents the proportion of external equity to internal equity in the capital structure of the firm. The external equity represents the amount of debts/liabilities to outsiders. It includes both short term and long term liabilities. On the other hand owners' equity includes all such liabilities that belong to the shareholders, e.g., share capital(both preferential as well as equity), reserves and surpluses, however accumulated losses and deferred expenses are to be deducted from the owners' equity to calculate debt equity ratio.

Either too high or too low a ratio may be disadvantageous. Too high suggests that management is not taking advantages of opportunities to maximise profits through borrowing. Too low suggests undue exposure to risk of bankruptcy and to a fixed burden of interest expense in the event of a period of relatively low profit (when the rate of return on total capital is less than the interest rate on borrowed capital). As a rule of thumb, debt – equity ratio of less than 2:1 is taken as acceptable, but this is not based on any scientific analysis, however many financial analysts prefer to consider 1:1 as safe. As the ratio increases, the amount of risk assumed by creditors increases, because the ratio indicates decreasing solvency. In fact, the acceptable level of ratio will vary from firm to firm. For e.g., banking institutions will have much higher debt – equity ratio as compared to manufacturing or trading concerns.

TABLE 5.9 DEBT EQUITY RATIO OF THE SELECTED REFINERY INDUSTRY UNDER THE STUDY FOR THE PERIOD OF (2007-08 TO 2012-13)

	2012-13	2011-12	2010-11	2009-10	2008-09	2007-08	AVERAGE	STD DEV	COV(%)
BPCL	1.42	1.42	1.17	1.7	1.75	1.29	1.46	0.23	15.57
HPCL	2.36	2.09	1.99	1.84	2.12	1.59	2.00	0.26	13.16
IOCL	1.02	1.22	0.95	0.88	1.02	0.86	0.99	0.13	13.17
MRPL	1.08	0.8	0.24	0.31	0.42	0.55	0.57	0.32	56.49
ONGC	0.04	0.04	0.05	0.19	0.2	0.18	0.12	0.08	69.14
RIL	0.3	0.36	0.46	0.49	0.65	0.46	0.45	0.12	26.53
AVG	1.04	0.99	0.81	0.90	1.03	0.82	0.93	0.68	72.58

Source: Compiled and computed from ' Capitalline Corporate Database' of Capital market Publishers (I) Ltd., Mumbai

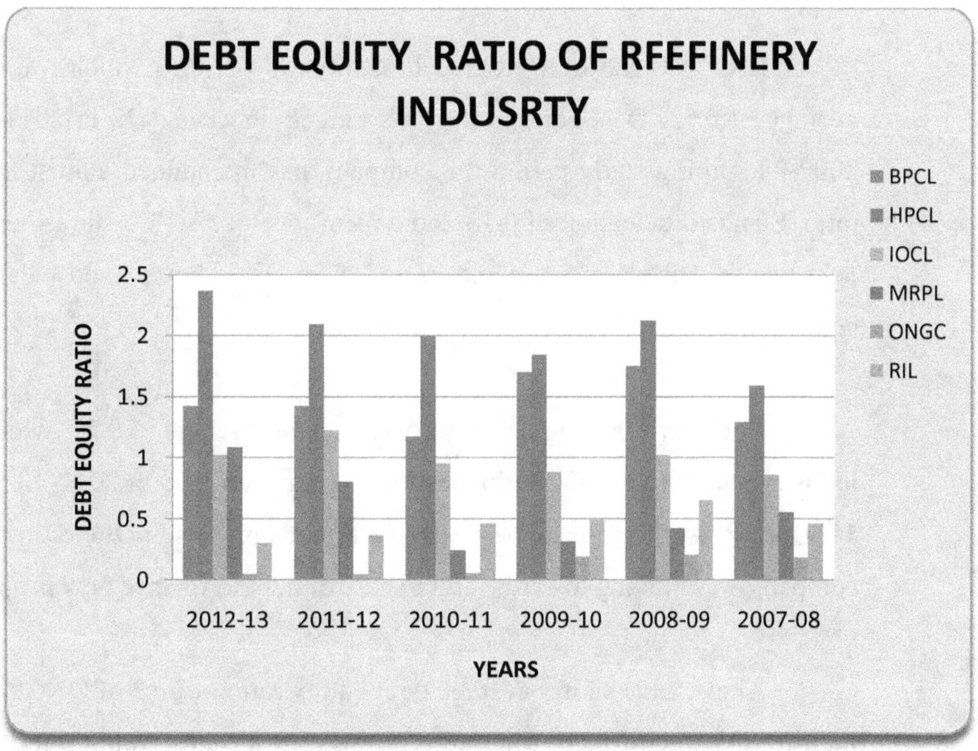

The above table no. 5.5 shows Debt Equity ratio of refinery industries taken under sample. BPCL has maintained average debt equity ratio at 1.46 during period of study, which was slightly less than industry average of 0.93. Debt equity ratio was ranged between 1.75 in 2008-09 to 1.17 in 2010-11. Standard deviation of 0.23 shows less variation in ratio as industry average was of 0.68. the ratio shows greater portion of debt to equity in company, which means company is having more debt fund compared to owners' equity, on the other hand company at a greater side to take advantage of trading on equity.

HPCL was having the highest proportion of debt equity ratio during period of study i.e. 2, as compared to industry average of 0.93. It means that company was having twice proportion of debt compare to its equity. Debt equity ratio was ranged between 2.36 in 2012-13 to 1.59 in 2007-08. Standard deviation of 0.26 was less than industry average of 0.68, it means that there was less inconsistency in debt equity ratio during study period. Greater portion of debt will adversely affect profitability during slag period, however proper utilization of debt funds may improve return to share holders.

IOCL has shown average debt equity ratio of 0.99 which was near to industry average of 0.93. Debt equity ratio was ranged between 1.22 in 2011-12 and 0.86 in 2007-08. During study period the company has maintained almost ideal debt equity ratio. Standard deviation of 0.13 and co variance of 13.17% shows less fluctuation in debt equity ratio during research period. Overall it shows good balance of debt and equity.

MRPL was having debt equity ratio at an average of 0.57, which was less than industry average of 0.93. Ratio was ranged between 1.08 in 2012-13 to 0.24 in 2010-11. During last three years there was continuous increase in the ratio. This shows that company was moving towards larger share of debt to finance new projects.

Above table shows average debt equity ratio of 0.12 of ONGC as compared to industry average of 0.93. The ratios show very meagre proportion of debt in capital structure. The ratio was ranged between 0.2 in 2008-09 to 0.04 in 2012-13. During last three years it was almost negligible that means there was a greater control of owners. Capital structure was not balanced one but lean towards equity share holders. It also means very little chance of trading on equity.

RIL has maintained average debt equity ratio at 0.45. industry average was of 0.93, which means company has been maintaining lower level of debt compare to other companies under study. The ratio was ranged between 0.65 in 2008-09 to 0.30 in 2012-13. Standard deviation of 0.12 and co variance of 26.53% suggests less fluctuation in debt equity ratio.

ANOVA TEST ON DEBT EQUITY RATIO

Null Hypothesis: - There is no significant difference in debt equity ratio of selected refinery Industries during study period

Alternative Hypothesis: - There is significant difference in debt equity ratio of selected refinery Industries during the study period.

Level of significance: 5% Level

Table 5.10 ANOVA TEST ON DEBT EQUITY:-

RATIO

ANOVA					
Source of Variation	*SS*	*df*	*MS*	*F*	*F crit*
SS between companies	14.67	5	2.93	73.36	2.60
SS between years	0.31	5	0.06	1.53	2.60
Error	1	25	0.04		
Total	15.98	35			

Calculated F value: 73.36

Table F value: 2.6

Result: Significant

The analysis showed the significant result. It can be seen from the table, that the calculated value of F was found as 73.36, while the table value of F was 2.6, AT 5%

level of significance. The calculated value of F, being more than the table value of F, the alternate Hypothesis stood accepted and the null hypothesis got rejected at 5% level of significance. So it proves that the differences among the average of this group were much significant and the average liquidity of the groups of the refinery Industries differ much.

Fixed assets turnover

The ratio measures the efficiency in the utilization of fixed assets. The ratio of sales to fixed assets measures the turnover of the plant and machinery, it compares the sales revenue of a company with its net fixed assets. **According to J.R. Monga, "Assets are the economic resources owned by the business which can be conveniently expressed in monetary terms."**This ratio describes how efficiently company is using its fixed assets to generate revenue. If company has high fixed assets turnover it shows that company is efficient at managing its fixed assets as fixed assets are important because they usually represent the largest component of fixed assets and is expressed as under;

Fixed assets turnover = sales / net fixed assets

TABLE 5.11 FIXED ASSETS TURNOVER RATIO OF THE SELECTED REFINERY INDUSTRY UNDER THE STUDY FOR THE PERIOD OF (2007-08 TO 2012-13)

	2012-13	2011-12	2010-11	2009-10	2008-09	2007-08	AVG	SD	COV(%)
BPCL	7.17	6.72	5.19	4.75	5.98	5.15	5.83	0.96	16.55
HPCL	5.63	5.38	4.53	4.32	6.22	5.35	5.24	0.71	13.48
IOCL	4.2	4.49	3.61	3.78	4.98	4.38	4.24	0.50	11.74
MRPL	5.8	5.97	5.11	4.29	5.17	4.42	5.13	0.69	13.42
ONGC	0.86	0.85	0.85	0.85	1.05	1.05	0.92	0.10	11.11
RIL	2.24	2.05	1.58	1.24	1.01	1.29	1.57	0.49	30.98
AVG	4.32	4.24	3.48	3.21	4.07	3.61	3.82	2.00	52.44

Source: Compiled and computed from ' Capitalline Corporate Database' of Capital market Publishers (I) Ltd., Mumbai

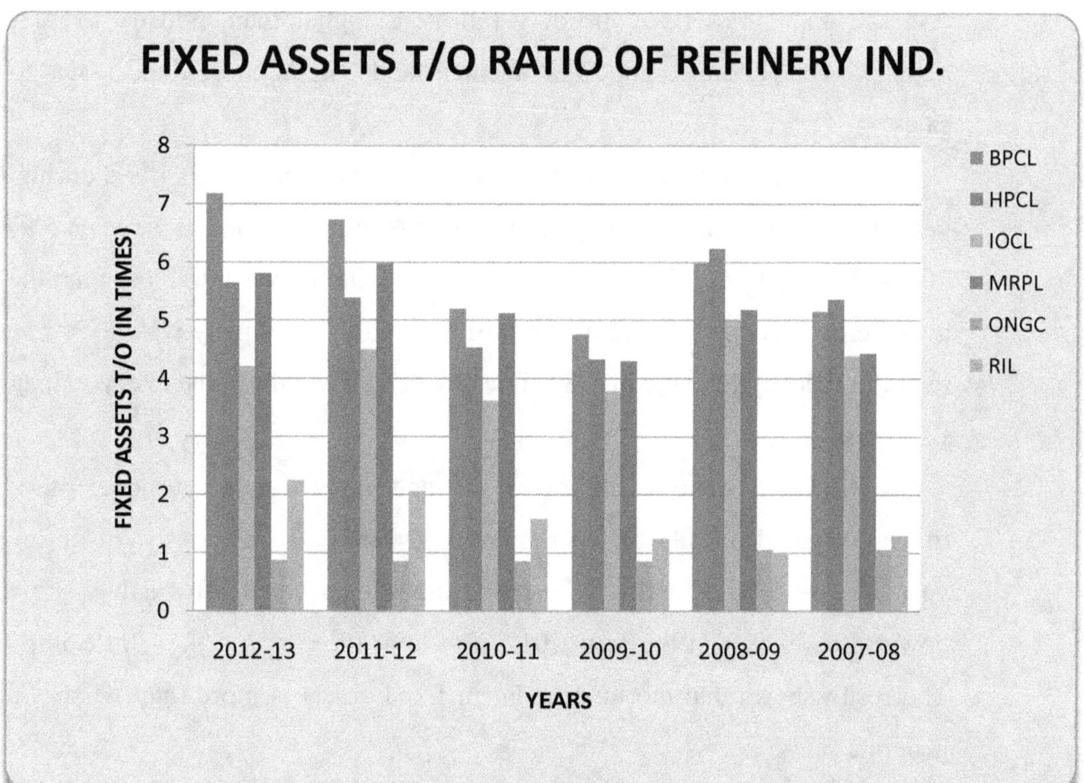

The above table no. 5.6 shows Fixed Assets Turnover ratio of refinery industries taken under sample. The table shows fixed assets turnover ratio of BPCL. The company has shown increasing trend after year 2007-08. The fixed assets turnover ratio of BPCL was ranged between 7.17 times in 2012-13 to 5.15 times in 2007-08. Standard deviation of 0.96 shows less fluctuations compared to industry average of 2. The average fixed assets turnover ratio of BPCL was 5.83 times which was also the highest among all sample companies under study. It means higher efficiency. Company is more efficient in using fixed assets to generating sales.

The fixed assets turnover ratio of HPCL has shown fluctuating trend during research period. Highest 6.22 times in 2008-09, whereas the lowest 4.32 times in 2009-10. The standard deviation was 0.71 times which was less than the industry average. The mean ratio of company was 5.24 times, higher than industry average of 3.82 times. Thus it shows that the company has managed its fixed assets efficiently.

With an average of 4.34 times, IOCL has maintained mix trend of fixed assets turnover ratio during research period. The ratio ranged between 4.98 times in 2008-09 to 3.61 times in 2010-11. Standard deviation was 0.50, less than the industry average. Average 4.35 times fixed turnover ratio was higher than industry average of 3.82 times. Overall it shows good management and utilization of fixed assets to produce sales.

The fixed assets turnover ratio of MRPL has shown mix trend during fist three years then after it has shown upward trend, the ratio was ranged between 5.97 times in 2011-12 to 4.29 times in 2009-10. Standard deviation was 0.69, less than the industry average of 2. Average fixed assets turnover ratio of company was 5.13 times, higher than the industry average of 3.82 times, which shows the satisfactory management of fixed assets.

ONGC has shown the lowest average of fixed assets turnover ratio, i.e. 0.92 times compared to industry average of 3.82 times. It was consistent during fist two years i.e. 1.05 times and was also the highest and then after it has shown almost downtrend, except in the year 2012-13 where there was a very little improvement. The result shows that the investment in fixed assets is more than what is needed to generate sales.

RIL has maintained average fixed assets turnover ratio of 1.57 times which is less than the industry average, the company has shown improvements in fixed assets turnover ratio after 2007-08. It was maximum in 2012-13 i.e. 2.24 times which indicates that necessary steps were taken to improve the ratio.

ANOVA TEST ON FIXED ASSETS TURNOVER RATIO

Null Hypothesis: - There is no significant difference in fixed assets turnover ratio of selected refinery Industries during study period
Alternative Hypothesis: - There is significant difference in fixed assets turnover ratio of selected refinery Industries during the study period.
Level of significance: 5% Level

Table 5.12 ANOVA TEST ON FIXED ASSETS TURNOVER RATIO:-

ANOVA					
Source of Variation	*SS*	*df*	*MS*	*F*	*F crit*
SS between companies	128.470	5	25.69	110.50	2.60
SS between years	6.170	5	1.23	5.31	2.60
Error	5.810	25	0.23		
Total	140.450	35			

FIXED ASSETS TURNOVER RATIO :-

Calculated F value: 110.50

Table F value: 2.6

Result: Significant

The analysis showed the significant result. It can be seen from the table, that the calculated value of F was found as 110.50, while the table value of F was 2.6, AT 5% level of significance. The calculated value of F, being more than the table value of F, the alternate Hypothesis stood accepted and the null hypothesis got rejected at 5% level of significance. So it proves that the differences among the average of this group were much significant and the average liquidity of the groups of the refinery Industries differs much.

BIBLIOGRAPHY

1. Archer, S H., and Ambrosio'D, C. A. (1972): "Business Finance – Theory and Management ", p-445.
2. Banerjee, B. (2008): "Financial Policy and Management Accounting", Prentice-Hall of India Ltd., New Delhi, p-114.
3. Bardia, S.C. (2004): " Liquidity Management: A Case study of Steel Authority of India Ltd.", The Management Accountant, ICWAI, Kolkata, June, pp -463-467.
4. Bhattacharya, H. (2007): "Working Capital Management –Strategies and Techniques ", Prentice-Hall of India Pvt. Ltd., New Delhi, pp-279-282.
5. Chorafas, D. N. (2002): "Liabilities, Liquidities, and Cash Management-
6. Balancing Financial Risk", John Wiley& Sons., New York, U.S.A., pp-119-124.
7. Chowdhury, Anil B. R. (1987): "Working Capital Management – A Workbook on Corporate Liquidity", Management Technologists, Calcutta, pp-1-2,
8. Gentry, J.A., Mehta, D.R., Bhattacharya, S.K., Cobbaut, R., and Scaringella,J.L. (1979):" An introduction study of management perceptions of the working capital process", Journal of International Business Studies, Vol-10(1), pp-28-38.
9. Gentry, E J.(1976): " management Perceptions of the Working Capital Process", Faculty Working Paper, College of Commerce and Business Administration, The University of Illinois, p-32.
10. Gupta, R.K. (1990): "Profitability, Financial Structure and Liquidity", Printwell Publishers, Jaipur, p-133.
11. Handerson J. W. and Maness, T. S. (1989): "The Financial Analyst's Desk Book; A Cash Flow approach to Liquidity", Van Nostrand Reinhold, New York, pp-95-96.(WEB VERSION)
12. Hampton, J.J. (1979): "Financial Decision Making", The Prentice- Hall of India Pvt. Ltd., p-12.

INDEX

Sr.no	Title	Page no.
6.1	Introduction	168
6.2	Comparison of liquidity vis a vis profitability ratios	169- 205
6.3	Multiple correlation matrix	206

6.1.Introduction

LIQUDITY VS PROFITABILITY : RISK – RETURN TANGLE

The firm would make just enough invetment in current assets if it were possible to estimate working capital needs exactly. Under perfect cetainty, current assets holdings would be at the minimum level. A larger investment in current assets under cetainity would mean a low rate of return on investment for the firm, as excess investment in current assets will not earn enogh return. A smaller investment in current assets, on the other hand, would mean interuupted production and sales, due to frequent stock outs and inability to pay crediotors in time due to lack of liquidity.

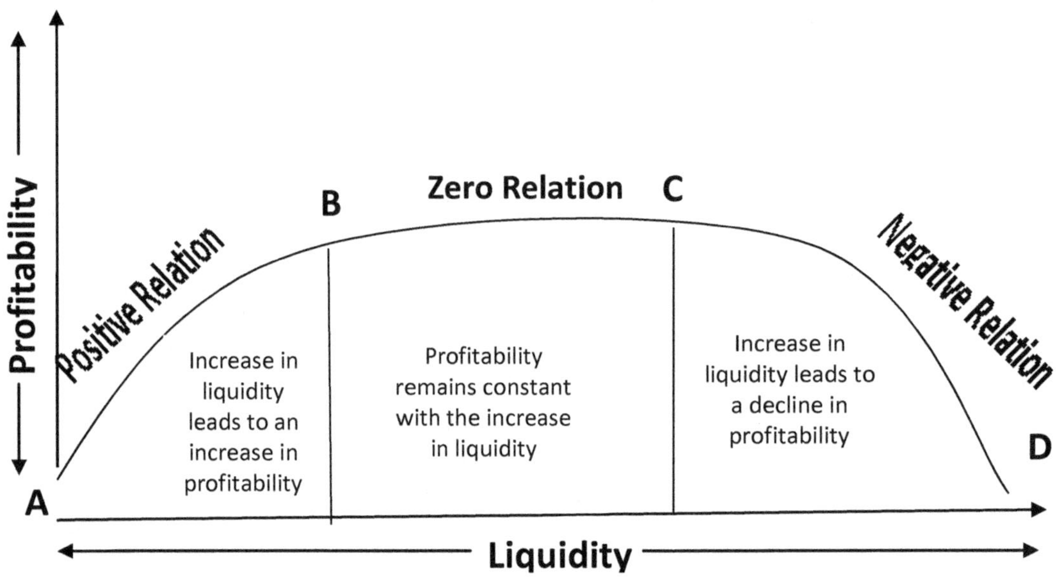

As it is not possible to estimate the quantum of liquidity in business, the firm must decide about levels of liqudity to be maintanied in business and it depends upon working capital policy. It may follow a conservative, or an aggressive or may be average policy. These policies have different risk return implications as mentioned in detail by ***Van Horne, J.C. in "A risk return analysis of a firm's working capital position."***

Two important aims of the working captial mangement are : ***profitability and liquidity/solvency***. Liquidity or solvency used in technical sense, refers to the firm's ability to meet maturing obligations and fulfill the day to day requirment of cash. Lenders and creditors expect prompt settlements of thier claims as and when due. ***To***

ensure solvency, the firm should be very liquid, which means larger current assets holding. If the firm maintains a relatively large investment in current assets holdings. Thus a liquid firm has less risk of insolvency. However, there is a cost assoicated with the firm's funds will be tied up in current assets, and to the extent this investment is idle, the firms' profitability will suffer.

6.2.Liquditiy vis a vis Profitability Matrix

Under liqudity – profitability matrix analysis, companies were classified according to its liquidity and profitability criterion. And according to thsese values they are put in different cells viz. cell 1, cell 2, cell 3, cell 4, so the companies will receive a classification according to the place they occupy.

Table Division of companies in liqudity profitability matrix

	Profitability		
Liquidity	CR \ GP	**High**	**Low**
	High	Cell 1	Cell 2
	Low	Cell 3	Cell 4

Classification is made, considering following aspects :

a) For measuring liquidity, one liquidity ratio as a parameter is considered. For e.g. current ratio (CR).
b) For measuring profitability, one ratio from profitability criterion is considered as parameter for e.g. Gross profit ratio (GP).
c) Each liqudiity ratio is compared to each profitability ratio.
d) All sample companies are included for evaluating liquidity profitability matrix.
e) The position is decided by taking average of indusry as a 'benchmark' for all companies to evaluate the perfomance.

f) Cell – 2 and cell -3 are traditioally known as ***profitability liquidity trade off situatiions***, as increase in one corresponding reduction in other occurs.

g) A company with high profitability and high liquidity goes to cell – 1, with high liquidity but low profitability goes to cell – 2. Whereas company with low liquidty but high profitability goes to cell -3 and company with low liquidity and low profitability goes to cell – 4.

According to Pimentel (2005), the companies in cell – 1 are considered to be in good finanicial position, on the other side, the company located to cell – 4 are considered as in bad financial position.

Table 6. 1 Liquidity – Profitability status of the selected refinery industries based on the combination of Current ratio and Gross profit ratio.

	→ Profitability ←		
↑ Liquidity ↓	GP / CR	**High (>= 10)**	**Low (< 10)**
	High (>= 1)	ONGC	MRPL, RIL
	Low (< 1)		BPCL, HPCL, IOCL

Table No. 6.1 shows the liquidity – profitability matrix of the selected refinery industries with reference to short term liquidity and overall profitability. Current Ratio was taken as the measurement of short term liquidity capacity,while Gross Profit was used as profitability indicator. Indusry average of 10% is considered as a standard for Gross profit. Industry average current ratio of 1 is considered as standard to evaluate Current ratio.The table discloses that the ONGC has a strong position being in high profitability and high liquidity cell. While MRPL and RIL are having high liquidity but at the cost of low profitabilty. BPCL, HPCL and IOCL do not perform well, are come under cell -4, which denotes low liquidity low profitability.

Table 6.2 Liquidity – Profitability status of the selected refinery industries based on the combination of Current ratio and Net profit ratio.

	Profitability		
Liquidity	CR / NP	High (>= 6)	Low (< 6)
	High (>= 1)	ONGC, RIL	MRPL
	Low (< 1)		BPCL, HPCL, IOCL

Table No. 6.2 shows the liquidity – profitability matrix of the selected refinery industries with reference to short term liquidity and overall profitability. Current Ratio was taken as the measurement of short term liquidity capacity,while Net Profit was used as profitability indicator. Indusry average of 6% is considered as a standard for Net profit. Industry average current ratio of 1 is considered as standard to evaluate Current ratio. ONGC and RIL were in cell -1 showing high liquidity and highe profitabiity, where as MRPL has maintained high current ratio but profitability in the form of net profit was low, hence occupied cell – 2. While BPCL, HPCL, and IOCL were in cell – 4 due to low current ratio and low net profit margin showing poor performance.

Table 6.3 Liquidity – Profitability status of the selected refinery industries based on the combination of Current ratio and Earning Per Share.

→ Profitability ←			
↓ Liquidity ↑	EPS / CR	High (>= 39)	Low (< 39)
	High (>= 1)	ONGC, RIL	
	Low (< 1)	BPCL	HPCL, IOCL, MRPL

Table No. 6.3 shows the liquidity – profitability matrix of the selected refinery industries with reference to short term liquidity and overall profitability. Curent Ratio was taken as the measurement of short term debt paying capacity,while Earning Per Share was used as profitability indicator. Indusry average of Rs.39 per share is considered as a standard for EPS. Industry average current ratio of 1 is considered as standard to evaluate Current ratio. ONGC and RIL has maintained high current ratio and also managed profitability well in the form of EPS thus occupied cell -1, while BPCL shows profitability liquidity trade off situation by maintaing low liquidity and earning well, company was placed in cell – 3. HPCL, IOCL and MRPL were not performing well in both, they maintained low current ratio but couldn't improve profitability and hence occupied cell -4.

Table 6.4 Liquidity – Profitability status of the selected refinery industries based on the combination of Current ratio and Dividend Per Share.

→ Profitability ←			
Liquidity	DPS / CR	High (>= 9)	Low (< 9)
	High (>= 1)	ONGC, RIL	MRPL
	Low (< 1)	BPCL	HPCL, IOCL

Table No. 6.4 shows the liquidity – profitability matrix of the selected refinery industries with reference to short term liquidity and overall profitability. Current Ratio was taken as the measurement of short term debt paying capacity,while Dividend Per Share was used as profitability indicator. Indusry average of Rs. 9 per share is considered as a standard for DPS. Industry average current ratio of 1 is considered as standard to evaluate Current ratio. ONGC and RIL has maintained liquidity profitability well and occupied the best position at cell – 1, MRPL has traditionally fit at liquidity profitability trade off, maitaining high liquidity at a cost low profitability. BPCL on other hand at cell -3 maintained low liquidity at a cost of high profitability. HPCL and IOCL didn't perform well, had a low currnet ratio as well as low DPS.

Table 6.5 Liquidity – Profitability status of the selected refinery industries based on the combination of Current ratio and Return on Capital Employed.

	Profitability		
Liquidity	CR \ ROCE	High (>= 16)	Low (< 16)
	High (>= 1)	MRPL, ONGC	RIL
	Low (< 1)		BPCL, HPCL, IOCL

Table No. 6.5 shows the liquidity – profitability matrix of the selected refinery industries with reference to short term liquidity and overall profitability. Current Ratio was taken as the measurement of short term debt paying capacity,while Return On Capital Employed was used as profitability indicator. Indusry average of 16% is considered as a standard for ROCE. Industry average current ratio of 1 is considered as standard to evaluate Current ratio. MRPL and ONGC has maintianed high CR as well as ROCE and placed at cell -1. RIL struggling little for ROCE, had maintained high CR, therfore placed at cell -2. BPCL, HPCL and IOCL were low at CR as well as ROCE placed at cell -4 indicating poor performance

Table 6.6 Liquidity – Profitability status of the selected refinery industries based on the combination of Current ratio and Return on Net Worth.

	Profitability		
Liquidity	**RONW** / **CR**	**High (>= 13)**	**Low (< 13)**
	High (>= 1)	MRPL, ONGC, RIL	
	Low (< 1)		BPCL, HPCL, IOCL

Table No. 6.6 shows the liquidity – profitability matrix of the selected refinery industries with reference to short term liquidity and overall profitability. Current Ratio was taken as the measurementment of short term debt paying capacity,while Return On Net Worth was used as profitability indicator. Indusry average of 13% is considered as a standard for RONW. Industry average ratio of 1 is considered as standard to evaluate Current ratio. MRPL, ONGC and RIL performed well at both level showing high CR and high RONW, were placed at cell -1. While no companies were at liquidity profitability trade off zone. BPCL, HPCL and IOCL registerd low CR and low RONW therefore continued at cell -4. MRPL was excepitonal at cell -1, because during 2012-13 the company has shown negative return on net worth.

Table 6.7 Liquidity – Profitability status of the selected refinery industries based on the combination of Inventory Turnover ratio and Gross profit ratio.

Profitability			
Liquidity	GP / ITR	High (>= 10)	Low (< 10)
	High (>= 19)	ONGC	
	Low (< 19)		BPCL, HPCL, IOCL, MRPL, RIL

Table No. 6.7 shows the liquidity – profitability matrix of the selected refinery industries with reference to short term liquidity and overall profitability. Inventory Turnover Ratio was taken as the measurementment of efficiency,while Gross Profit was used as profitability indicator. Indusry average of 10% is considered as a standard for Gross profit. Industry average ratio of 19 times is considered as standard to evaluate ITR. ONGC was the only company which could maintain high ITR as well as high GP at cell -1. All other companies viz. BPCL, HPCL, IOCL, MRPL, RIL were registerd low ITR as well as low GP and were placed at cell -4.

Table 6.8 Liquidity – Profitability status of the selected refinery industries based on the combination of Inventory Turnover ratio and Net profit ratio.

	→ Profitability ←		
↑ Liquidity ↓	ITR \ NP	High (>= 6)	Low (< 6)
	High (>= 19)	ONGC	
	Low (< 19)	RIL	BPCL, HPCL, IOCL, MRPL

Table No. 6.8 shows the liquidity – profitability matrix of the selected refinery industries with reference to short term liquidity and overall profitability. Inventory Turnover Ratios was taken as the measurementment of efficiency,while Net Profit was used as profitability indicator. Indusry average of 6% is considered as a standard for Net profit. Industry average ratio of 19 times is considered as standard to evaluate ITR. ONGC was only company maintained high ITR as well as high NP, RIL at liquidity profitability trade off zone maintained low liquidity and high profitability. All other companies viz. BPCL, HPCL, IOCL, MRPL has shown very weak perfomance, as companies have maintained low ITR as well as low NP.

Table 6.9 Liquidity – Profitability status of the selected refinery industries based on the combination of Inventory Turnover ratio and Return on Capital Employed.

Profitability			
Liquidity	ROCE / ITR	High (>= 16)	Low (< 16)
	High (>= 19)	ONGC	
	Low (< 19)	MRPL	BPCL, HPCL, IOCL, RIL

Table No. 6.9 shows the liquidity – profitability matrix of the selected refinery industries with reference to short term liquidity and overall profitability. Inventory Turnover Ratio was taken as the measurementment of efficiency,while Return On Capital Employed was used as profitability indicator. Indusry average of 16% is considered as a standard for ROCE. Industry average ratio of 19 times is considered as standard to evaluate ITR. ONGC has maintained high ITR and high ROCE, hence set at cell -1, MRPL at profitability liquidity trade off, has shown low ITR and high ROCE at cell 3. Whereas BPCL, HPCL, IOCL and RIL couldnt perform well and occupied position at cell – 4 for having low ITR and low ROCE.

Table 6.10 Liquidity – Profitability status of the selected refinery industries based on the combination of Inventory Turnover ratio and Return on Net Worth ratio.

	→ **Profitability** ←		
↓ Liquidity ↑	ITR \ RONW	**High (>= 13)**	**Low (< 13)**
	High (>= 19)	ONGC	
	Low (< 19)	MRPL, RIL	BPCL, HPCL, IOCL

Table No. 6.10 shows the liquidity – profitability matrix of the selected refinery industries with reference to short term liquidity and overall profitability. Inventory Turnover Ratio was taken as the measurementment of efficiency,while Return On Net Worth was used as profitability indicator. Indusry average of 13% is considered as a standard for RONW. Industry average ratio of 19 times is considered as standard to evaluate ITR. ONGC again being market leader, sustained high ITR and high RONW set at cell -1, MRPL and RIL could maintain high RONW, but failed to achieve proper ITR hence set at cell -3. BPCL, HPCL, and IOCL struggling for both liquidity as well as profitability, maintained low ITR and low RONW, therecome occupied cell – 4.

Table 6.11 Liquidity – Profitability status of the selected refinery industries based on the combination of Inventory Turnover ratio and Dividend Per Share.

Liquidity ↓↑	ITR \ DPS → Profitability	High (>= 9)	Low (< 9)
	High (>= 19)	ONGC	
	Low (< 19)	BPCL, RIL	HPCL, IOCL, MRPL

Table No. 6.11 shows the liquidity – profitability matrix of the selected refinery industries with reference to short term liquidity and overall profitability. Inventory Turnover Ratio was taken as the measurementment of efficiency,while Dividend Per Share was used as profitability indicator. Indusry average of Rs. 9 per share is considered as a standard for DPS. Industry average ratio of 19 times is considered as standard to evaluate ITR. ONGC has performed well in both categories, having high ITR and more than indusry average DPS, set at cell -1. BPCL and RIL has successfully maintained high DPS, but having low ITR, set at cell – 3. HPCL, IOCL and MRPL did not perform well and could not maintain both liquidity as well as prfoitability having low ITR and low DPS placed at cell – 4.

Table 6.12 Liquidity – Profitability status of the selected refinery industries based on the combination of Inventory Turnover ratio and Earning Per Share.

		Profitability	
Liquidity	ITR \ EPS	**High (>= 39)**	**Low (< 39)**
	High (>= 19)	ONGC	
	Low (< 19)	BPCL, RIL	HPCL, IOCL, MRPL

Table No. 6.12 shows the liquidity – profitability matrix of the selected refinery industries with reference to short term liquidity and overall profitability. Inventory Turnover Ratio was taken as the measurementment of efficiency,while Earning Per Share was used as profitability indicator. Indusry average of Rs. 39 per share is considered as a standard for EPS. Industry average ratio of 19 times is considered as standard to evaluate ITR. ONGC has maintained both liquidiy as well profitability criterion very well, having high ITR as well as high EPS occupied the best position i.e. cell – 1. No companies were at cell -2. BPCL and RIL couldn't maintain high ITR but managed to get EPS above industry average and hence occupied place at cell – 3. HPCL, IOCL and MRPL failed in both categories, maintained low ITR as well as low EPS fall at cell – 4.

Table 6.13 Liquidity – Profitability status of the selected refinery industries based on the combination of Debtors Turnover ratio and Gross profit ratio.

	→ Profitability ←		
↓ Liquidity ↑	GP / DTR	High (>= 10)	Low (< 10)
	High (>= 36)	ONGC	BPCL, HPCL, IOCL
	Low (< 36)		MRPL, RIL

Table No. 6.13 shows the liquidity – profitability matrix of the selected refinery industries with reference to short term liquidity and overall profitability. Debtors Turnover Ratio was taken as the measurement of short term liquidity,while Gross Profit was used as profitability indicator. Indusry average of 10% is considered as a standard for Gross profit. Industry average of 36 times considered as standard to evaluate DTR. ONGC has shown the best performance having high GP and high DTR, got the position at cell – 1. BPCL, HPCL and IOCL set at profitability liquidity trade off due to high DTR but low GP, no companies were at cell – 3. MRPL and RIL could't maintain the industry standard and therefore placed at cell – 4.

Table 6.14 Liquidity – Profitability status of the selected refinery industries based on the combination of Debtors Turnover ratio and Net profit ratio.

Liquidity ↕ / Profitability ↔	NP / DTR	High (>= 6)	Low (< 6)
	High (>= 36)		BPCL, HPCL, IOCL
	Low (< 36)	ONGC, RIL	MRPL

Table shows No. 6.14 the liquidity – profitability matrix of the selected refinery industries with reference to short term liquidity and overall profitability. Debtors Turnover Ratio was taken as the measurement of short term liquidity,while Net Profit was used as profitability indicator. Indusry average of 6% is considered as a standard for Net profit. Industry average ratio of 36 times considered as standard to evaluate DTR. No companies were at cell – 1. BPCL, HPCL and IOCL were at cell – 2, having high profitablility and low net profit, due to high DTR and low NP. ONGC and RIL were at liquidity profitability trade off, showing low DTR and high high NP. MRPL has shown the worst performance and was not able to maintain both liquidty as well as profitability at industry average and fall in to cell -4 due to low DTR and low NP.

Table 6.15 Liquidity – Profitability status of the selected refinery industries based on the combination of Debtors Turnover ratio and Retrun on Capital Employed.

Profitability			
Liquidity	ROCE / DTR	**High (>= 16)**	**Low (< 16)**
	High (>= 36)		BPCL, HPCL, IOCL
	Low (< 36)	MRPL, ONGC	RIL

Table No. 6.15 shows the liquidity – profitability matrix of the selected refinery industries with reference to short term liquidity and overall profitability. Debtors Turover Ratio was taken as the measurement of short term liquidity,while Return On Capital Employed was used as profitability indicator. Indusry average of 16% is considered as a standard for ROCE. Industry average ratio of 36 times is considered as standard to evaluate DTR. There was not a single company at cell -1, BPCL, HPCL and IOCL have maintained high DTR but at cost of low ROCE therefore set at cell -2. On the other hand MRPL, ONGC were at cell -3 due to high ROCE and low DTR. RIL has shown exceptionally low DTR as well as low ROCE hence got the worst position at cell -4.

Table 6.16 Liquidity – Profitability status of the selected refinery industries based on the combination of Debtors Turnover ratio and Return on Net Worth.

→ Profitability ←			
↓ Liquidity ↑	RONW / DTR	High (>= 13)	Low (< 13)
	High (>= 36)		BPCL, HPCL, IOCL
	Low (< 36)	MRPL, ONGC, RIL	

Table No. 6.16 shows the liquidity – profitability matrix of the selected refinery industries with reference to short term liquidity and overall profitability. Debtors Turnover Ratio was taken as the measurement of short term liquidity,while Return On Net Worth was used as profitability indicator. Indusry average of 13% is considered as a standard for RONW. Industry average current ratio of 36 times is considered as standard to evaluate DTR. There was not a single company at the best position i.e. cell -1 as well as the worst one i.e. cell -4. All companies were struggling to maintaining liquidity profitability trade off. BPCL, HPCL and IOCL were at cell -2 due to high DTR and low RONW. MRPL, ONGC and RIL were occupied cell – 3 due to low DTR and high RONW.

Table 6.17 Liquidity – Profitability status of the selected refinery industries based on the combination of Debtors Turnover ratio and Dividend Per share.

	Profitability		
Liquidity	DTR / DPS	High (>= 9)	Low (< 9)
	High (>= 36)	BPCL	HPCL, IOCL
	Low (< 36)	ONGC, RIL	MRPL

Table No. 6.17 shows the liquidity – profitability matrix of the selected refinery industries with reference to short term liquidity and overall profitability. Debtors Turnover Ratio was taken as the measurement of short term liquidity,while Dividend Per Share was used as profitability indicator. Indusry average of Rs. 9 per share is considered as a standard for DPS. Industry average ratio of 36 times is considered as standard to evaluate DTR. BPCL significantly occupied cell – 1 due to high DTR as wll as high DPS. HPCL and IOCL were at cell -2 as the companies have maintained high DTR at cost of low DPS, on other side at cell -3, there were ONGC and RIL both companies succeeded in maintaining high DPS, but coludn't maintain industry average of DTR. MRPL didn't perform well in both DTR as well as DPS, due to low DTR and low DPS, company got position at cell – 4.

Table 6.18 Liquidity – Profitability status of the selected refinery industries based on the combination of Debtors Turnover ratio and Earning Per Share.

Profitability			
Liquidity	DTR \ EPS	**High (>= 39)**	**Low (< 39)**
	High (>= 36)	BPCL	HPCL, IOCL
	Low (< 36)	ONGC, RIL	MRPL

Table No. 6.18 shows the liquidity – profitability matrix of the selected refinery industries with reference to short term liquidity and overall profitability. Debtors Turnover Ratio was taken as the measurement of short term liquidity,while Earning Per Share was used as profitability indicator. Indusry average of 36 times is considered as a standard for DTR. Industry average ratio of Rs. 39 per share is considered as standard to evaluate EPS. BPCL has performed well under both cases, as the company maintained high DTR as well as high EPS. While HPCL, IOCl were at profitability liquidity trade off have maintained high DTR and low EPS, set at cell - 2. Whereas ONGC and RIL, on other side have maintained high EPS at a cost of low DTR, so got postion at cell -3. MRPL couldn't perform well showing low DTR and low EPS got the worst position at cell – 4.

Table 6.19 Liquidity – Profitability status of the selected refinery industries based on the combination of Quick ratio and Gross profit ratio.

→ Profitability ←			
↑ Liquidity ↓	GP / QK	**High (>= 10)**	**Low (< 10)**
	High (>= 0.78)	ONGC	RIL
	Low (< 0.78)		BPCL, HPCL, IOCL, MRPL

Table No. 6.19 shows the liquidity – profitability matrix of the selected refinery industries with reference to short term liquidity and overall profitability. Quick ratio was taken as the measurement of short term liquidity,while Gross Profit was used as profitability indicator. Indusry average of 10% is considered as a standard for Gross profit. Industry average ratio of 0.78 is considered as standard to evaluate quick ratio. ONGC has performed well and has shown high QR as well as high GP, and got the best position at cell – 1. RIL at liquidity profitability trade off occupied cell -2 as the company maintained high QR but low GP. Whereas BPCL, HPCL , IOCL and MRPL couldn't perform as per expectations and all companies have failed to maintain industry average of QR and GP. Due to low GP and low QR all companies were located at cell -4.

Table 6.20 Liquidity – Profitability status of the selected refinery industries based on the combination of Quick ratio and Net profit ratio.

	Profitability		
Liquidity	QK / NP	High (>= 6)	Low (< 6)
	High (>= 0.78)	ONGC, RIL	
	Low (< 0.78)		BPCL, HPCL, IOCL, MRPL

Table No. 6.20 shows the liquidity – profitability matrix of the selected refinery industries with reference to short term liquidity and overall profitability. Quick Ratio was taken as the measurement of short term liquidity,while Net Profit was used as profitability indicator. Indusry average of 6% is considered as a standard for Gross profit. Industry average current ratio of 0.78 is considered as standard to evaluate Quick ratio. ONGC and RIL have performed well and succeded in maintaining both QR and NP above the industry average, hence got postion at cell – 1. There was not a single company at liqudity profitability trade off positons. BPCL, HPCL, IOCL and MRPL were below the industry average in both QR and NP, therefore located at cell – 4.

Table 6.21 Liquidity – Profitability status of the selected refinery industries based on the combination of Quick ratio and Retrun On Capital Employed.

	Profitability		
Liquidity	ROCE / QK	High (>= 16)	Low (< 16)
	High (>= 0.78)	ONGC	RIL
	Low (< 0.78)	MRPL	BPCL, IOCL, HPCL

Table No. 6.21 shows the liquidity – profitability matrix of the selected refinery industries with reference to short term liquidity and overall profitability. Quick Ratio was taken as the measurement of short term liquidity,while Return on Capital Employed was used as profitability indicator. Indusry average of 16% is considered as a standard for Return on Capital Employed. Industry average ratio of 0.78 is considered as standard to evaluate Quick ratio. ONGC was the only company which has maintained both QR and ROCE above the industry average, the company has got cell -2 due to high QR and high ROCE. RIL was at liqudity profitability trade off due to low ROCE and high QR and hence occupied cell – 2. On the other hand MRPL has maintained low QR and high ROCE. All remaining companies BPCL, IOCL and HPCL couldn't perform as per industry expectations, the companies have shown low QR and low ROCE , thus got position at cell – 4.

Table 6.22 Liquidity – Profitability status of the selected refinery industries based on the combination of Quick ratio and Return On Net Worth.

	→ Profitability ←		
Liquidity ↑↓	RONW / QK	High (>= 13)	Low (< 13)
	High (>= 0.78)	ONGC, RIL	
	Low (< 0.78)	MRPL	BPCL, HPCL , IOCL

Table No. 6.22 shows the liquidity – profitability matrix of the selected refinery industries with reference to short term liquidity and overall profitability. Quick Ratio was taken as the measurement of short term liquidity,while Return on Net Worth was used as profitability indicator. Indusry average of 13% is considered as a standard for Return on Net Worth. Industry average ratio of 0.78 is considered as standard to evaluate Quick ratio. ONGC and RIl have performed exceptionally well, and have successful maintained both RONW and QR above industry average, due to high QR and high RONW, companies were placed at cell -1. MRPL at liqudity profitability trade off point maintained high RONW but at a cost of low QR, thus got placed at cell -3. BPCL, HPCL and IOCL were at cell -4 due to low QR and low RONW.

Table 6.23 Liquidity – Profitability status of the selected refinery industries based on the combination of Quick ratio and Dividend Per Share.

Profitability			
Liquidity	DPS / QK	High (>= 9)	Low (< 9)
	High (>= 0.78)	ONGC, RIL	
	Low (< 0.78)	BPCL	HPCL, IOCL, MRPL

Table No. 6.23 shows the liquidity – profitability matrix of the selected refinery industries with reference to short term liquidity and overall profitability. Quick Ratio was taken as the measurement of short term liquidity,while Dividend Per Share was used as profitability indicator. Indusry average of Rs. 9 per share is considered as a standard for Return on Net Worth. Industry average ratio of 0.78 is considered as standard to evaluate Quick ratio. ONGC and RIL have maintained both QR and DPS at above industry average and therefore got placed at cell -1. BPCL have maintained high DPS but at cost of low QR, therfore occupied cell – 3. HPCL, IOCL and MRPL didn't perform well, due to low QR and low DPS, these companies placed at cell -4.

Table 6.24 Liquidity – Profitability status of the selected refinery industries based on the combination of Quick ratio and Earning Per Share.

→ Profitability ←			
↓ Liquidity ↑	EPS / QK	High (>= 39)	Low (< 39)
	High (>= 0.78)	ONGC, RIL	
	Low (< 0.78)	BPCL	HPCL, IOCL, MRPL

Table No. 6.24 shows the liquidity – profitability matrix of the selected refinery industries with reference to short term liquidity and overall profitability. Quick Ratio was taken as the measurement of short term liquidity,while Earning Per Share was used as profitability indicator. Indusry average of Rs. 39 per share is considered as a standard for Return on Net Worth. Industry average ratio of 0.78 is considered as standard to evaluate Quick ratio. ONGC and RIL have maintained both QR and EPS at above industry average and therefore got placed at cell -1. BPCL have maintained high EPS but at cost of low QR, therfore occupied cell – 3. HPCL, IOCL and MRPL didn't perform well, due to low QR and low EPS, these companies placed at cell -4. There was not a single company set at cell-2.

Table 6.25 Liquidity – Profitability status of the selected refinery industries based on the combination of Debt Equity ratio and Gross Profit.

	Profitability		
Liquidity	DE \ GP	High (>= 10)	Low (< 10)
	High (>= 0.93)		BPCL, HPCL, IOCL
	Low (< 0.93)	ONGC	MRPL, RIL

Table 6.25 shows the liquidity – profitability matrix of the selected refinery industries with reference to short term liquidity and overall profitability. Debt Equity ratio was taken as the measurement of short term debt paying capacity,while Gross Profit was used as profitability indicator. Indusry average of 10% is considered as a standard for Gross profit. Industry average ratio of 0.93 is considered as standard to evaluate Debt Equity ratio. There was not a single company at the best position i.e. at cell – 1. BPCL, HPCL and IOCL were at liquidity profitability trade off zone, as having low GP but high DE, these companies were placed at cell – 2. ONGC on the other hand couldn't maitain DE ratio above industry average, but had GP more than the industry average which led the company to cell -3. MRPL and RIL did not perform up to thier standard, and having low DE and low GP, these companies were placed at cell – 4.

Table 6.26 Liquidity – Profitability status of the selected refinery industries based on the combination of Debt Equity ratio and Net profit ratio.

	→ **Profitability** ←		
Liquidity (↕)	**DE** \ **NP**	**High (>= 6)**	**Low (< 6)**
	High (>= 0.93)		BPCL, HPCL, IOCL
	Low (< 0.93)	ONGC, RIL	MRPL

Table 6.26 shows the liquidity – profitability matrix of the selected refinery industries with reference to short term liquidity and overall profitability. Debt Equity ratio was taken as the measurement of short term debt paying capacity,while Net Profit was used as profitability indicator. Indusry average of 6% is considered as a standard for Net profit. Industry average ratio of 0.93 is considered as standard to evaluate Debt Equity ratio. There was not a single company at cell – 1. BPCL, HPCL and IOCL were at cell – 2 due to high DE but low NP, whereas ONGC and RIL at cell – 3 due to having low DE and high NP. MRPL did not maintain DE as well as NP up to industry average and hence placed at cell – 4.

Table 6.27 Liquidity – Profitability status of the selected refinery industries based on the combination of Debt Equity and Return On Capital Employed.

	Profitability		
Liquidity	ROCE / DE	High (>= 16)	Low (< 16)
	High (>= 0.93)		BPCL, HPCL, IOCL
	Low (< 0.93)	ONGC, RIL	MRPL

Table 6.27 shows the liquidity – profitability matrix of the selected refinery industries with reference to short term liquidity and overall profitability. Debt Equity ratio was taken as the measurement of short term debt paying capacity,while Return on Capital Employed was used as profitability indicator. Indusry average of 16% is considered as a standard for Return on Capital Employed. Industry average ratio of 0.93 is considered as standard to evaluate Debt Equity ratio. No companies were placed at cell – 1. BPCL, HPCL and IOCL were at liquidity profitability trade off point, as these companies were having high DE at cost of low ROCE, on the other hand RIL and ONGC were having high ROCE at a cost of low DE and hence set at cell – 3. MRPL having low DE as well as low ROCE occupied position at cell – 4.

Table 6.28 Liquidity – Profitability status of the selected refinery industries based on the combination of Debt Equity ratio and Return On Net Worth.

	Profitability		
Liquidity	DE \ RONW	High (>= 13)	Low (< 13)
	High (>= 0.93)		BPCL, HPCL, IOCL
	Low (< 0.93)	MRPL, ONGC, RIL	

Table 6.28 shows the liquidity – profitability matrix of the selected refinery industries with reference to short term liquidity and overall profitability. Debt Equity ratio was taken as the measurement of short term debt paying capacity,while Return on Net Worth was used as profitability indicator. Indusry average of 13% is considered as a standard for Return On Net Worth. Industry average ratio of 0.93 is considered as standard to evaluate Debt Equity ratio. There was not a single company at the best position i.e. cell – 1, as well as the worst at cell -4. All the comapnies were positioned at liquidtiy profitabiltiy trade off points. BPCL, HPCL and IOCL were having high DE at a cost of low RONW. Whereas MRPL, ONGC and RIL differently had high RONW at a cost of low DE.

Table 6.29 Liquidity – Profitability status of the selected refinery industries based on the combination of Debt Equity ratio and Dividend Per Share.

→ Profitability ←			
↑ Liquidity ↓	DPS / DE	High (>= 9)	Low (< 9)
	High (>= 0.93)	BPCL	HPCL, IOCL
	Low (< 0.93)	ONGC, RIL	MRPL

Table 6.29 shows the liquidity – profitability matrix of the selected refinery industries with reference to short term liquidity and overall profitability. Debt Equity ratio was taken as the measurement of short term debt paying capacity,while Dividend Per Share was used as profitability indicator. Indusry average of Rs. 9 per share is considered as a standard for Dividend Per Share. Industry average ratio of 0.93 is considered as standard to evaluate Debt Equity ratio. BPCL has performed exceptionally well in both liquidity and profitability, the company was having high DE as well as high DPS, so got placed at cell – 1. HPCL and IOCL were at cell-2 due to high DE but low DPS, ONGC and RIL on the other hand, at cell -3, maintained high DPS but at a cost of low DE. MRPL continue withe poor level, at cell -4, couldn't find the proper balance between liquidity as well as profitability, as having low DE and low DPS, it was placed at cell – 4.

Table 6. 30 Liquidity – Profitability status of the selected refinery industries based on the combination of Debt Equity ratio and Earning Per Share.

		Profitability	
Liquidity	DE / EPS	High (>= 39)	Low (< 39)
	High (>= 0.93)	BPCL	HPCL, IOCL
	Low (< 0.93)	ONGC, RIL	MRPL

Table 6. 30 shows the liquidity – profitability matrix of the selected refinery industries with reference to short term liquidity and overall profitability. Debt Equity ratio was taken as the measurement of short term debt paying capacity,while Earning Per Share was used as profitability indicator. Indusry average of Rs. 39 per share is considered as a standard for Earning Per Share. Industry average ratio of 0.93 is considered as standard to evaluate Debt Equity ratio. BPCL had maintained both liquidity as well as profitability at its best, due to high DE and high EPS company was placed at cell – 1. HPCL and IOCL were at liquidity profitability trade off point, having low EPS and high DE, placed at cell – 2. While ONGC and RIL have maintained high EPS at cost of low DE. MRPL continued with below industry average liquidity as well as profitability placed at cell -4. The company was having low DE as well as low EPS.

Table 6.31 Liquidity – Profitability status of the selected refinery industries based on the combination of Fixed Assets Turnover ratio and Gross profit ratio.

	→ Profitability ←		
↓ Liquidity ↑	GP / FATO	**High (>= 10)**	**Low (< 10)**
	High (>= 3)		BPCL, HPCL, IOCL, MRPL
	Low (< 3)	ONGC	RIL

Table 6.31 shows the liquidity – profitability matrix of the selected refinery industries with reference to short term liquidity and overall profitability. Fixed Assets Turn Over ratio was taken as the measurement of short term efficiency,while Gross Profit was used as profitability indicator. Indusry average of 10% is considered as a standard for Gross profit. Industry average ratio of 3 times is considered as standard to evaluate Fixed Assets Turn Over ratio. There was not a single company at cell – 1. BPCL, HPCL, IOCL, and MRPL were at liquidity profitability trade off point, have shown low GP and high FATO and therefore placed at cell – 2. ONGC, on the flip side had high GP but at a cost of low FATO, so got placed at cell – 3. RIL exceptioanally couldn't maintain its standard and being not succeded in both liquidity as well profitability level, placed at cell -4. RIL was having low FATO as well as low GP during research period.

Table 6.32 Liquidity – Profitability status of the selected refinery industries based on the combination of Fixed Assets Turnover ratio and Net profit ratio.

	Profitability		
	NP / FATO	High (>= 6)	Low (< 6)
Liquidity	High (>= 3)		BPCL, HPCL, IOCL, MRPL
	Low (< 3)	ONGC, RIL	

Table 6.31 shows the liquidity – profitability matrix of the selected refinery industries with reference to short term liquidity and overall profitability. Fixed Assets Turn Over ratio was taken as the measurement of short term efficiency,while Net Profit was used as profitability indicator. Indusry average of 6% is considered as a standard for Net profit. Industry average ratio of 3 times is considered as standard to evaluate Fixed Assets Turn Over ratio. There was not a single company at the best position cell – 1 as well as the worst one at cell – 4. BPCL, HPCL, IOCL and MRPL had a low FATO but maintained NP above the industry average and thus placed at cell – 2. ONGC and RIL on other hand had low FATO and high NP, and thus placed at cell – 3.

Table 6.33 Liquidity – Profitability status of the selected refinery industries based on the combination of Fixed Assets Turnover ratio and Return On Capital Employed.

Profitability			
Liquidity	ROCE / FATO	High (>= 16)	Low (< 16)
	High (>= 3)	MRPL	BPCL, HPCL, IOCL
	Low (< 3)	ONGC	RIL

Table 6.33 shows the liquidity – profitability matrix of the selected refinery industries with reference to short term liquidity and overall profitability. Fixed Assets Turn Over ratio was taken as the measurement of short term efficiency,while Return On Capital Employed was used as profitability indicator. Indusry average of 16% is considered as a standard for Return On Capital Employed. Industry average ratio of 3 times is considered as standard to evaluate Fixed Assets Turn Over ratio. MRPL had performed exceptionally well got placed at cell – 1. The company had sussessfully maintained high FATO and high ROCE. BPCL, HPCL and IOCL had maintained high FATO but low low ROCE, thus placed at cell – 2. ONGC, on the other hand, had maintained high ROCE at a cost of low FATO, and occupied place at cell – 3. RIL had performed the worst, as having both FATO and ROCE below industry average, occupied place at cell – 4.

Table 6.34 Liquidity – Profitability status of the selected refinery industries based on the combination of Fixed Assets Turnover ratio and Return On Net Worth.

	Profitability		
Liquidity	FATO \ RONW	**High (>= 13)**	**Low (< 13)**
	High (>= 3)	MRPL	BPCL, HPCL, IOCL
	Low (< 3)	ONGC, RIL	

Table 6.34 shows the liquidity – profitability matrix of the selected refinery industries with reference to short term liquidity and overall profitability. Fixed Assets Turn Over ratio was taken as the measurement of short term efficiency,while Return On Net Worth was used as profitability indicator. Indusry average of 13% is considered as a standard for Return On Net Worth. Industry average ratio of 3 times is considered as standard to evaluate Fixed Assets Turn Over ratio. MRPL had high RONW as well as high FATO, thus placed at cell -1, but during 2012-13, the company has shown negative return and that was considered as an exceptional situation for research work under this case. There was not a single company at the worst position i.e. at cell – 4. BPCL, HPCL and IOCL were at liquidity profitability trade off points, having low RONW but high FATO placed at cell – 2. ONGC and RIL, on flip side maintained high RONW but at a cost of low FATO, and thus occupied place at cell – 3.

Table 6.35 Liquidity – Profitability status of the selected refinery industries based on the combination of Fixed Assets Turnover ratio and Dividend Per Share.

	→ Profitability ←		
↑ Liquidity ↓	DPS / FATO	High (>= 9)	Low (< 9)
	High (>= 3)	BPCL	HPCL, IOCL, MRPL
	Low (< 3)	ONGC, RIL	

Table 6.35 shows the liquidity – profitability matrix of the selected refinery industries with reference to short term liquidity and overall profitability. Fixed Assets Turn Over ratio was taken as the measurement of short term efficiency,while Dividend Per Share was used as profitability indicator. Indusry average of Rs. 9 per share is considered as a standard for Dividend Per Share. Industry average ratio of 3 times is considered as standard to evaluate Fixed Assets Turn Over ratio. BPCL had performed well and maintained both DPS and FATO above the industry average. HPCL, IOCL and MRPL were having low DPS and high FATO and occupied position at cell – 2. ONGC and RIL, on the other hand at liquidity profitability trade off point, maintained high DPS and low FATO, and thus occupied position at cell – 3. There was not a single company at cell – 4.

Table 6.36 Liquidity – Profitability status of the selected refinery industries based on the combination of Fixed Assets Turnover ratio and Earning Per Share.

Liquidity ↕	Profitability ↔		
	FATO \ EPS	**High (>= 39)**	**Low (< 39)**
	High (>= 3)	BPCL	HPCL, IOCL, MRPL
	Low (< 3)	ONGC, RIL	

Table 6.36 shows the liquidity – profitability matrix of the selected refinery industries with reference to short term liquidity and overall profitability. Fixed Assets Turn Over ratio was taken as the measurement of short term efficiency,while Earning Per Share was used as profitability indicator. Indusry average of Rs. 39 per share is considered as a standard for Earning Per Share. Industry average ratio of 3 times is considered as standard to evaluate Fixed Assets Turn Over ratio. BPCL had performed well, and maintained both liquidity as well as profitability above industry average, thus placed at cell – 1. There was not single company at the worst point of cell – 4. HPCL, IOCL and MRPL were at liquidity and profitability trade off point, maintained EPS below the industry average and FATO at above industry average, thus occupied place at cell -2. ONGC and RIL, on the other hand, had successfully maintaind EPS above the industry average, and FATO at below industry average. These companies were placed at cell – 3.

6.3. Analysis of Correlation

The anlaysis of liquidity – profitability status of the selected refinery industries through the presentation of matrices is not sufficient to draw a definite conclusion on the nature and degree of association between liquidity and profitability. In reality, it fails to examine actual impact of liquidity mangement on profitabiliity. To cover this limitaion of Profitability – Liquidity Matrices, correlation analysis was done, and further to varify its magnitude and level of significance t test was used. The nature and degree of retionship between liquidity and profitability were assessed through correlation coefficients between selected measures of liquidity management (viz. CR, QR, ITR, DTR, FATO, DE) and the selected profitability indicators (viz. GP, NP, ROCE, RONW, EPS, DPS) after taking into account their magnitude by using Pearson's correlation coefficient. In order to examine whether the computed values of correlation coefficients are statistically significant or not, t test was used.

H0 = There is no signifant relationship between two ratios.

H1 = There is a significant relationship between two ratios

Confidence interval 95% amd 99%

Table no. showing correlatioship between liqudity and prfitability ratios of refinery industries

	CR	INVTTO	DRTO	QK	DERAT	FATO	GP	NP	ROCE	RONW	DPS	EPS
CR	1											
INVTTO	0.783674	1										
DRTO	-0.87891	-0.48147	1									
QK	**0.92333	*0.888553	-0.66877	1								
DERAT	-0.8424	-0.55517	**0.92292	-0.7539	1							
FATO	-0.87391	-0.64858	0.730002	-0.88297	0.768423	1						
GP	*0.877289	**0.97456	-0.60635	0.955203	-0.67239	-0.80181	1					
NP	**0.911388	**0.940787	-0.65241	0.980394	-0.71746	-0.86592	**0.992017	1				
ROCE	*0.83427	**0.883964	-0.7324	0.81316	-0.78431	-0.58135	*0.873532	*0.845889	1			
RONW	**0.917876	0.768199	-0.8892	*0.851485	-0.93714	-0.72773	*0.826774	*0.840197	**0.94278	1		
DPS	0.568373	*0.843566	-0.15984	0.811962	-0.31301	-0.68354	*0.851184	*0.843374	0.532012	0.450485	1	
EPS	0.356675	0.204029	-0.1325	0.533992	-0.27384	-0.70121	0.351986	0.442855	-0.03483	0.148034	0.591432	1

* Correlation is significant at the 0.05 level . (Source: Authors own calculations) ** Correlation is significant at the 0.01 level..

BIBLIOGRAPHY

1. Agarwal, J.D. (1988), "A goal programming model for working capital management," Finance India, Vol. 2, Issue 2.
2. Aksoy, Y. (1990), "Interactive Multiple Objective Decision Making: A Bibliography (1965–1988)," Management Research News, Vol. 13, Issue 2.
3. Chakraborty, K. (2008), "Working Capital and Profitability: An Empirical Analysis of Their Relationship with Reference to Selected Companies in the Indian Pharmaceutical Industry," The Icfai Journal of Management Research
4. Chakraborty, P.K. and Bandopadhyay, K. (2007), "Strategic Working Capital Management: Case of a Turnaround Company," ICFAI Reader
5. Coskun, S., Basligil, H. and Baracli, H. (2008), "A weakness determination and analysis model for business process improvement," Business Process Management Journal, Vol. 14, Issue 2.
6. Cote, J.M. and Latham, C.K. (1999), "The Merchandising Ratio: A Comprehensive Measure of Working Capital Strategy," Issues in Accounting Education; Vol. 14, Issue 2 7.
7. Filbeck, G., Krueger, G. and Krueger, T.M. (2005), "An Analysis of Working Capital Management Results across Industries," Mid-American Journal of Business, Vol. 20,Issue 2.
8. Garcia-Teruel, P.J. and Martinez-Solano, P. (2007), "Effects of working capital management on SME profitability," International Journal of Managerial Finance, Vol.3, Issue 2.
9. Jafar, A. and Sur, D. (2006), "Efficiency of Working Capital Management in Indian Public Enterprises during the Post-liberalization Era: A Case Study of NTPC," The Icfai Journal of Management Research
10. Khorram Shahgol, R. and Okoruwa, A. (1994), "A goal programming approach to investment decisions: A case study of fund allocation among different shopping malls in Atlanta," Operational Research, Vol. 73, Issue 1.

INDEX

SR.NO	TITLE	PAGE NO.
7.1	INTRODUTION	210
7.2	MAIN FINDINGS CHAPTER 1 OVERVIEW OF OIL INDUSTRY CHAPTER 2 RESEARCH METHODOLOGY CHAPTER 3 SAMPLE PROFILE CHAPTER 4 ANALYSIS OF PROFITABILITY CHAPTER 5 ANALYSIS OF LIQUIDITY CHAPTER 6 PROFITABILITY VIS A VIS LIQUIDTY ANALYSIS	211- 252
7.33	SUMMARY AND FINDINGS	253

INTRODUCTION

India has one of the fastest growing economies in the world, and the demand for oil and gas is rising at a matching rate. Not only is India's market potential huge, but in recent years India has emerged as one of the most prospective regions in the world with major oil and gas discoveries, both onshore and offshore.

India has total reserves (proved & indicated) of 1,201 million metric tonnes (MMT) of crude oil and 1,437 billion cubic metres (BCM) of natural gas as on April 1, 2010, according to the basic statistics released by the Ministry of Petroleum and Natural Gas. Against a crude oil production of about 37 million tonnes per annum (MTPA), India's consumption currently exceeds 138 million tonnes. In 2010, 194 MMT of crude oil was refined and actual natural gas production was 31.0 BCM. By the end of 2012, the refinery capacity is expected to reach 240.96 million metric tonnes per annum (MMTPA).

The refining capacity of the oil refineries in India has undergone nearly a three-fold increase in 2010. The country exported 50.974 MMT of petroleum products during 2009-10. To provide energy security, the Government of India is seeking private and foreign investments in excess of $250 billion in both the upstream and the downstream sectors during the next 10 years. India's petroleum product consumption has grown by 4-5% over the past 10 years and the oil demand in India is expected to rise to 368 MMTPA by 2025. With widening gap between demand and supply, both for oil and gas, the outlook for the upstream sector is extremely positive. While oil and gas will continue to play a substantial role in the total energy mix, the need for harnessing alternate energy sources like Coal Bed Methane (CBM), Underground Coal Gasification (UCG) and Shale Gas (gas locked in sedimentary rocks) will become crucial to balance the demand and supply.

The Government of India approved the New Exploration Licensing Policy (NELP) on April 9, 2009, to tackle the increasing demand supply gap of energy in India. In the eighth round of the NELP-VIII, 1.62 km2 areas will be covered comprising of 70 oil and gas blocks and 10 areas for the extraction of coal bed methane (CBM) gas from below the coal fields under CBM-IV. Petroleum & Natural Gas Ministry launched the ninth round of NELP (NELP-IX) in New Delhi on October 15, 2010. NELP-IX offered 34 exploration blocks comprising of 8 deepwater blocks,

7 shallow water blocks and 19 on land blocks. Moreover, the government is planning its first ever offer of shale gas exploration permits in 2012. Shale gas (gas locked in sedimentary rocks) is an emerging area and has become an important source of energy in a few countries which have been able to commercially exploit this resource.

In this report an attempt has been made to provide the broad understanding of the oil and gas sector in India across the industries. The upstream and downstream processing sectors, key players, key market, transportation and distribution network, fuel retailing, Indian taxation systems have been presented. The Western Australian capability/ level of interest in the market have also been described. Oil has been used for lighting purposes for many thousands of years. In areas where oil is found in shallow reservoirs, seeps of crude oil or gas may naturally develop, and some oil could simply be collected from seepage or tar. ponds. Historically we know the tales of eternal firs where oil and gas seeps ignited and burned. For e.g. famous oracle of Delphi was built around 1,000 B.C. written sources from 500 B.C. describe how Chinese used natural gas to boil water. It was not until 1859 that "Colonel" Edwin Drake drilled the first successful oil well, with the sole purpose of finding oil. The Drake well was located in the middle of quiet farm country in northwestern Pennsylvania, and sparked the international search for an industrial use for petroleum. Electricity did not emerge as an illuminant till the Edison Electric Light Company was founded in 1878. Well into the 20th century, kerosene, gas and electricity continued to compete as illuminants. Whilst the use of gas as an illuminant has virtually disappeared, a large population, especially in India, continues to use kerosene as illuminant. In 1890 Canadian Geologist Abraham Gesner has found Kerosene, which was extracted from coal and oil. Kerosene was most common energy source during that time as was used in lighting of the lamp which would in return the increase the value of kerosene.

MAIN FINDINGS

CHAPTER 1 OVERVIEW OF OIL INDUSTRY

We all know that motor – oil and gasoline come from crude oil, what many people do not realize is that crude oil is also the starting point for many diverse products such as clothes, medical equipment, electronics, vitamin capsules and tires. Whether land or under the ocean crude oil comes from deep underground where the remains of plant and animals (fossil) from millions of years ago have been heated – pressurized over time. Generally blackish in colour, crude oil has a characteristic odour that comes from the presence of small quantities of chemical compounds containing sulphur and nitrogen. There are different grades of crude oil. Each has a specific composition that is determined by the original decomposed source, materials as well as the properties of surrounding soil or rock formation.

It can be light or heavy, referring to density and sweet or sour referring to its sulphur content, however in row state, crude oil is of little use, it must be refined to make it into useable products. Depending upon the type of crude oil, it is treated via different refining process to turn it into fuels, lubricating oils, waxes, chemicals, plastics, and many other products used every day in society.

In order to meet ever growing demand for petroleum products, the government has consistently endeavoured to enhance exploration and exploitation of petroleum resources, along with developing a concrete and structured distribution and marketing system. Despite this crude oil production for 2013-14 remained stagnant at around 37.8 million metric tonnes (MMT) as against 37.9 MMT in 2012-13, showing a marginal decrease of about 0.20%. The bulk of crude oil production is from ageing fields, with the exception of Krishana Godavari (KG) basin and Rajasthan blocks. Production of crude oil was also affected by environmental issue, bandhs/blockades, lower base potential and delay in production from wells in some states. The average natural gas production for 2013-14 was about 35.4 BCM as against 40.7 BCM for 2012-13, showing a decline of about 13%. India has an estimated sedimentary area of 3.14 million sq. Km. Comprising 26 sedimentary basin. A total of 254 production sharing contracts have so far been singed under nine rounds of New Exploration Licensing Policy (NELP) bidding, of which 148 blocks are currently operational and the remaining 106 have been relinquished by the contractors. An area of 1.5 million sq. Km. Has so far been awarded under the NELP, which works out to almost 48% of the total sedimentary area in the country. Current average oil production from the NELP blocks is about 6938 barrels per day. Activities related to the 10th round NELP bidding (NELP – X) have been initiated. A total of 86 blocks (30 deep water, 23 shallow water and 33 on land) have been tentatively proposed

- According to a report released by McKinsey a global consultancy firm at the VI Asia Gas Partnership Summit, India's natural gas demand is expected to nearly double to 320 million metric standard cubic metres per day (mmscmd) by 2015. According to the analysis the current demand of 166 mmscmd—made up of nearly 132 mmscmd supplies from domestic fields and the rest from imported liquefied natural gas (LNG)—is likely to rise to at least a minimum of 230 mmscmd and a maximum of 320 mmscmd by 2015.
- The government is planning for its first ever offer of shale gas exploration in 2012. Shale gas (gas locked in sedimentary rocks) is an emerging area. It has become an important source of energy in a few countries that have been able to commercially exploit this resource.
- Economic survey 2011-12: India's oil refining capacity likely to rise 15% to 214 MT
- Out of the 21 refineries operating in the country, 17 are in public sector, three in private sector, and one is a joint venture of BPCL and Oman Oil Company (6 MT a year refinery at Bina in Madhya Pradesh).
- "The refinery capacity is further expected to increase to 214.07 million tonnes per annum by the end of 2011-12," it said.
- Though the document did not name the new units that would be commissioned, it may be alluding to almost complete 9 MT Bhatinda refinery that has been built by a joint venture of state-owned Hindustan Petroleum and steel baron Lakhsmi Mittal-controlled Mittal Investment Sarl.
- Also, Essar Oil is expanding its Vadinar refinery in Gujarat to 18 MT from current 14 MT.
- The Survey said refinery production (crude throughput) during 2010-11 had reached 206.15 MT (including Jamnagar Refinery under a special economic zone by Reliance

Industries Ltd), showing an increase of 6.9 per cent compared to 192.77 MT in 2009-10.

- During the current financial year (April-December), refinery production was 158.26 MT.
- "The country is not only self-sufficient in refining capacity for its domestic consumption but also substantially exports petroleum products," it said.
- During 2010-11, the country exported 59.13 MT of petroleum products worth Rs 1,96,112 crore.

OIL TRADING

On average, 52 mbpd of oil were moved internationally in 2006. The USA, Europe and Japan were responsible for more than 60% of world oil imports, while the Middle East, Africa and former Soviet Union accounted for more than 65% of world oil exports.

The crude oil spot price averaged $US 72 per barrel in 2007, more than triple the average price in 2002. Towards the end of 2007, the price of crude oil breached US$ 100 per barrel and, in May 2008, US$ 120 per barrel.

REFINING

According to the 2007 BP Statistical Energy Survey, world 2006 refinery capacity was 87 mbpd and 2006 refinery throughput was 75 mbpd on average. The countries with the largest oil refining capacity are, in order, the USA, China, Russia, Japan, India, South Korea, Germany, Italy and Saudi Arabia. Saudi Arabia is currently doubling its refinery capacity before 2012.

EXPLORATION AND DEVELOPMENT

In June 2007, OPEC announced plans to invest US$ 130 billion in expanded production between then and 2012. Excluding Iraq, production is forecast to increase from 35.7 million bpd to 39.7 million bpd in 2010. Between 2013 and 2020 OPEC plans to spend a further US$ 500 billion provided biofuels doesn't change economics. Saudi Arabia alone is investing US$ 50 billion to increase crude production capacity from 10.5 million barrels a day in 2007 to 12 million bpd in 2009 and 15 million bpd after 2025.

A Harrison Lovegrove study of 200 non state-owned oil and gas companies found 2005 development costs rose 30% to US$ 159 billion, yet only yielded a 2% increase in proved reserves and a 1% increase in production. Part of the reason is that countries rich in oil are increasingly excluding foreign companies from participation. A later study showed spending by 228 oil and gas companies increased 45% in 2006 to US$ 400 billion but again only increased reserves by 2%.

A March 2007 report by Harrison Lovegrove estimated that state owned oil and gas companies invested US$ 75 billion in oil and gas asset acquisitions in 2006, 33% of the total of US$ 166 billion. Average 2006 prices paid were US$ 12.86 per barrel of proved oil / gas reserves, an increase of 34% on 2005.

Only three major fields have been discovered worldwide since 1969 and none since 1976. A study by Simmons found that since 1980, only three fields out of all of the new discoveries are producing over 200,000 barrels a day. In the 1990's, over 420 fields were discovered, but only 11 have production that exceeds 100,000 barrels per day.

To raise the interest of foreign companies in the E&P sector. The government decided to award some small and medium fields for development to the private and joint sectors respectively, and came out with two rounds in 1992 and 1993. These rounds evinced tremendous response from foreign players. Also in order to upgrade the information on the hydrocarbon potential of India's unexplored sedimentary basins, the government offered blocks for geophysical survey during 1993 to 1995.

SWOT Analysis of the Indian oil and gas industry Strengths

SWOT Analysis of the Indian oil and gas industry Strengths	
STRENGTH •India is the world's fifth biggest energy consumer and continues to grow rapidly •Major natural gas discoveries by a number of domestic companies hold significant medium- to long-term potential. •Demand for petroleum products •Increase in demand for oil and gas •High exploration portfolio	**WEAKNESS** •The oil and gas sector is dominated by state-controlled enterprises, although the government has taken steps in recent years to deregulate the industry and encourage greater foreign participation •Increase in oil prices •Inadequate and slowly developing infrastructure •Lack of awareness in safety issues •Environmental issues
OPPORTUNITY •Liquefied natural gas (LNG) imports are still set to grow rapidly over the longer term as domestic consumption expands •India has freed gasoline retail price controls •Untapped domestic oil and gas potential •Strong domestic energy demand growth •High recovery rates from existing projects	**THREATS** Increased competition within government and private players •Continuing government interference •Changes in national energy policies

The Indian Oil and Gas industry plays an important role in the Indian economy with major refineries and gas companies in the country. Indian oil and gas sector is majorly controlled by state owned Oil and Natural Gas Corporation (ONGC) which accounts for approx. 60% of India's crude oil output. The Indian Oil industry consumption was around 3.27 mn barrels per day (b/d) in 2011 compared to around 3.15 mn b/d in 2010 and is expected to reach around 4.08 mn b/d by 2016. Indian refinery industry has around 21 refineries with total oil refinery capacity being around 3.6 mn b/d which is expected to reach around 4.29 mn b/d by 2016.India imports around 70% of the total oil needed, from countries like Saudi Arabia, Iran, UAE, etc, and has spent around US$ 91,490 million (mn) in 2011 on imports. India has a largely state-controlled oil and gas sector. The main government upstream vehicle is ONGC, which accounts for two-thirds of India's crude oil and natural gas production. It is diversifying into refining and oil distribution. Privately owned domestic conglomerate Reliance Industries also participates in the Indian exploration and refining segments, with BP set to be a key partner in domestic upstream activities.

CHAPTER 2 RESEARCH METHODOLOGY

An Introduction to Oil Industry in India

Oil exploration and production in India is done by companies like NOC or National Oil Corporation, ONGC or Oil and Natural Gas Corporation and OIL who are actually the oil companies in India that are owned by the government under the Industrial Policy Rule. The National Oil Corporation during the 1970s used to produce and supply more than 70 percent of the domestic need for the petroleum but by the end of this amount dropped to near about 35 percent. This was because the demand on the one hand was increasing at a good rate and the production was declining at a steady rate.

CONCEPT OF PROFITABILITY

The word 'profitability' is composed of two words, namely; profit and ability. The term profit has already been discussed at length in detail. The term ability indicates the power of a firm to earn profits. The ability of an enterprise also denotes its earning power or operating performance. Also, that the business ability points towards the financial and operational ability of the business. So, on this basis profitability may be defined as —the ability of a given instrument to earn a return from its use Weston and Brigham defines profitability as "the net surplus of a large number of policies and decisions.". Profit being an absolute figure fails to indicate the adequacy of income or changes in efficiency resulting from financial and operational performance of an enterprise

CONCEPT OF LIQUIDITY

By the term 'liquidity' is meant the debt-repaying capacity of an undertaking. It refers to the firm's ability to meet the claims of suppliers of goods, services and capital. According to Archer and D'Ambrosio, liquidity means cash and cash availability, and it is from current operations and previous accumulations that cash is available, to take care of the claims of both the short-term suppliers of capital and the long-term ones. It has two dimensions; the short-term and the long-term liquidity

SCOPE OF THE STUDY

The scope or area of the study includes the analysis of profitability vis a vis liquidity of oil refinery industry in india for the period of 2007-08 to 2012-13. The research has been focused on top seven refinery companies on the basis of paid up capital as on 31st march 2012

UNIVERSE OF THE STUDY

The universe of the study consists of all the limited oil refinery companies working in India and listed in Bombay Stock Exchange.

SAMPLING DESIGN

There are total numbers of 21 oil refinery companies working in India, out of which 17 are public sector units, 3 are private sectors and 1 is Joint Venture Company. The sample of seven oil refinery were selected considering the following factors

- Listed on Bombay Stock exchange
- Paid up capital during the year as on year ended 31st march 2012
- For the period form 2007-08 to 2012-13.

SOURCES AND COLLECTION OF DATA

The main source of data was published financial reports, statistical figures, economic survey; central statistical organization survey etc, for the purpose of research secondary data will be considered.

SAMPLE SIZE

Out of the 21 oil refinery companies following six companies on the bases of their paid up capital (as on 31st March 2012) were selected for the research work.

Following companies were selected

Sr.no.	**Company name**	***Paid up capital (Rs.Cr)**
1	ONGC	4277.76
2	RIL	3271
3	IOCL	2427.95
4	MRPL	1752.60
5	BPCL	361.54
6	HPCL	338.63

(*paid up capital as on 31-3-2012)

ANALYSIS OF DATA

For the analysis of data, various tools techniques were taken into consideration, for analytical purpose ratio analysis was used. For checking profitability position of the companies gross profit,net profit, return on capital employed, earning per share, dividend per share, return on net worth ratios were used. Further, for verifying significance level F test was used. While to verify liquidity position of the companies current ratio, quick ratio, inventory turnover, debtors turnover, debt to equity, fixed assets turnover ratio were used, to evaluate significance level, F test was used. While comparing profitability vis a vis liquidity position of companies, liquidity – profitability matrix was constructed, to further evaluating interrelationship multiple correlation was used. To verify interrelationship significance t test was applied.

LIMITATIONS OF STUDY

- The study is based upon the secondary data taken from published annual accounts and reports of selected companies
- There are different methods to measure the profitability and liquidity of an industry in these context views of experts can differ from one to another.
- The study is limited to period from 2007-08 to 2012-13.

CHAPTER 3 SAMPLE PROFILE

Bharat Petroleum Corporation Ltd

Bharat Petroleum Corporation Ltd (BPCL) operates in the petroleum industry in India. The company operates in a single segment - Refinery and Marketing activities, which includes Downstream petroleum sector. They are also engaged in the Exploration and Production of Hydrocarbons (E&P). BPCL on a regular basis imports their LPG requirements mainly from the Middle East. Occasional there are import requirements of Gasoil, Kerosene, Gasoline and Base Oil. The company refineries consist of Mumbai Refinery, Kochi Refinery, Numaligarh Refinery and Bina Refinery. BPCL exports Fuel Oil and Naphtha and Base Oil (Group II). During the year 2001-02, the company commissioned the Gas Turbine and Heat Recovery Steam Generator project at a cost of Rs.1750 million. Refinery Modernization Project was being implemented at a cost of Rs 18,310 million. This project besides improve distillate yield and energy efficiency of the company. The company had Allied Retail Business (ARB) also apart from the regular business, making them not only the largest non-fuel revenue generator in the oil industry, but also amongst the leading retail networks in the country, offering a basket of services ranging from C-stores, Quick Service Restaurants to financial and travel related services. In August 2010, Indian Oil Corporation Ltd, Bharat Petroleum Corporation Ltd and Hindustan Petroleum Corporation Limited entered into a memorandum of understanding (MoU) with Gujarat State Petroleum Corp Ltd to form a joint venture for trunk gas pipelines. In February 2011, the company signed an initial agreement with the provincial government of Rajasthan to sell fuel products from the state's proposed refinery. The company will sell at least 75% of the volume of the products from the proposed Rajasthan refinery under the agreement. The company plans to rise the capacity at its just commissioned Bina refinery in Madhya Pradesh to nine million tonne and is looking at the right time for a public offering of the unit. The company is planning to bid for city-gas projects in Kochi (Kerala) and Hyderabad (Andhra Pradesh) and plans to launch 600 new fuel retail outlets this fiscal, according to S Vardarajan, director, corporate finance. The company has lined up investments of Rs 50,000 crore ($11 billion) to expand their capacities in refining, retail and upstream projects over the next five years.

Hindustan Petroleum Corporation Ltd,

Hindustan Petroleum Corporation Ltd, a fortune 500 company, is one of the major integrated oil refining and marketing companies in India. The company is a Mega Public Sector Undertaking (PSU) with Navaratna status. The company operates in two business segments: Downstream, and exploration and production of hydrocarbons. The Downstream segment is engaged in refining and marketing of petroleum products. They operate two coastal refineries, one at Mumbai (West Coast) of 6.5 million metric tonnes per annum (MMTPA) and the other in Vishakapatnam, (East Coast) with a capacity of 8.3 MMTPA. They also hold an equity stake of 16.95% in Mangalore Refinery & Petrochemicals Ltd (MRPL), a refinery at Mangalore with a capacity of 9 MMTPA. The company owns the country's Lube Refinery with a capacity of 335,000 Metric Tonnes. The company's products and services include Refineries, aviation, bulk fuels & specialities, international trade, liquefied petroleum gas (LPG) - HP gas, Lubes - HP lubes. The company's subsidiaries include HPCL Biofuels Ltd and HPCL-Mittal Energy Ltd. In December 2000, the 'Guru Gobind Singh Refineries' was incorporated as a wholly owned subsidiary company. The company completed the Rs 378 crore pipeline project from Vijayawada to Secunderabad, which was commissioned on March 2002. They set up a new LPG Bottling plant with capacity of 44 TMTPA in Kota. The company implemented 15 company tank trucks in the year 2004. During the year 2008-09, the installation of facilities for production of Euro III / IV Petrol (Motor Spirit) at both the Refineries was completed. In pursuit of promoting alternate fuels, CREDA-HPCL Biofuel Ltd (CHBL) was incorporated on October 14, 2008, as a subsidiary company with equity shareholding of 74% by the company and 26% by Chhattisgarh State Renewable Energy Development Agency (CREDA). CHBL is to undertake cultivation of Jatropha plant, an energy crop used for production of bio- diesel, on 15,000 hectares of land leased by the Government of Chhattisgarh. In April 2011, the company approved the acquisition of balance 50% shares held by other joint venture partners in Prize Petroleum Company Ltd. In November 2011, the company entered into an MoU with Greater Calcutta Gas Supply Corporation Ltd (GCGSCL) and Gas Authority of India Ltd (GAIL) to carry out Natural Gas business in the City of Kolkata and its adjoining districts. The company is setting up a state of the art Green R&D Centre at Bangalore with an objective to become a technology leader through continuous &

innovative R&D efforts. The projects is being executed in a phase manner with a phase-I capital investment of Rs 210 crore.

Indian Oil Corporation Ltd

Indian Oil Corporation Ltd (Indian Oil) is India's flagship national oil company with business interests straddling the entire hydrocarbon value chain - from refining, pipeline transportation and marketing of petroleum products to exploration & production of crude oil & gas, marketing of natural gas and petrochemicals. The company is the leading Indian corporate in the Fortune 'Global 500' listing, ranked at the 98th position in the year 2011. Indian Oil Corporation Ltd was established in the year 1959 as Indian Oil Company Ltd. In the year 1964, Indian Refineries Ltd merged with Indian Oil Corporation Ltd. Indian Oil Blending Ltd a wholly owned subsidiary was merged with IndianOil on May 2006. The company transferred their entire equity holding in Indian Strategic Petroleum Reserves Ltd (ISPRL) to the Oil Industry Development Board, a government body functioning under the Ministry of Petroleum & Natural Gas. Consequently, ISPRL ceased to be a wholly owned subsidiary in May 2006. In the year 2007, the company received plenty of awards, Oil Industry Safety Directorate Awards, 'Most Admired Retailer of the Year' award, 'CIO 100 Award 2007', SAP ACE - Awards for Customer Excellence and the only petroleum company as 'The Most Trusted Brand' in ET's Brand Equity's annual survey. The SERVO acquires prestigious MAN Global approvals, Indian Oil's R&D Centre gets special recognition for Bioremediation and also SERVO secures entry into NSF White Book - H1 Category during the period. The company won Retailer of the Year - Rural Impact Award and their XtraPower won Loyalty Summit Award during the year 2008. During the year 2010-11, the company enrolled about 46.8 lakh new Indane LPG customers and commissioned 245 new Indane distributors taking their total to 618.3 lakh and 5,311 respectively. The LPG Bottling capacity was enhanced to 5,518 TMTPA with capacity addition of 326 TMT. In order to provide LPG to rural India, the company commissioned 145 distributors under the Rajiv Gandhi Gramin LPG Vitaran Yojana under the auspices of Ministry of Petroleum & Natural Gas. As a part of their CSR activity, 10,052 new connections were released to BPL families. During the year, the company formed a joint venture company was formed with Nuclear Power Corporation of India Ltd (NPCIL) for setting up Nuclear power plants. In July

2010, the company commissioned their first gas pipeline between Dadri and Panipat and thus they commenced gas supplies to Panipat Refinery. In a bid to scale up their gas infrastructure, a 5 MMTPA LNG Import & Re-gassification Terminal Project was planned at Ennore, Tamil Nadu. This LNG Terminal would be the first of its kind on the East coast of India. Furthermore, in consortium with GSPC, HPCL and BPCL, the company won gas pipeline bids for Mallavaram to Bhilwara and Vijaypur via Bhopal, Mehsana to Bhatinda and Bhatinda to Jammu and Srinagar

Mangalore Refinery and Petrochemicals Limited

Mangalore Refinery and Petrochemicals Limited (MRPL), a Mini Ratna company was incorporated in 7th March of the year 1988 and commenced a business in 2nd August as a joint venture oil refinery promoted by Hindustan Petroleum Corporation and Indian Rayon & Industries Limited (IRIL) & Associates (AV Birla Group), now it is a subsidiary company of ONGC. MRPL is the only refinery in India to have two CCRs producing unleaded petrol of high octane. The refinery was conceived to maximize middle distillates with the capability to process light to heavy and sour to sweet crudes with 24 to 46 API gravity. In 2003, ONGC and MRPL had signed a Memorandum of Understanding for the supply of crude oil. As at 28th March of the year 2003, ONGC acquired the total shareholding of 37.39% held by A.V. Birla Group and further infused equity capital of Rs.600 crores consequently made MRPL a majority held subsidiary of ONGC. The Company had contributed Rs 20 crore to New Mangalore Port Trust towards construction of new jetty at the port for exclusive use of the company. Further it is participating as an equity shareholder in the 364 km long cross country multi product Mangalore-Hassan-Bangalore pipeline which will help the company in accessing wider consumption areas for its products. The Hassan-Bangalore Pipeline project of 367 KM long was operational and the first parcel of HSD was transported through this pipeline and was delivered at Bangalore on 1st August of the year 2003. The Centre for High Technology (CHT) selected the MRPL for the Jawaharlal Nehru centenary awards under energy performance of refineries for the year 2003-04. Shell made tie-up with MRPL for Petro products in the year 2004. During the year 2004-05, based on the MOU with ONGC the company purchased 3.7 MMT Mumbai High Crude on pricing formula applicable to other PSU Refineries. MRPL had signed a pact with Saudi, Iran firms for crude supply in the year 2005, also in the same year; the company had forged alliance with Ashok Leyland for retail outlets. MRPL plans to initiate plant-scale experiments on spent caustic treatment with chlorine dioxide to treat phenols, conduct a study on ONGC-Hazira HCR samples on producing Gasoline using ONGC Hazira naphtha and MRPL reformate, and analyse the feasibility of producing US Military grade ATF-JP5. The company also plans to augment refining capacity from the present rating of 9.69 TPA to 15 TPA. Studies have been initiated to add fresh capacities to the tune of 15 TPA. Also the company plans to launch its unique branded petrol and diesel in very soon.

Oil & Natural Gas Corp. Ltd

During March 1999, ONGC, Indian Oil Corporation (IOC) and Gas Authority of India Limited (GAIL) both of three agreed to have cross holding in each other's stock to pave the way for Long-term strategic alliance amongst themselves for the domestic and overseas business opportunities in the energy value chain. The ONGIO International Pvt Ltd was incorporated in the year 2001 as 50:50 joint venture projects with Indian Oil Corporation Ltd with aim of providing Training, Consultancy & Services in Hydrocarbon Sector and later company has decided to wind up ONGIO due to loss. During 2001-02 the augment recovery from onshore fields of 13 projects 2 were resourcefully commissioned. By the end of the same year 2001-02 the company 's subsidiary unit ONGC Videsh Ltd commenced its commercial production of gas. In the year of 2004 ONGC initiated Phase-I of a collaborative project on CBM in Jharia Field and successfully completed the same in 2005. During 2004-05 the company discovered its third deep-water exploration campaign 'Sagar Samriddhi' in Krishna-Godavari (KG) Basin at the location Vashistha (VA-1A) in block KG-OS-DW-IV. In the western offshore a shallow-water oil and gas was recorded in D-33, about 60 Kilometers South-West of Mumbai High, Onshore, Oil and Gas was found in Tiphuk-1 in North Assam Shelf and Oil was struck at Wamaj in Cambay Basin. Offshore, four new Platforms (2 Well Platforms, 1 Process Platforms and 1 Clamp-on) were Commissioned for enhancing production. New trunk pipelines are being laidsub-sea from Mumbai High Field to Urban Oil and Gas processing facility. In March 2005 ONGC launched its retail marketing business with commissioning of its first autofuels outlet at Manglore under the brand 'ONGC Values' and 'Shopp'njoy' for fuel and non-fuel business respectively. The company has also received approval/license from the Government for marketing of non-subsidised LPG cooking gas, Kerosene and Aviation refueling sales. Tripura Power Development Company Pvt Ltd (TPDCL) was incorporated to set up a gas-based power-generating project in Tripura. TPDCL has been renamed as ONGC Tripura Power Company Pvt Ltd after the domination. In the same year the company has entered into various alliances in form of execution of Memorandum of Understanding with Kakinada Seaport & IL&FS with 26% equity stake for development of Port based SEZ at Kakinada, Andhra Pradesh. During the year 2006 the company was awarded 60 out of 110 exploration blocks by the Government in the five NELP rounds. Out of these 60 NELP Blocks 35 are in the form of unincorporated joint ventures and remaining blocks are company's 100% participating interest. For the sake of its excellent concert, the company has received numerous awards every year. The highlights are NDTV Profit Business Leadership Award, Motilal Oswal CNBC TV18 Biggest Wealth Creator of India for the period of 2001-06, Golden Peacock Award 2006 for Corporate Governance in PSU category, is this award has been conferred to the company regularly. Dun & Bradstreet-American Express Corporate Awards 2006 in the oil and gas exploration sector and Greentech Gold Safety Award in petroleum sector apart from this, the company listed and ranked in Indian level also in global level by various evaluators.

Reliance Industries Ltd

Reliance Industries Ltd is an India-based company. The company is India's largest private sector company on all major financial parameters. They are the first private sector company from India to feature in the Fortune Global 500 list of 'World's Largest Corporations' and ranks 117th amongst the world's Top 200 companies in terms of profits. The company operates world-class manufacturing facilities across the country at Allahabad, Barabanki, Dahej, Hazira, Hoshiarpur, Jamnagar, Nagothane, Nagpur, Naroda, Patalganga, Silvassa and Vadodara. The company operates in three business segments: petrochemicals, refining, and oil and gas. The petrochemicals segment includes production and marketing operations of petrochemical products. The refining segment includes production and marketing operations of the petroleum products. The oil and gas segment includes exploration, development and production of crude oil and natural gas. The other segment of the company includes textile, retail business and special economic zone (SEZ) development. In the year 1966 the RIL was founded by Shri Dhirubhai H.Ambani, it was started as a small textile manufacturer unit. In May 8, 1973 RIL was incorporated and conformed their name as RIL in the year 1985. Over the years, the company has transformed their business from manufacturing of textiles products into a petrochemical major. The company has set up a texturising / twisting facilities in 1979, RIL has also set up plants for Polyester Staple Fiber (PSF) in 1986 and for Linear Alkyl Benzene (LAB) & Purified Terephthalic Acid (PTA) in 1988. RIL has setup a petrochemical facility to produce HDPE and PVC at Hazira, Gujarat in technical collaboration with DuPont and BF Goodich respectively. The Hazira petrochemical plant was commissioned in 1991-92. In the year 1995-96, the company entered the telecom industry through a joint venture with NYNEX, USA and promoted Reliance Telecom Private Limited in India. Reliance became the first corporate in Asia to issue bonds in the U.S at the year of 1996-97. The company commissioned an 80,000 tonne bottle grade PET chip plant at Hazira manufacturing complex. Reliance's PET chips has been accepted internationally due to their high quality during the year 1997-98 and in the same year Reliance Industries Planned to invest around Rs. 5000 crores (USD 1,250 million) in building two world-scale plants at the site of the Jamnagar refinery in Gujarat. In 1998-99, RIL introduced packaged LPG in 15 kg cylinders under the brand name Reliance Gas. In 1999-2000, RIL commissioned the world's largest 1.4 million tonnes per annum Paraxylene (PX) plant at its new integrated petrochemicals complex at Jamnagar which was planned at 1997-98. Reliance Petroleum Limited (RPL) was amalgamated with Reliance Industries Ltd in the year 2002-03.

CHAPTER 4 ANALYSIS OF PROFITABILITY

Gross profit margin ratio

During study period BPCL has maintained average gross profit margin of 1.70%, which was very low compare to industry average of 10.75%, the margin was ranged between 2.58% in 2008-09 to 0.93% in 2011-12, the standard deviation was 0.57 as compared to industry average of 16.06 which means there was a less fluctuation in gross profit margin during period of research. Overall the company has shown satisfactory gross profit margin. Gross profit margin of HPCL varied between 2% in 2009-10 to 1.1% in 2012-13. Average gross profit margin was 1.44% which was also the lowest among the average of other companies' as well as industry average of 16.06%. Overall it was clear that company has maintained very poor gross profit margin on sales due to high cost of production and direct expenses. During period of study gross profit margin of IOCL was showing mix trend, ranged between 3.47% in 2007-08 to 1.9% in 2012-13. The company has maintained average gross profit margin of 3.13% which was less than the industry average of 16.06%. Overall the company has maintained satisfactory gross profit margin. MRPL was the only exception showing negative return of gross profit on sales. Although company has maintained average return of 3.60%, during last year it was negative. Highest return was in 2008-09 which was 6.21%. Due to heavy cost of production company couldn't maintain positive return on sales. ONGC has shown very sound profitability position. It has shown average of 44.76% which was more than the industry average of 10.75%. Gross profit margin was ranged between 53.87% in 2009-10 to 30.34% in 2012-13. Standard deviation of 8.16% compared to industry average of 16.06% which means there was a less fluctuations in gross profit margin during period of research. RIL has shown downtrend in gross profit during research period, ranged between 13.35% in 2008-09 to 5.91% in 2011-12, during last four years of study, there was a continuous decrease in gross profit margin, which shows negative future profitability position. The company has managed average 9.85% return on gross profit which was also less than the industry average.

Net profit margin ratio

BPCL. has maintained average 0.99% net profit margin which was less than industry average of 6.85%. The margin was ranged between 1.26% in 2009-10 to 0.54% in 2008-09. It was fluctuating during research period. Standard deviation was 0.35% which was less than the industry average of 9.36%. Overall it shows very low net profit margin as compared to other industry players of research sample. HPCL had the lowest average of net profit margin among other companies, i.e. 0.80% whereas average industry net profit margin was 6.85%, the margin was ranged between 1.2% in 2009-10 to 0.43% in 2012-13. During research period, the net profit margin has shown mix trend. In short the company had maintained poor net profit margin during research period. During study period, net profit margin of IOCL was ranged between 3.74% in 2009-10 to 0.95% in 2008-09. Average net profit margin was 1.96% which was below industry average of 6.85%. Overall it shows satisfactory net profit margin. MRPL had shown good net profit margin during the first three years of research, ranged between 3.89% in 2007-08 to 3% in 2010-11, but during last two years of study there was a downtrend in net profit margin, moreover it was negative 1.15% in 2012-13. Due to high cost of production company couldn't maintain net profit margin.ONGC has shown better net profit margin during research period. The company was having the highest average of net profit margin i.e. 26.14% far better than the industry average of just 6.85%, margin was ranged between 31.02% in 2011-12 to 23.5% in 2008-09. The company is having very strong profitability prospectus RIL had maintained average 8.67% net profit margin slightly more than industry average of 6.85%, the margin was ranged between 14.45% in 2007-08 to 5.7% in 2012-13. The company was having very sound profitability position, except the constraint that negative trend of net profit margin will lead to adverse profitability condition in future.

Return on net worth

Return on net worth of BPCL. The ratio showed mix trend during research period. The average was 11.17% which was little less than industry average of 13.92%. The ratio was ranged between 15.88% in 2012-13 to 6.06% in 2008-09. The standard deviation was 3.46 which also less than the industry average of 7.79 showing less fluctuation in return on net worth of company. In short the company has maintained good ratio of return on net worth. The ratio of return on net worth of HPCL shows fluctuating trend. The company had given average return of 8.86% as compared to industry average of 13.92%, which was the lowest return compare to other companies included in research study. The ratio was ranged between 12.26% in 2010-11 to 5.35% in 2008-09. Overall the company has given satisfactory return on net worth during period of study.The ratio of return on net worth of IOCL has also shown mix trend, ranged between 20.22% in 2009-10 to 6.71% in 2008-09. Overall the company has maintained average return of 12.06% which was little less than industry average of 13.92. overall the company could maintain satisfactory return on net worth during period of study.The ratio of return on net worth of MRPL has shown exceptionally negative return in 2012-13 i.e. 11.7% due to negative profit after tax. However the company has managed average return of 16.30% on net worth which was more than the industry average of 13.92%, but as far as company is showing negative trend it was adverse for future profitability.ONGC has given the highest return on net worth at an average of 20.39% compared to industry average of 13.92%, ratio was ranged between 22.24% in 2011-12 to 16.81% in 2012-13. Standard deviation was mere 2.47 which mean less fluctuation in return. Overall the company has performed well and given good returns to shareholders.RIL has maintained return on net worth with an average of 14.75% which was better than industry average of 13.92%, although the ratio has shown decreasing trend during last three years of study period. The ratio was ranged between 24.66% in 2007-08 to 11.66% in 2012-13. Overall the company has given satisfactory return to their shareholders.

Return on capital employed

Return on capital employed of BPCL average return was 12.27% which was less than industry average of 16.24%. Standard deviation of 1.96 means there was a less fluctuations during research period of study. The average was between 14.86% in 2008-09 to 10.18% in 2011-12. Return on capital employed of HPCL was satisfactory at an average of 8.19% with industry average of 16.24% almost half of the industry average, which shows poor return on capital employed as compare to other companies, ratio was ranged between 9.91% in 2009-10 to 6.23% in 2007-08. Standard deviation of 1.36, less than the industry average means less fluctuation in return on capital employed during study period. Ratio of return on capital employed of IOCL was ranged between 15.83% in 2009-10 to 8.64% in 2012-13. The ratio has shown mixed trend. The average return was 12.76% which was also less than industry average of 16.24%. Overall the company has maintained satisfactory return on capital employed.MRPL was the only company which had given negative return to capital employed due to heavy loss after tax and high expenses to revenue. In 2012-13, it has shown negative return of 1.43%, however company could maintain average ratio of 20.55% which was unexpectedly higher than the industry average of 16.24%.ONGC has given the highest average return on capital employed i.e. 31.11%, ranged between 36.3% in 2007-08 to 24.6% in 2012-13. Standard deviation was 4.59 which was also less than the industry average of 9.6 which means there was less uncertainty in return on capital employed during study period. Overall the company is having good prospects in return on capital employed. RIL has maintained 12.55% average return on capital employed. The ratio was ranged between 15.68% in 2007-08 to 10.96% in 2008-09, however during last two years of research period, company has maintained upward trend in return on capital employed. Standard deviation was 1.67 compared to industry average of 9.6 means less deviation in return on capital employed.

Dividend Per Share

The Dividend Per Share of BPCL has shown increasing trend during firs four years of study period, whereas during last two years company could maintain DPS of rs.11 per share. Average DPS of BPCL was 10.17 rs. Per share, which was little more than the industry average of Rs.9.67 per share. Overall it shows positive and satisfactory dividend per share.HPCL, has maintained increasing trend of DPS during first four years, whereas during last two years, company had shown constant DPS of rs. 8.5 per share. The average DPS was rs. 8.54, which was less than the industry average of rs.9.67 per share. Standard deviation of 4.08 shows less fluctuations in dividend per share of a company.During study period, IOCL has maintained the average DPS of rs. 7.78 per share, ranged between 13 in 2009-10 to rs. 5 per share in 2011-12. Standard deviation was 3.02 which is less than industry average of 8.05 which means less changes in dividend payment during research period.

MRPL has shown average DPS of 0.97 per share, which was far below than the industry average of rs.9.67 per share. During first four years of research company had constant DPS of rs. 1.2, gradually it decreased to 1 re. per share and nil. Due to negative earnings after tax , company couldn't maintain proper dividend policy.ONGC has shown the highest average of rs. 20.83 per share, as compared to industry average of rs. 9.67 per share, it was ranged between 33 rs. Per share in 2009-10 to 8.75 per share in 2010-11. But dividend during last two years of study were near to industry average. Moreover the standard deviation is 12.61 which is also more than the industry average of 8.05, which means inconsistency in payment of dividend during study period. During period of study, Dividend Per Share of RIL was ranged between rs.13 per share in 2007-08 to rs.8 per share in 2010-11. Company has maintained average DPS of 9.75, which was also more than the industry average of rs.9.67 per share. Standard deviation was 2.60, less than the industry average of 8.05, which means less change in dividend payment during study period. Overall the company has maintained satisfactory dividend payment policy.

Earnings Per Share

EPS of BPCL with an average of rs. 41.78 per share, which was more than the industry average of rs. 39.90 per share. EPS was ranged between rs. 65.05 per share in 2012-13 to 36.27 rs. Per share in 2011-12, standard deviation is 14.40 which was also less than the industry average of 29.18. Overall EPS of company was satisfactory. HPCL has shown average EPS of rs. 31.34 per share, which was less than industry average of rs.39.90 per share. The highest EPS was rs.45.45 in 2010-11, where as it was minimum in 2008-09 i.e. rs.16.98. standard deviation was 10.01, less than the industry average showing less changes in EPS. IOCL has shown average EPS of 32.13, which was lower than the industry average of rs.39.90 per share. EPS was ranged between 58.39 in 2007-08 to 16.29 in 2011-12. Standard deviation of 15.68, below the industry average shows consistency in EPS.MRPL has shown negative EPS in the year 2012-13 i.e. -4.32 rs. Per share. Moreover, the company has shown the lowest average of rs.4.66 per share which was far below than the industry average of rs.39.90. EPS was ranged between 7.26 per share in 2007-08 to -4.32 per share in 2012-13. Overall it was very dissatisfactory. ONGC has maintained EPS of rs.78 to rs.75 during first three years then after it was ranged between rs.22.12 per share to rs.29.36 per share during last three years. The average was rs.51.30 per share which was more than the industry average of rs.39.90 per share. Standard deviation was 28.59 slightly less than the industry average of rs.29.18 per share. RIL, has performed well during research period showing average EPS of rs.78.18 per share, which was almost double than the industry average of 39.90 per share. The EPS was ranged between 133.86 per share in 2007-08, which was also the highest among all companies to rs.49.64 per share in 2009-10, overall the company has given good EPS.

CHAPTER 5 ANALYSIS OF LIQUIDITY

Current ratio

During research period, current ratio of BPCL was ranged between 0.78 in 2012-13 to 0.5 in 2008-09. The ratio shows fluctuating trend. The average ratio during the period was 0.69 which was the lowest one compare to other industry average. Company couldn't maintain the ideal current ratio during the study period, hence not able to pay its current liabilities in time. During period of study current ratio of HPCL was between 1.03 in 2007-08 to 0.68 in 2012-13, with an average of 0.80 which was near to ideal current ratio, but below to industry average of 1.01. During most of the years company was not able pay its current liabilities as ratio was less than 1. The above table shows the current ratio of IOCL, which was the highest 0.84 in 2007-08 and the lowest in 2008-09 i.e. 0.61, trend shows very little fluctuations with an industry average of 0.78. liquidity position was good, but exact standard ratio couldn't be maintained. While, MRPL shows ideal current ratio during most of the period, the ratio was ranged between 1.36 in 2008-09 to 0.92 in 2012-13. The company has also maintained average current ratio of 1.06 which was more than the industry average. ONGC was leading the race, maintaining standard current ratio throughout the research period, maximum 2.37 in 2012-13, to minimum 1.13 in 2011-12, with the highest average of 1.51. overall the company has shown good liquidity position during period of study. RIL has also maintained the standard current ratio. The company has kept average current ratio at 1.19. the data shows very less fluctuations in current ratio. Current ratio was ranged between 1.44 in 2011-12 to 0.98 in 2007-08.

Stock turnover ratio or stock velocity ratio

Inventory turnover ratio of BPCL, the data shows fluctuating trend in ratio. It was 11.64 times in 2007-08, then the highest 21.91 times in 2008-09, and further declined to 11.09 times and lowest 9.86 times in the 2009-10 and 2010-11 respectively. The company has maintained average turnover at 13.70 times which was below to industry average of 19.61 times. Overall the company has maintained satisfactory turnover ratio. The inventory turnover ratio of HPCL has also shown mix trend. The turnover was ranged between 15.31 times in 2008-09 to 8.68 times in 2010-11. During study period, company has maintained average turnover at 10.93 times less than the industry average of 19.61 times. Overall the company has kept moderate inventory turnover ratio. Whereas IOCL was having the lowest average of 9.17 times of inventory turnover. IOCL was struggling to move inventory faster as compare to other companies of sample study. The company has figured out the lowest turnover ratio of 7.56 times in 2010-11, and highest was 13.98 times in 2008-09. Overall it was dissatisfactory result for company. Inventory turnover ratio of MRPL shows fluctuating trend ranged between 23.6 times in 2008-09 to 7.32 times in 2011-12. The company has shown the lowest inventory turnover ratio to other companies under study. Overall it was dissatisfactory result of company. ONGC has shown tremendous inventory turnover ratio and also the highest among others. The company has shown the average of 61.42 times, almost 3.20 times more than the industry average of 19.61 times. This shows the company was very efficient in converting inventory to sales. During study period RIL has shown mix trend ranged between 12.92 times in 2008-09 to 8.29 times in 2009-10. The company could maintain 10.57 times inventory turnover during period of research which was less than industry average of 19.61 times.

Debtor's turnover ratio

Average ratio was of 61.63 times more than the industry average of 36.08 times. Company's average debtor's turnover ratio was higher among all companies under study. The turnover was ranged between 88.37 times in 2008-09 to 46.16 times in 2012-13. Standard deviation was 15.80 and co variance was 25.64% shows greater fluctuations in debtors turnover ratio during study period. BPCL was quick to convert credit sales into cash and has implemented good collection policy. HPCL was next to BPCL in context to average debtors turnover ratio during study period. It was 55.18 times, more than the industry average of 36.08. the ratio was ranged between 63.44 times in 2007-08 to 48.7 in 2012-13. Standard deviation of 7.42 and co variance of 13.44% show fewer fluctuations in debtors turnover ratio. Overall the company has maintained good credit collection policy. The average debtors turnover ratio of IOCL was 41.49 times. It was also more than the industry average of 36.08 times. The turnover ratio was less fluctuating as standard deviation was 5.49 and co variance was 13.23%. Debtors turnover ratio was ranged between 48.15 times in 2008-09 to 36.01 times in 2011-12.Overall the company has maintained satisfactory collection policy. MRPL has maintained average debtors turnover ratio at 19.50 times, which was less than the industry average of 36.08 times. The ratio was maximum of 21.93 times in

2008-09 and minimum of 17.68 times in 2012-13. Standard deviations of 1.85 and co variance of 9.47% were the least among all companies under study. It means that there was a very little fluctuation in debtors turnover ratio during study period. Overall it shows moderate collection policy. ONGC has exceptionally shows the least turnover ratio among all companies under study. It shows average of 16 times. The debtors turnover ratio was ranged between 19.38 in 2010-11 to 12.71 times in 2012-13. Standard deviation was 2.26 and covariance was 14.09% shows major fluctuations in debtors turnover ratio. Overall it was very dissatisfactory result for a company as lower turnover ratio adversely affects the liquidity position of a company. It also leads to major blockage of working capital in the form of receivables. Average debtors turnover ratio of 22.68 times of RIL. The ratio was more than the industry average of 36.08 times. It was ranged between 26.87 in 2007-08 to 18.4 times in 2011-12. Standard deviation was 4.07 whereas covariance of 17.94% shows fewer fluctuations in debtors turnover ratio during period of study. Overall it shows good collection policy.

Liquid/quick/acid test ratio

BPCL has shown average quick ratio of 0.64 during research period, which was less than the industry average of 0.93. the ratio was mostly consistent during research period except the lowest one 0.45 in 2010-11. During last two years it was consistent as well as maximum i.e. 0.71. the company has also shown the lowest variation of 15.55% from average.HPCL had lowest average of quick ratio i.e. 0.52 among other companies. Moreover the company has shown the fluctuating trend in quick ratio, ranged between 0.52 in 2011-12 to 0.71 in 2012-13. The standard deviation was 0.10 which was also less than industry average of 0.37, means less inconsistency in ratio. IOCL has maintained mix trend of quick ratio during period of study showing average of 0.54 at a covariance of 19.67%, the company couldn't maintain ideal quick ratio. The ratio was ranged between 0.74 in 2011-12 to 0.45 in 2009-10. MRPL had quick ratio ranged between 0.98 in 2008-09 to 0.5 in 2012-13. The company has maintained average of 0.64 which was less than industry average of 0.78. Standard deviation of 0.18 compared to industry average of 0.78 shows less fluctuations in quick ratio during study period. ONGC has maintained quick ratio well, showing average quick ratio of 1.41 highest among all sample companies. Quick ratio was ranged between 2.26 in 2012-13 to 1.08 in 2010-11. ONGC was also having the highest co variance of 30.55% means there were greater fluctuations in trend of quick ratio throughout the research period. Overall it was a good management of working capital. During research period RIL has shown average quick ratio of 0.95, ranged between 1.17 in 2011-12 to 0.69 in 2009-10. Standard deviation was 0.18 less than industry average of 0.37. the company was the second highest in maintenance of quick ratio among all sample companies during period of study.

Debt – equity ratio

BPCL has maintained average debt equity ratio at 1.46 during period of study, which was slightly less than industry average of 0.93. Debt equity ratio was ranged between 1.75 in 2008-09 to 1.17 in 2010-11. Standard deviation of 0.23 shows less variation in ratio as industry average was of 0.68. the ratio shows greater portion of debt to equity in company, which means company is having more debt fund compared to owners' equity, on the other hand company at a greater side to take advantage of trading on equity. HPCL was having the highest proportion of debt equity ratio during period of study i.e. 2, as compared to industry average of 0.93. It means that company was having twice proportion of debt compare to its equity. Debt equity ratio was ranged between 2.36 in 2012-13 to 1.59 in 2007-08. Standard deviation of 0.26 was less than industry average of 0.68, it means that there was less inconsistency in debt equity ratio during study period. Greater portion of debt will adversely affect profitability during slag period, however proper utilization of debt funds may improve return to share holders. IOCL has shown average debt equity ratio of 0.99 which was near to industry average of 0.93. Debt equity ratio was ranged between 1.22 in 2011-12 and 0.86 in 2007-08. During study period the company has maintained almost ideal debt equity ratio. Standard deviation of 0.13 and co variance of 13.17% shows less fluctuation in debt equity ratio during research period. Overall it shows good balance of debt and equity. MRPL was having debt equity ratio at an average of 0.57, which was less than industry average of 0.93. Ratio was ranged between 1.08 in 2012-13 to 0.24 in 2010-11. During last three years there was continuous increase in the ratio. This shows that company was moving towards larger share of debt to finance new projects. Above table shows average debt equity ratio of 0.12 of ONGC as compared to industry average of 0.93. The ratios show very meagre proportion of debt in capital structure. The ratio was ranged between 0.2 in 2008-09 to 0.04 in 2012-13. During last three years it was almost negligible that means there was a greater control of owners. Capital structure was not balanced one but lean towards equity share holders. It also means very little chance of trading on equity. RIL has maintained average debt equity ratio at 0.45. industry average was of 0.93, which means company has been maintaining lower level of debt compare to other companies under study. The ratio was ranged between 0.65 in 2008-09 to 0.30 in 2012-13. Standard deviation of 0.12 and co variance of 26.53% suggests less fluctuation in debt equity ratio.

Fixed assets turnover

Fixed assets turnover ratio of BPCL. The company has shown increasing trend after year 2007-08. The fixed assets turnover ratio of BPCL was ranged between 7.17 times in 2012-13 to 5.15 times in 2007-08. Standard deviation of 0.96 shows less fluctuations compared to industry average of 2. The average fixed assets turnover ratio of BPCL was 5.83 times which was also the highest among all sample companies under study. It means higher efficiency. Company is more efficient in using fixed assets to generating sales. The fixed assets turnover ratio of HPCL has shown fluctuating trend during research period. Highest 6.22 times in 2008-09, whereas the lowest 4.32 times in 2009-10. The standard deviation was 0.71 times which less than the industry average was. The mean ratio of company was 5.24 times, higher than industry average of 3.82 times. Thus it shows that the company has managed its fixed assets efficiently. With an average of 4.34 times, IOCL has maintained mix trend of fixed assets turnover ratio during research period. The ratio ranged between 4.98 times in 2008-09 to 3.61 times in 2010-11. Standard deviation was 0.50, less than the industry average. Average 4.35 times fixed turnover ratio was higher than industry average of 3.82 times. Overall it shows good management and utilization of fixed assets to produce sales. The fixed assets turnover ratio of MRPL has shown mix trend during fist three years then after it has shown upward trend, the ratio was ranged between 5.97 times in 2011-12 to 4.29 times in 2009-10. Standard deviation was 0.69, less than the industry average of 2. Average fixed assets turnover ratio of company was 5.13 times, higher than the industry average of 3.82 times, which shows the satisfactory management of fixed assets. ONGC has shown the lowest average of fixed assets turnover ratio, i.e. 0.92 times compared to industry average of 3.82 times. It was consistent during fist two years i.e. 1.05 times and was also the highest and then after it has shown almost downtrend, except in the year 2012-13 where there was a very little improvement. The result shows that the investment in fixed assets is more than what is needed to generate sales. RIL has maintained average fixed assets turnover ratio of 1.57 times which is less than the industry average, the company has shown improvements in fixed assets turnover ratio after 2007-08. It was maximum in 2012-13 i.e. 2.24 times which indicates that necessary steps were taken to improve the ratio.

LIQUIDITY PROFITABILITY STATUS OF THE SELECTED REFINERY INDUSTRIES BASED ON THE COMBINATION OF CURRNET RATIO AND GROSS PROFIT RATIO

The table discloses that the ONGC has a strong position being in high profitability and high liquidity cell. While MRPL and RIL are having high liquidity but at the cost of low profitability. BPCL, HPCL and IOCL do not perform well, are come under cell -4, which denotes low liquidity low profitability.

LIQUIDITY PROFITABILITY STATUS OF THE SELECTED REFINERY INDUSTRIES BASED ON THE COMBINATION OF CURRNET RATIO AND NET PROFIT RATIO

Industry average of 6% is considered as a standard for Net profit. Industry average current ratio of 1 is considered as standard to evaluate Current ratio. ONGC and RIL were in cell -1 showing high liquidity and higher profitability, where as MRPL has maintained high current ratio but profitability in the form of net profit was low, hence occupied cell – 2. While BPCL, HPCL, and IOCL were in cell – 4 due to low current ratio and low net profit margin showing poor performance.

LIQUIDITY PROFITABILITY STATUS OF THE SELECTED REFINERY INDUSTRIES BASED ON THE COMBINATION OF CURRNET RATIO AND EARNING PER SHARE

Current Ratio was taken as the measurement of short term debt paying capacity,while Earning Per Share was used as profitability indicator. Industry average of Rs.39 per share is considered as a standard for EPS. Industry average current ratio of 1 is considered as standard to evaluate Current ratio. ONGC and RIL has maintained high current ratio and also managed profitability well in the form of EPS thus occupied cell -1, while BPCL shows profitability liquidity trade off situation by maintain low liquidity and earning well, company was placed in cell – 3. HPCL, IOCL and MRPL were not performing well in both, they maintained low current ratio but couldn't improve profitability and hence occupied cell -4.

LIQUIDITY PROFITABILITY STATUS OF THE SELECTED REFINERY INDUSTRIES BASED ON THE COMBINATION OF CURRNET RATIO AND DIVIDEND PER SHARE

Current Ratio was taken as the measurement of short term debt paying capacity,while Dividend Per Share was used as profitability indicator. Indusry average of Rs. 9 per share is considered as a standard for DPS. Industry average current ratio of 1 is considered as standard to evaluate Current ratio. ONGC and RIL has maintained liquidity profitability well and occupied the best position at cell – 1, MRPL has traditionally fit at liquidity profitability trade off, maitaining high liquidity at a cost low profitability. BPCL on other hand at cell -3 maintained low liquidity at a cost of high profitability. HPCL and IOCL didn't perform well, had a low currnet ratio as well as low DPS.

LIQUIDITY PROFITABILITY STATUS OF THE SELECTED REFINERY INDUSTRIES BASED ON THE COMBINATION OF CURRNET RATIO AND RETURN ON NET WORTH

Current Ratio was taken as the measurement of short term debt paying capacity,while Return On Net Worth was used as profitability indicator. Indusry average of 13% is considered as a standard for RONW. Industry average ratio of 1 is considered as standard to evaluate Current ratio. MRPL, ONGC and RIL performed well at both level showing high CR and high RONW, were placed at cell -1. While no companies were at liquidity profitability trade off zone. BPCL, HPCL and IOCL registered low CR and low RONW therefore continued at cell -4. MRPL was exceptional at cell -1, because during 2012-13 the company has shown negative return on net worth.

LIQUIDITY PROFITABILITY STATUS OF THE SELECTED REFINERY INDUSTRIES BASED ON THE COMBINATION OF CURRNET RATIO AND RETURN ON CAPITAL EMPLOYED

Current Ratio was taken as the measurement of short term debt paying capacity,while Return On Capital Employed was used as profitability indicator. Indusry average of 16% is considered as a standard for ROCE. Industry average current ratio of 1 is considered as standard to evaluate Current ratio. MRPL and ONGC has maintianed high CR as well as ROCE and placed at cell -1. RIL struggling little for ROCE, had maintained high CR, therfore placed at cell -2. BPCL, HPCL and IOCL were low at CR as well as ROCE placed at cell -4 indicating poor performance

LIQUIDITY PROFITABILITY STATUS OF THE SELECTED REFINERY INDUSTRIES BASED ON THE COMBINATION OF STOCK TURNOVER RATIO AND GROSS PROFIT RATIO

Inventory Turnover Ratio was taken as the measurement of efficiency, while Gross Profit was used as profitability indicator. Industry average of 10% is considered as a standard for Gross profit. Industry average ratio of 19 times is considered as standard to evaluate ITR. ONGC was the only company which could maintain high ITR as well as high GP at cell -1. All other companies viz. BPCL, HPCL, IOCL, MRPL, RIL were registered low ITR as well as low GP and were placed at cell -4.

LIQUIDITY PROFITABILITY STATUS OF THE SELECTED REFINERY INDUSTRIES BASED ON THE COMBINATION OF STOCK TURNOVER RATIO AND NET PROFIT RATIO

Inventory Turnover Ratios was taken as the measurement of efficiency, while Net Profit was used as profitability indicator. Indusry average of 6% is considered as a standard for Net profit. Industry average ratio of 19 times is considered as standard to evaluate ITR. ONGC was only company maintained high ITR as well as high NP, RIL at liquidity profitability trade off zone maintained low liquidity and high profitability. All other companies viz. BPCL, HPCL, IOCL, MRPL has shown very weak performance, as companies have maintained low ITR as well as low NP.

LIQUIDITY PROFITABILITY STATUS OF THE SELECTED REFINERY INDUSTRIES BASED ON THE COMBINATION OF STOCK TURNOVER RATIO AND EARNING PER SHARE

Inventory Turnover Ratio was taken as the measurementment of efficiency,while Earning Per Share was used as profitability indicator. Indusry average of Rs. 39 per share is considered as a standard for EPS. Industry average ratio of 19 times is considered as standard to evaluate ITR. ONGC has maintained both liquidiy as well profitability criterion very well, having high ITR as well as high EPS occupied the best position i.e. cell – 1. No companies were at cell -2. BPCL and RIL couldn't maintain high ITR but managed to get EPS above industry average and hence occupied place at cell – 3. HPCL, IOCL and MRPL failed in both categories, maintained low ITR as well as low EPS fall at cell – 4.

LIQUIDITY PROFITABILITY STATUS OF THE SELECTED REFINERY INDUSTRIES BASED ON THE COMBINATION OF STOCK TURNOVER RATIO AND DIVIDEND PER SHARE

Inventory Turnover Ratio was taken as the measurementment of efficiency,while Dividend Per Share was used as profitability indicator. Indusry average of Rs. 9 per share is considered as a standard for DPS. Industry average ratio of 19 times is considered as standard to evaluate ITR. ONGC has performed well in both categories, having high ITR and more than indusry average DPS, set at cell -1. BPCL and RIL has successfully maintained high DPS, but having low ITR, set at cell – 3. HPCL, IOCL and MRPL did not perform well and could not maintain both liquidity as well as prfoitability having low ITR and low DPS placed at cell – 4.

LIQUIDITY PROFITABILITY STATUS OF THE SELECTED REFINERY INDUSTRIES BASED ON THE COMBINATION STOCK TURNOVER RATIO AND RETURN ON NET WORTH

Inventory Turnover Ratio was taken as the measurementment of efficiency,while Return On Net Worth was used as profitability indicator. Indusry average of 13% is considered as a standard for RONW. Industry average ratio of 19 times is considered as standard to evaluate ITR. ONGC again being market leader, sustained high ITR and high RONW set at cell -1, MRPL and RIL could maintain high RONW, but failed to achieve proper ITR hence set at cell -3. BPCL, HPCL, and IOCL struggling for both liquidity as well as profitability, maintained low ITR and low RONW, therefore occupied cell – 4

LIQUIDITY PROFITABILITY STATUS OF THE SELECTED REFINERY INDUSTRIES BASED ON THE COMBINATION OF STOCK TURNOVER RATIO AND RETURN ON CAPITAL EMPLOYED

Inventory Turnover Ratio was taken as the measurementment of efficiency,while Return On Capital Employed was used as profitability indicator. Indusry average of 16% is considered as a standard for ROCE. Industry average ratio of 19 times is considered as standard to evaluate ITR. ONGC has maintained high ITR and high

ROCE, hence set at cell -1, MRPL at profitability liquidity trade off, has shown low ITR and high ROCE at cell 3. Whereas BPCL, HPCL, IOCL and RIL couldnt perform well and occupied position at cell – 4 for having low ITR and low ROCE.

LIQUIDITY PROFITABILITY STATUS OF THE SELECTED REFINERY INDUSTRIES BASED ON THE COMBINATION OF DEBTORS TURNOVER RATIO AND GROSS PROFIT RATIO

Debtors Turnover Ratio was taken as the measurement of short term liquidity,while Gross Profit was used as profitability indicator. Indusry average of 10% is considered as a standard for Gross profit. Industry average of 36 times considered as standard to evaluate DTR. ONGC has shown the best performance having high GP and high DTR, got the position at cell – 1. BPCL, HPCL and IOCL set at profitability liquidity trade off due to high DTR but low GP, no companies were at cell – 3. MRPL and RIL could't maintain the industry standard and therefore placed at cell – 4.

LIQUIDITY PROFITABILITY STATUS OF THE SELECTED REFINERY INDUSTRIES BASED ON THE COMBINATION OF DEBTORS TURNOVER RATIO AND NET PROFIT RATIO

Debtors Turnover Ratio was taken as the measurement of short term liquidity,while Net Profit was used as profitability indicator. Indusry average of 6% is considered as a standard for Net profit. Industry average ratio of 36 times considered as standard to evaluate DTR. No companies were at cell – 1. BPCL, HPCL and IOCL were at cell – 2, having high profitablility and low net profit, due to high DTR and low NP. ONGC and RIL were at liquidity profitability trade off, showing low DTR and high NP. MRPL has shown the worst performance and was not able to maintain both liquidty as well as profitability at industry average and fall in to cell -4 due to low DTR and low NP.

LIQUIDITY PROFITABILITY STATUS OF THE SELECTED REFINERY INDUSTRIES BASED ON THE COMBINATION OF DEBTORS TURNOVER RATIO AND EARNING PER SHARE

Debtors Turnover Ratio was taken as the measurement of short term liquidity, while Earning Per Share was used as profitability indicator. Indusry average of 36 times is considered as a standard for DTR. Industry average ratio of Rs. 39 per share is considered as standard to evaluate EPS. BPCL has performed well under both cases, as the company maintained high DTR as well as high EPS. While HPCL, IOCl were at profitability liquidity trade off have maintained high DTR and low EPS, set at cell - 2. Whereas ONGC and RIL, on other side have maintained high EPS at a cost of low DTR, so got position at cell -3. MRPL couldn't perform well showing low DTR and low EPS got the worst position at cell – 4.

LIQUIDITY PROFITABILITY STATUS OF THE SELECTED REFINERY INDUSTRIES BASED ON THE COMBINATION OF DEBTORS TURNOVER AND DIVIDEND PER SHARE

Debtors Turnover Ratio was taken as the measurement of short term liquidity,while Dividend Per Share was used as profitability indicator. Indusry average of Rs. 9 per share is considered as a standard for DPS. Industry average ratio of 36 times is considered as standard to evaluate DTR. BPCL significantly occupied cell – 1 due to high DTR as wll as high DPS. HPCL and IOCL were at cell -2 as the companies have maintained high DTR at cost of low DPS, on other side at cell -3, there were ONGC and RIL both companies succeeded in maintaining high DPS, but coludn't maintain industry average of DTR. MRPL didn't perform well in both DTR as well as DPS, due to low DTR and low DPS, company got position at cell – 4.

LIQUIDITY PROFITABILITY STATUS OF THE SELECTED REFINERY INDUSTRIES BASED ON THE COMBINATION OF DEBTORS TURNOVER RATIO AND RETURN ON NET WORTH

Debtors Turnover Ratio was taken as the measurement of short term liquidity,while Return On Net Worth was used as profitability indicator. Indusry average of 13% is considered as a standard for RONW. Industry average current ratio of 36 times is considered as standard to evaluate DTR. There was not a single company at the best position i.e. cell -1 as well as the worst one i.e. cell -4. All companies were struggling to maintaining liquidity profitability trade off. BPCL, HPCL and IOCL were at cell -2 due to high DTR and low RONW. MRPL, ONGC and RIL were occupied cell – 3 due to low DTR and high RONW.

LIQUIDITY PROFITABILITY STATUS OF THE SELECTED REFINERY INDUSTRIES BASED ON THE COMBINATION OF DEBTORS TURNOVER RATIO AND RETURN ON CAPITAL EMPLOYED

Debtors Turnover Ratio was taken as the measurement of short term liquidity,while Return On Capital Employed was used as profitability indicator. Indusry average of 16% is considered as a standard for ROCE. Industry average ratio of 36 times is considered as standard to evaluate DTR. There was not a single company at cell -1, BPCL, HPCL and IOCL have maintained high DTR but at cost of low ROCE therefore set at cell -2. On the other hand MRPL, ONGC were at cell -3 due to high ROCE and low DTR. RIL has shown exceptionally low DTR as well as low ROCE hence got the worst position at cell -4.

LIQUIDITY PROFITABILITY STATUS OF THE SELECTED REFINERY INDUSTRIES BASED ON THE COMBINATION OF QUICK RATIO AND GROSS PROFIT RATIO

Quick ratio was taken as the measurement of short term liquidity,while Gross Profit was used as profitability indicator. Indusry average of 10% is considered as a standard for Gross profit. Industry average ratio of 0.78 is considered as standard to evaluate quick ratio. ONGC has performed well and has shown high QR as well as high GP, and got the best position at cell – 1. RIL at liquidity profitability trade off occupied cell -2 as the company maintained high QR but low GP. Whereas BPCL, HPCL , IOCL and MRPL couldn't perform as per expectations and all companies have failed to maintain industry average of QR and GP. Due to low GP and low QR all companies were located at cell -4.

LIQUIDITY PROFITABILITY STATUS OF THE SELECTED REFINERY INDUSTRIES BASED ON THE COMBINATION OF QUICK RATIO AND NET PROFIT RATIO

Quick Ratio was taken as the measurement of short term liquidity,while Net Profit was used as profitability indicator. Indusry average of 6% is considered as a standard for Gross profit. Industry average current ratio of 0.78 is considered as standard to evaluate Quick ratio. ONGC and RIL have performed well and succeded in maintaining both QR and NP above the industry average, hence got postion at cell –

1. There was not a single company at liqudity profitability trade off positons. BPCL, HPCL, IOCL and MRPL were below the industry average in both QR and NP, therefore located at cell – 4.

LIQUIDITY PROFITABILITY STATUS OF THE SELECTED REFINERY INDUSTRIES BASED ON THE COMBINATION OF QUICK RATIO AND EARNING PER SHARE RATIO

Quick Ratio was taken as the measurement of short term liquidity,while Earning Per Share was used as profitability indicator. Indusry average of Rs. 39 per share is considered as a standard for Return on Net Worth. Industry average ratio of 0.78 is considered as standard to evaluate Quick ratio. ONGC and RIL have maintained both QR and EPS at above industry average and therefore got placed at cell -1. BPCL have maintained high EPS but at cost of low QR, therfore occupied cell – 3. HPCL, IOCL and MRPL didn't perform well, due to low QR and low EPS, these companies placed at cell -4. There was not a single company set at cell-2.

LIQUIDITY PROFITABILITY STATUS OF THE SELECTED REFINERY INDUSTRIES BASED ON THE COMBINATION OF QUICK RATIO AND DIVIDEND PER SHARE

Quick Ratio was taken as the measurement of short term liquidity,while Dividend Per Share was used as profitability indicator. Indusry average of Rs. 9 per share is considered as a standard for Return on Net Worth. Industry average ratio of 0.78 is considered as standard to evaluate Quick ratio. ONGC and RIL have maintained both QR and DPS at above industry average and therefore got placed at cell -1. BPCL have maintained high DPS but at cost of low QR, therfore occupied cell – 3. HPCL, IOCL and MRPL didn't perform well, due to low QR and low DPS, these companies placed at cell -4.

LIQUIDITY PROFITABILITY STATUS OF THE SELECTED REFINERY INDUSTRIES BASED ON THE COMBINATION OF QUICK RATIO AND RETURN ON NET WORTH

Quick Ratio was taken as the measurement of short term liquidity,while Return on Net Worth was used as profitability indicator. Indusry average of 13% is considered as a standard for Return on Net Worth. Industry average ratio of 0.78 is considered as standard to evaluate Quick ratio. ONGC and RIl have performed exceptionally well, and have successful maintained both RONW and QR above industry average, due to high QR and high RONW, companies were placed at cell -1. MRPL at liqudity profitability trade off point maintained high RONW but at a cost of low QR, thus got placed at cell -3. BPCL, HPCL and IOCL were at cell -4 due to low QR and low RONW.

LIQUIDITY PROFITABILITY STATUS OF THE SELECTED REFINERY INDUSTRIES BASED ON THE COMBINATION OF QUICK RATIO AND RETURN ON CAPITAL EMPLOYED

Quick Ratio was taken as the measurement of short term liquidity,while Return on Capital Employed was used as profitability indicator. Indusry average of 16% is considered as a standard for Return on Capital Employed. Industry average ratio of 0.78 is considered as standard to evaluate Quick ratio. ONGC was the only company which has maintained both QR and ROCE above the industry average, the company has got cell -2 due to high QR and high ROCE. RIL was at liqudity profitability trade off due to low ROCE and high QR and hence occupied cell – 2. On the other hand MRPL has maintained low QR and high ROCE. All remaining companies BPCL, IOCL and HPCL couldn't perform as per industry expectations, the companies have shown low QR and low ROCE , thus got position at cell – 4.

LIQUIDITY PROFITABILITY STATUS OF THE SELECTED REFINERY INDUSTRIES BASED ON THE COMBINATION OF DEBT EQUITY RATIO AND GROSS PROFIT RATIO

Debt Equity ratio was taken as the measurement of short term debt paying capacity,while Gross Profit was used as profitability indicator. Indusry average of 10% is considered as a standard for Gross profit. Industry average ratio of 0.93 is considered as standard to evaluate Debt Equity ratio. There was not a single company at the best position i.e. at cell – 1. BPCL, HPCL and IOCL were at liquidity profitability trade off zone, as having low GP but high DE, these companies were placed at cell – 2. ONGC on the other hand couldn't maitain DE ratio above industry average, but had GP more than the industry average which led the company to cell -3. MRPL and RIL did not perform up to thier standard, and having low DE and low GP, these companies were placed at cell – 4.

LIQUIDITY PROFITABILITY STATUS OF THE SELECTED REFINERY INDUSTRIES BASED ON THE COMBINATION OF DEBT EQUITY AND NET PROFIT RATIO

Debt Equity ratio was taken as the measurement of short term debt paying capacity,while Net Profit was used as profitability indicator. Indusry average of 6% is considered as a standard for Net profit. Industry average ratio of 0.93 is considered as standard to evaluate Debt Equity ratio. There was not a single company at cell – 1. BPCL, HPCL and IOCL were at cell – 2 due to high DE but low NP, whereas ONGC and RIL at cell – 3 due to having low DE and high NP. MRPL did not maintain DE as well as NP up to industry average and hence placed at cell – 4.

LIQUIDITY PROFITABILITY STATUS OF THE SELECTED REFINERY INDUSTRIES BASED ON THE COMBINATION OF DEBT EQUITY AND EARNING PER SHARE

Debt Equity ratio was taken as the measurement of short term debt paying capacity,while Earning Per Share was used as profitability indicator. Indusry average of Rs. 39 per share is considered as a standard for Earning Per Share. Industry average ratio of 0.93 is considered as standard to evaluate Debt Equity ratio. BPCL had maintained both liquidity as well as profitability at its best, due to high DE and high EPS company was placed at cell – 1. HPCL and IOCL were at liquidity profitability trade off point, having low EPS and high DE, placed at cell – 2. While ONGC and RIL have maintained high EPS at cost of low DE. MRPL continued with below industry average liquidity as well as profitability placed at cell -4. The company was having low DE as well as low EPS.

LIQUIDITY PROFITABILITY STATUS OF THE SELECTED REFINERY INDUSTRIES BASED ON THE COMBINATION OF DEBT EQUITY RATIO AND DIVIDEND PER SHARE

Debt Equity ratio was taken as the measurement of short term debt paying capacity,while Dividend Per Share was used as profitability indicator. Indusry average of Rs. 9 per share is considered as a standard for Dividend Per Share. Industry average ratio of 0.93 is considered as standard to evaluate Debt Equity ratio. BPCL has performed exceptionally well in both liquidity and profitability, the company was having high DE as well as high DPS, so got placed at cell – 1. HPCL and IOCL were at cell-2 due to high DE but low DPS, ONGC and RIL on the other hand, at cell -3, maintained high DPS but at a cost of low DE. MRPL continue withe poor level, at cell -4, couldn't find the proper balance between liquidity as well as profitability, as having low DE and low DPS, it was placed at cell – 4.

LIQUIDITY PROFITABILITY STATUS OF THE SELECTED REFINERY INDUSTRIES BASED ON THE COMBINATION OF DEBT EQUITY RATIO AND RETURN ON CAPITAL EMPLOYED

Debt Equity ratio was taken as the measurement of short term debt paying capacity,while Return on Capital Employed was used as profitability indicator. Industry average of 16% is considered as a standard for Return on Capital Employed. Industry average ratio of 0.93 is considered as standard to evaluate Debt Equity ratio. No companies were placed at cell – 1. BPCL, HPCL and IOCL were at liquidity profitability trade off point, as these companies were having high DE at cost of low ROCE, on the other hand RIL and ONGC were having high ROCE at a cost of low DE and hence set at cell – 3. MRPL having low DE as well as low ROCE occupied position at cell – 4.

LIQUIDITY PROFITABILITY STATUS OF THE SELECTED REFINERY INDUSTRIES BASED ON THE COMBINATION OF DEBT EQUITY RATIO AND RETURN ON NET WORTH

Debt Equity ratio was taken as the measurement of short term debt paying capacity,while Return on Net Worth was used as profitability indicator. Indusry average of 13% is considered as a standard for Return On Net Worth. Industry average ratio of 0.93 is considered as standard to evaluate Debt Equity ratio. There was not a single company at the best position i.e. cell – 1, as well as the worst at cell - 4. All the comapnies were positioned at liquidtiy profitabiltiy trade off points. BPCL, HPCL and IOCL were having high DE at a cost of low RONW. Whereas MRPL, ONGC and RIL differently had high RONW at a cost of low DE.

LIQUIDITY PROFITABILITY STATUS OF THE SELECTED REFINERY INDUSTRIES BASED ON THE COMBINATION OF FIXED ASSETS TURNOVER RATIO AND GROSS PROFIT RATIO

Fixed Assets Turn Over ratio was taken as the measurement of short term efficiency,while Net Profit was used as profitability indicator. Indusry average of 6% is considered as a standard for Net profit. Industry average ratio of 3 times is considered as standard to evaluate Fixed Assets Turn Over ratio. There was not a single company at the best position cell – 1 as well as the worst one at cell – 4. BPCL, HPCL, IOCL and MRPL had a low FATO but maintained NP above the industry average and thus placed at cell – 2. ONGC and RIL on other hand had low FATO and high NP, and thus placed at cell – 3.

LIQUIDITY PROFITABILITY STATUS OF THE SELECTED REFINERY INDUSTRIES BASED ON THE COMBINATION OF FIXED ASSETS TURNOVER RATIO AND NET PROFIT RATIO

Fixed Assets Turn Over ratio was taken as the measurement of short term efficiency,while Net Profit was used as profitability indicator. Indusry average of 6% is considered as a standard for Net profit. Industry average ratio of 3 times is considered as standard to evaluate Fixed Assets Turn Over ratio. There was not a single company at the best position cell – 1 as well as the worst one at cell – 4. BPCL, HPCL, IOCL and MRPL had a low FATO but maintained NP above the industry average and thus placed at cell – 2. ONGC and RIL on other hand had low FATO and high NP, and thus placed at cell – 3.

LIQUIDITY PROFITABILITY STATUS OF THE SELECTED REFINERY INDUSTRIES BASED ON THE COMBINATION OF FIXED ASSETS TURNOVER RATIO AND EARNING PER SHARE

Earning Per Share was used as profitability indicator. Indusry average of Rs. 39 per share is considered as a standard for Earning Per Share. Industry average ratio of 3 times is considered as standard to evaluate Fixed Assets Turn Over ratio. BPCL had performed well, and maintained both liquidity as well as profitability above industry average, thus placed at cell – 1. There was not single company at the worst point of cell – 4. HPCL, IOCL and MRPL were at liquidity and profitability trade off point, maintained EPS below the industry average and FATO at above industry average, thus occupied place at cell -2. ONGC and RIL, on the other hand, had successfully maintaind EPS above the industry average, and FATO at below industry average. These companies were placed at cell – 3.

LIQUIDITY PROFITABILITY STATUS OF THE SELECTED REFINERY INDUSTRIES BASED ON THE COMBINATION OF FIXED ASSETS TURNOVER RATIO AND DIVIDEND PER SHARE

Fixed Assets Turn Over ratio was taken as the measurement of short term efficiency,while Dividend Per Share was used as profitability indicator. Indusry average of Rs. 9 per share is considered as a standard for Dividend Per Share. Industry average ratio of 3 times is considered as standard to evaluate Fixed Assets Turn Over ratio. BPCL had performed well and maintained both DPS and FATO above the industry average. HPCL, IOCL and MRPL were having low DPS and high FATO and occupied position at cell – 2. ONGC and RIL, on the other hand at liquidity profitability trade off point, maintained high DPS and low FATO, and thus occupied position at cell – 3. There was not a single company at cell – 4.

LIQUIDITY PROFITABILITY STATUS OF THE SELECTED REFINERY INDUSTRIES BASED ON THE COMBINATION OF FIXED ASSETS TURNOVER RATIO AND RETURN ON NET WORTH

Fixed Assets Turn Over ratio was taken as the measurement of short term efficiency,while Return On Net Worth was used as profitability indicator. Indusry average of 13% is considered as a standard for Return On Net Worth. Industry average ratio of 3 times is considered as standard to evaluate Fixed Assets Turn Over ratio. MRPL had high RONW as well as high FATO, thus placed at cell -1, but during 2012-13, the company has shown negative return and that was considered as an exceptional situation for research work under this case. There was not a single company at the worst position i.e. at cell – 4. BPCL, HPCL and IOCL were at liquidity profitability trade off points, having low RONW but high FATO placed at cell – 2. ONGC and RIL, on flip side maintained high RONW but at a cost of low FATO, and thus occupied place at cell – 3.

LIQUIDITY PROFITABILITY STATUS OF THE SELECTED REFINERY INDUSTRIES BASED ON THE COMBINATION OF CURRNET RATIO AND RETURN ON CAPITAL EMPLOYED

Fixed Assets Turn Over ratio was taken as the measurement of short term efficiency,while Return On Capital Employed was used as profitability indicator. Indusry average of 16% is considered as a standard for Return On Capital Employed. Industry average ratio of 3 times is considered as standard to evaluate Fixed Assets Turn Over ratio. MRPL had performed exceptionally well got placed at cell – 1. The company had sussessfully maintained high FATO and high ROCE. BPCL, HPCL and IOCL had maintained high FATO but low low ROCE, thus placed at cell – 2. ONGC, on the other hand, had maintained high ROCE at a cost of low FATO, and occupied place at cell – 3. RIL had performed the worst, as having both FATO and ROCE below industry average, occupied place at cell – 4.

SUGGESTIONS AND FUTURE RECOMMENDATIONS

1. Every company should increase its production as well as plant capacity to get the benefit of economies of scale, larger the refineries, more will be the output and less will be the cost of refining
2. To increase the profitability, there must be reduction in high administrative as well as raw materials cost. High cost of crude at international level may decrease the profitability but by considering and focusing on other cost of production, company can increase its profitability
3. Increase the stock turn over ration which in return lead towards increase in return on capital employed.
4. Companies are not paying constant or regular dividend which adversely affect the shareholders' confidence, company should try to make regular dividend by taking proper care of profitability and liquidity position
5. Refinery industry is a capital intensive industry, which requires heavy capital expenditure; all capital expenditure for acquiring the assets should be taken after considering all the probable factors.
6. Use of non conventional sources of energy can also reduce the cost of refining and even positively help the environmental concern.
7. Company should properly observe sales and liquidity position, when its necessary to take proper steps for working capital crisis.
8. To improve the liquidity position in the business, the company should invest into long term interest generating assets, instead of any short run purpose.
9. For proper cash management in the company, it is better to take care of cost of inventory as well as size of inventory; even proper care should be taken at the time of collection. The company should be quick at collection of dues.
10. The policy of getting finance is also not proper, the company should try to get finance through competitive commercial bidding, and even should go for other options like debentures, equity etc. to finance their long term as well as short term needs. The companies are at present rely upon the conventional system of borrowing from governments
11. By the proper use of operating assets, and reduction in non operative expenses, companies can increase their profitability.

12. To be at international market, the companies should focus on quality of output, even the government should promote the export oriented units, and should export the final product to less developed as well as developing countries of the world.
13. For continuous production at proper quality level, the companies need decent infrastructure to satisfy their inventory storage needs.
14. Government, to promote the industry, can reduce the power rate, excise duty, corporate taxes and should also promote special economic zones.
15. Cost audit of refinery companies should be made compulsory, for better findings of facts and figures.
16. This research is based upon the refineries in india only, one can further compare these to other country's refinery and can find out deviation in research.
17. This research has been carried out on the basis of annual reports and statistics from the government portals and sponsored magazines.
18. There are different methods for evaluating profitability and liquidity and are having their own limitations in analysis,
19. There are ideal ratios in general, but one should by proper research should develop the ideal ratios for refinery industry only.
20. There are also some erroneous facts in published reports of the company, therefore proper care should be taken in publishing financial data.
21. The business of refinery industry is not confined to geographical borders of the country, it is having international issues, various micro as well as macro factors should be considered.
22. Refinery industry is highly affected by dollar pricing, therefore mechanism of foreign trade should be considered
23. Geopolitical factors play a vital role, military exercise, embargo, restrictions, banned etc. may at regular intervals affecting the oil industry in general.

LIST OF ABBREVIATIONS

AOC	ASSAM OIL COMPANY
APM	ADMINISTERED PRICE MECHANISM
b/cd.	BILLIONS PER CALENDAR DAY
BBD	BILLION BARREL PER DOLLAR
BPCL	BHARAL PETROLEUM LTD.
COGS	COST OF GOODS SOLD
CR	CURRENT RATIO
DPS	DIVIDEND PER SHARE
EBIT	EARNING BEFORE INTEREST AND TAX
EPS	EARNING PER SHARE
HPCL	HINDUSTAN PETROLEUM LTD.
IOCL	INDIAN OIL CORPORATION LTD.
ITR	INVENTORY TURNOVER RATIO
MENA	MIDDLE EASTERN AND NORTH AFRICAN
MRPL	MANGLORE REFINERY LTD.
MT	METRIC TONNES
NCI	NELSON COMPLEXITY INDEX
NELP	NEW EXPLORATION POLICY
OCC	OIL COORDINATING COMMITTEE
OECD	ORGANIZATION FOR ECONOMIC CO OPERATION AND DEVELOPMENT
ONGC	OIL AND NATURAL GAS COMMISSION
OPEC	OIL AND PETROLEUM EXPORTING COUNTRIES
PAT	PROFIT AFTER TAX
QR	QUICK RATIO
R/P	RESERVE TO PRODUCTION
RIL	RELIANCE INDIA LTD.
ROCE	RETURN ON CAPITAL EMPLOYED
RONW	RETURN ON NET WORTH
WPI	WHOLESALE PRICE INDEX

BIBLIOGRAPHY

1. Anothoney Robert N – Management Accounting Tax and Cases –Thomson (2002)
2. B Ramchandra Rao – Balance *Sheet Analysis* – Progressive Corporation PVT Ltd, Mumbai – (1991)
3. B.K. Bhove – Cost Accounting Methods & Problems – Academic Publishers – Calcutta (2002)
4. B.N.Ahuja – Dictionary of Commoerce – Academic (India) Publication 19Pth PEdition 2005
5. C. R. Kothari – Research Methodology – Wishwa Prakashan – (1998)
6. Chandra Prasanna – Financial Management Theory & practice – Indian Publishing Co. Ltd, New Delhi (1997)
7. Chandra, Prasanna – *Financial Management* – Tata Mc.Graw Hill Publication – 5Pth P Edition 1997
8. Chopde,L. N. Choudhari D. H. and others – I*ntroduction to Management* accounting – Sheth Publishers Pvt. Ltd. Mumbai (1999)
9. Christian Crumlish – The Internet (No Experience Required) – BPB Publication 2nd P Edition
10. D K Bhattacharya – Research Methodology – Excel Books – 1Ps t Edition (2005)
11. Dr. Maheshwari S.N. – Financial Management Principal & Practice - Sultanchand & Sons – New Delhi (2002) – 3Prd P Edition
12. Dr. Maheshwari.S.N. – Principles of Management Accounting - Sultanchand & Sons. (Sixth edition-2002),333
13. E.F. Brigham, Michael C. Ehrhardt – Financial Management Theory & Prectice – Thomson – 10Pth PEdition 2004
14. Reliance Review of Energy Markets - A study conducted by Reliance Industries (2002)
15. Foulke, Roy A. – Practical Financial Statement Analysis – Tata Mc Graw Hill Publishing Co. Ltd., Bombay (Edition – 1996)
16. Gupta S. P. – Business Statistics – Sultanchand & Sons (Thirteenth Edition)
17. Hampton John and Cecilia Wagner – Working Capital Management – John Wiley Sons – New York (1989)
18. Jr. Stancill, James Men – Management of Working Capital – Intext Education Publishers – London (1971)

19. K. P. Singh, A. K. Sinha, S. C. Singh - Management of Working Capital – Janki Prakashan – New Delhi (1986)
20. Khan M.Y.and Jain P. K. – *Financial Management* – Tata Mc. Graw Hill Publishing Co. (1990)
21. Kishor M Ravi – cost and Management Accounting – Taxman's (second Edition)
22. M.N.Arora – Cost and Management Accounting – Theory and Problems Himalaya Publishing House – (First Edition-2004), 334
23. M.N.Arora – Management Accounting – Theory, Problems and Solutions – (First Edition-2004)
24. Maimbo S.M. – Interpretation of Financial Statements using Key Performance Ratios (1996)
25. Mindy C Martin, Steven M Hansen, Beth Klingher – Mastering Excel 2000 – BPB Publication – Premium Edition
26. P. C. Tripathy and P.N. Reddy – Principals of Management – Tata McGrow Hilll Publishing Company Ltd – New Delhi (1995)
27. P.P.Arya, Yesh Pal – Research Methodology in Management – Theory and Case Studies – Edition 2002
28. Pandey I. M. – *Financial Management* – Vikas Publishing House Pvt. Ltd – 8Pth P Edition 1999
29. Parag Diwan – Management – Principals and Practices – Excel Books – (2002)
30. Ravi M Kishore – Financial Management – New Delhi – (1996)
31. Robert E. Schellenberger – Managerial Analysis – D.B. Taraporevala & Sons & Co. Pvt. Ltd. (1969)
32. S K Bhattacharyya, John Dearden – Accounting for Management – Text and Cases – Vikas Publishing House Pvt Ltd – Revised Edition 1993
33. S. P. Gupta – Statistical Method – Sultanchand & Sons – Educational Publishers – New Delhi – (2001) 37.S.P. Gupta & M. P. Gupta - Business Statistics (10P th P Edition) – Sultanchand & Sons – New Delhi - (2005),335
34. Stevenson, William j., Harper & Row - Business statistics – (1978) 39.T. P. Ghosh – Accounting and Finance for Managers – Taxman allied Services Pvt. Ltd – New Delhi (2004)
35. Vanhorne – Fundamental of Financial Management – Prentice Hall of India Pvt. Ltd (1981)

36. Ravi M Kishore – Cost and Management Accounting – BPB Publication 2PndP Edition (1990)

Website visited

- http://www.capitaline.com
- http://www.capitalmarket.com/ier
- http://www.hindustanpetroleum.com
- http://www.bharatpetroleum.com
- http://www.cochirefinery.com
- http://www.iocl.com
- http://www.cpcl.co.in
- http://www.mrpl.co.in
- http://www.brpl.co.in
- http://www.Physics.csbju.edu/stasts/anova

www.ingramcontent.com/pod-product-compliance
Lightning Source LLC
LaVergne TN
LVHW080037210926
848481LV00011B/3216
9798233888908